READING THE BIBLE AGAIN FOR THE FIRST TIME

READING THE

BIBLE AGAIN

FOR THE FIRST TIME

Taking the Bible
Seriously
but Not Literally

MARCUS J. BORG

HarperOne
An Imprint of HarperCollinsPublishers

HarperOne

READING THE BIBLE AGAIN FOR THE FIRST TIME: *Taking the Bible Seriously but Not Literally.* Copyright © 2001 by Marcus J. Borg. All rights reserved. Printed in the United States of America. No part of this book may be used or reproduced in any manner whatsoever without written permission except in the case of brief quotations embodied in critical articles and reviews. For information address HarperCollins Publishers, 195 Broadway, New York, NY 10007.

HarperCollins books may be purchased for educational, business, or sales promotional use. For information please e-mail the Special Markets Department at SPsales@harpercollins.com.

HarperCollins website: http://www.harpercollins.com

HarperCollins®, ■®, and HarperOne™ are trademarks of HarperCollins Publishers.

FIRST HARPERCOLLINS PAPERBACK EDITION PUBLISHED IN 2002

Designed by Jessica Shatan

Library of Congress Cataloging-in-Publication Data
Borg, Marcus.
     Reading the Bible again for the first time : taking the Bible seriously but not literally / Marcus J. Borg.—1st ed.
         p. cm.
     Includes bibliographical references and index.
     ISBN 978–0–06–060919–1
     1. Bible—Criticism, interpretation, etc. 2. Metaphor in the Bible.
I. Title.
BS511.3.B67   2001
220.6'1—dc20   00—050599

23 24 25 26 27 LBC 48 47 46 45 44

FOR TOM HALLER
and the community at Ring Lake Ranch, Wyoming
August 2000

Contents

Preface

Conflict about the Bible is the single most divisive issue among Christians in North America today. And because of the importance of Christianity in the culture of the United States, conflict about the Bible is also central to what have been called "the culture wars."

The conflict is between two very different ways of reading the Bible. In language I will use later in the book, it is a conflict between a "literal-factual" way of reading the Bible and a "historical-metaphorical" way of reading it. The former is central to Christian fundamentalists and many conservative-evangelical Christians. The latter has been taught in seminaries of mainline denominations for the better part of a century. Most clergy have known about it for a long time. In the last few decades, the historical-metaphorical way of reading the Bible has become increasingly common among lay members of mainline churches.

This book represents the historical-metaphorical side of the debate. In its pages, I describe a way of seeing and reading the Bible that flows out of my life within two communities: the academic community of biblical scholarship and the scholarly study of religion, and the religious community of the church.

For over thirty-five years, I have been studying and teaching the Bible in private and public colleges, universities, and graduate schools. From the beginning, my special area of study has been Jesus and the gospels. But I have always had an abiding interest in the Hebrew Bible and have consistently taught it as well as the New Testament at the introductory and more advanced levels.

This book contains the most important and illuminating insights that I have learned about the Bible from this experience. It has three parts. Part One (three chapters) analyzes the present conflict and lays the foundation for a historical-metaphorical approach to the Bible. Parts Two and Three apply this approach and introduce the reader to major parts of the Bible. In Part Two, I treat portions of the Hebrew Bible in four chapters: creation stories, the Pentateuch, the prophets, and wisdom literature. In Part Three I explore major portions of the New Testament in three chapters: the gospels, Paul, and Revelation.

Because much of the book comes out of the experience of teaching at the undergraduate level, I trust that it may be of use in college and university courses. But I am also writing for a Christian audience, and I hope that this orientation will not get in the way of non-Christian readers. Readers in the latter category will sometimes find themselves listening to an intra-Christian conversation (and may perhaps find it interesting).

My desire to relate the book to Christianity flows out of the other community in which I live. For an even longer time than I have lived within the academy, I have lived in the Christian world. I was nurtured in the Lutheran church and remained Lutheran until about age thirty. Then, for almost a decade, my involvement with the institutional church was minimal. My reentry into its life was through a Presbyterian congregation in which I was a "kindred spirit" for a few years. That experience was very nourishing, but I realized that I desired a more liturgical and sacramental form of worship, and so I joined the Episcopal church, a denomination and tradition that I am very happy to call home. I describe myself as a nonliteralistic and nonexclusivistic Christian, committed to living my life with God within the Christian tradition, even as I affirm the validity of *all* the enduring religious traditions.

Thus, in addition to treating historical and literary matters, I have sought to explore the religious significance of the Bible—in particular, its significance for Christians. One of my central purposes in this book is to address the present conflict about the Bible within the church and to provide Christians with a persuasive way of seeing and reading their sacred scriptures, a way that takes the Bible seriously without taking it literally.

As I develop a historical-metaphorical approach to reading the Bible, I also offer an interpretation of the biblical tradition. What I present here is a way of seeing and reading the Bible that flows out of my total life experience: my education as a student of the Bible, my vocation as a teacher of biblical and religious studies, my journey as a Christian, and what I have learned from the journeys of others.

To say the obvious, the book reflects my own subjectivity. There is no point in pretending objectivity, as if I (or anybody) could have a vantage point outside of one's own personal and cultural history. The test of our subjectivities—whether they are primarily provincial, individualistic, or even narcissistic—is whether they make sense to others. And so I invite you into a way of seeing and reading the Bible that has made sense to me and encourage you to use your own discerning judgment about how much makes sense to you.

I am grateful to many people for what I have learned about the Bible. I am thankful for my socialization within the church. Though it included much that I have had to unlearn, it also instilled in me a love of the Bible and an abiding sense of its importance. I am indebted to professors from my past. In my undergraduate years, Paul Sponheim and Rod Grubb (both then professors at Concordia College in Moorhead, Minnesota) were most responsible for generating my adult interest in religion and the Bible. In my graduate education, George B. Caird, my primary professor at Oxford, was immeasurably important.

I am also indebted to authors of books on biblical scholarship from the last few centuries and contemporary colleagues within the academic guild. Some are acknowledged in footnotes, but some are not. Because this book comes out of over thirty years of teaching, I can no longer remember the source of many of the insights that I report. In virtually every case, I learned them from somebody; a completely original insight is a rare bird. I apologize for not being able to credit each contributor by name.

I conclude with a comment about the dedication of this book to Tom Haller and the community at Ring Lake Ranch, an ecumenical retreat center near DuBois, Wyoming. There my wife, Marianne, and I co-led a retreat for two weeks in late August, during which I also finished this book. On the first day of the retreat, Tom, a United Church of Christ clergyperson from St. Louis, was gravely injured in a horse-riding accident. For a day we did not know if he would live. His accident united the community of retreatants in a remarkably intimate way, especially as we prayed together for his recovery. In particular, I want to thank the staff at Ring Lake Ranch, especially Robert Hoskins, Ann Mebane, Elly Stewart, and its director, Joan Guntzelman. I am happy to say that Tom has recovered and very pleased to dedicate this book to him and the people with whom I lived for two rich weeks in the mountains of Wyoming.

Part One

FOUNDATIONS

1

Reading Lenses:
Seeing the Bible Again

The key word in the title of this book—*Reading the Bible Again for the First Time*—is "again." It points to my central claim. Over the past century an older way of reading the Bible has ceased to be persuasive for millions of people, and thus one of the most imperative needs in our time is a way of reading the Bible anew.

Reading and seeing go together. On the one hand, what we read can affect how we see. On the other hand, and more important for my immediate purpose, how we see affects how we read. What we bring to our reading of a text or document affects how we read it. All of us, whether we use reading glasses or not, read through lenses.

As we enter the twenty-first century, we need a new set of lenses through which to read the Bible. The older set, ground and polished by modernity, no longer works for millions of people. These lenses need to be replaced. The older way of seeing and reading the Bible, which I will soon describe, has made the Bible incredible and irrelevant for vast numbers of people.

This is so not only for the millions who have left the church in Europe and North America, but also for many Christians who continue to be active in the life of the church.

The need for new lenses thus exists within the church itself. The older lenses enabled Christians of earlier generations to experience the Bible as a lamp unto their feet, a source of illumination for following the Christian path. But for many Christians in our time, the older lenses have become opaque, turning the Bible into a stumbling block in the way.[1] Yet not all Christians agree about the need for new lenses. Many vigorously defend the older way of seeing the Bible. For them, what seems to be at stake is nothing less than the truth of the Bible and Christianity itself.

Conflicting Lenses

Conflict about how to see and read the Bible is the single greatest issue dividing Christians in North America today. On one side of the divide are fundamentalist and many conservative-evangelical Christians. On the other side are moderate-to-liberal Christians, mostly in mainline denominations.[2] Separating the two groups are two very different ways of seeing three foundational questions about the Bible: questions about its origin, its authority, and its interpretation.

The first group, who sometimes call themselves "Bible-believing Christians," typically see the Bible as the inerrant and infallible Word of God.[3] This conviction flows out of the way they see the Bible's origin: it comes from God, as no other book does. As a divine product, it is God's truth, and its divine origin is the basis of its authority. As a contemporary bumper sticker boldly puts it, "God said it, I believe it, that settles it." The sticker may be unfair to many who hold this position, but it was created by an advocate, not by a critic.

For these Christians, the Bible is to be interpreted literally, unless the language of a particular passage is clearly metaphorical. From their point of view, allowing nonliteral interpretation opens the door to evading the Bible's authority and making it say what we want it to say. They typically see themselves as taking the Bible with utmost seriousness and often criticize moderate-to-liberal Christians for watering it down and avoiding its authority. They also commonly see themselves as affirming "the old-time religion"—that is, Christianity as it was before the modern period. In fact, however, as we shall see, their approach is itself modern, largely the product of a particular form of nineteenth- and twentieth-century Protestant theology. Moreover, rather than allowing the Bible its full voice, their approach actually confines the Bible within a tight theological structure.[4]

The second group of Christians, most of whom are found in mainline churches, are less clear about how they *do* see the Bible than about how they do *not*. They are strongly convinced that many parts of the Bible cannot be taken literally, either as historically factual or as expressing the will of God. Some people who reach this conclusion leave the church, of course. But many continue within the church and are seeking a way of seeing the Bible that moves beyond biblical literalism and makes persuasive and compelling sense.

Their numbers are growing;[5] never before has there been so great an appetite for modern biblical scholarship among mainline Christians. They are responding strongly and positively to a more historical and metaphorical reading of the Bible. At the grass-roots level of mainline churches, a major de-literalization of the Bible is underway.

Though these Christians know with certainty that they cannot be biblical literalists, they are less clear about how they *do* see the origin and authority of the Bible. They are often uncertain what it means to say that the Bible is "the Word of God" or "inspired by God." Though they reject grounding the Bible's authority in its infallibility, they are unsure what "biblical authority" might mean.

Thus it is not surprising that even within mainline denominations, there is conflict about how to see and read the Bible. At the national level, most of these denominations have vocal minority

movements protesting what they perceive to be the loss of biblical authority. At the local level, some congregations are sharply
divided about how to see the Bible. The conflict also divides families. In many conservative Christian families, one or more members have either dropped out of church or become part of a
liberal church. The reverse is also true: many liberal Christian
families have seen one or more of their members become conservative Christians. Some families have been able to negotiate this
conflict with grace. But in many, it has been a source of division,
grief, and hand-wringing.

The conflict about the Bible is most publicly visible in discus-
sions of three issues. First, in some Christian circles, "creation
versus evolution" is the primary litmus test of loyalty to the
Bible. The second issue is homosexuality: May practicing gays
and lesbians be full members of the church? May the unions of
gay and lesbian couples be blessed? May gays and lesbians be ordained? This debate is often cast in the form of accepting or re-
jecting biblical authority.

A third lightning rod for the conflict is contemporary historical Jesus scholarship. For the last decade, the quest for the historical Jesus has attracted widespread media attention and public
interest, especially among mainline Christians. But it has generated a strongly negative reaction among fundamentalist and
conservative-evangelical Christians. From their point of view,
questioning the historical factuality of the gospels strikes at the
very foundations of Christianity.

The Roots of the Conflict

The border between fundamentalist and conservative-evangelical
Christians is hard to draw. A fundamentalist has been defined as
"an evangelical who is angry about something."[6] But some
conservative-evangelicals are not fundamentalists and have no
interest in defending, for example, the literal factuality of the
Bible's story of creation or the complete historical accuracy of
all the words attributed to Jesus. But what they share in

common is an understanding of the authority of the Bible grounded in its origin: it is true because it comes from God.

Fundamentalism itself—whether Christian, Jewish, or Muslim—is modern. It is a reaction to modern culture.[7] Christian fundamentalism as an identifiable religious movement originated early in the twentieth century in the United States, with its immediate roots in the second half of the nineteenth century.[8] It stressed the infallibility and inerrancy of the Bible in every respect, especially against Darwinism and what it called "the higher criticism" (by which it meant the scholarly study of the Bible as it had developed primarily in Germany in the nineteenth century).

The roots of the evangelical understanding of the Bible are older, going back to the Protestant Reformation of the sixteenth century. The Reformation replaced the authority of the church and church tradition with the sole authority of scripture. John Calvin and Martin Luther, the two most important leaders of the Reformation, both had a strong sense of biblical authority. But it was in the second and third generation of the Reformation that claims for the infallible truth of the Bible were made. "Plenary inspiration"—the notion that the words of the Bible were dictated by God and are therefore free from error—was emphasized by those later Reformers.[9]

The realization that these developments are relatively recent is important. The explicit description of the Bible as inerrant and infallible by fundamentalists and some conservative-evangelicals cannot claim to be the ancient and traditional voice of the church. Yet both fundamentalism and the notion of the Bible as "God's truth" (and thus without error) have their roots in an older, conventional way of seeing the Bible widely shared by most Christians for a long time.

An Older Way of Seeing the Bible

Ordinary people did not read the Bible until relatively recently. Until about five hundred years ago, the Bible could be read only

by the very few who knew Latin, Greek, or Hebrew and who
had access to handwritten manuscripts, which were expensive to
produce and therefore relatively scarce. Two developments
changed this. In the middle of the 1400s, the printing press was
invented. Less than a hundred years later, largely because of the
Protestant Reformation, the Bible was translated from ancient
"sacred" languages into contemporary languages.

The accessibility of the Bible to anybody who can read has
been a mixed blessing. Positively, it has resulted in a democrati-
zation of Christianity. No longer are the riches of the Bible
known only to an educated elite. But it has also had negative
consequences. It has made possible individualistic interpretation
of the Bible; and that, coupled with the elevated status given to
the Bible by the Protestant Reformation, has led to the fragmentation of Christianity into a multitude of denominations and sectarian movements, each grounded in different interpretations of
the Bible.

Moreover, prior to the invention of the printing press, virtually nobody had seen the books of the Bible bound together in a
single volume. Rather, the Bible was most commonly experienced as a collection of separate manuscripts. Indeed, during antiquity and the Middle Ages, the Bible was most often referred
to in the plural as "scriptures"—that is, as a collection of books.
Once the Bible was routinely bound as a single volume, it became easier to think of it as a single book with a single author
(namely, God).

Since then and until recently, the majority of Christians (especially Protestants) shared in common a set of lenses for seeing
and reading the Bible. Indeed, this way of seeing was so widespread that most Christians were not even aware of the lenses.

This older way of seeing the Bible has been called "natural literalism." In a state of natural literalism, the Bible is read and accepted literally without effort. Because someone in this state has
no reason to think differently, a literal reading of the Bible poses
no problems.

Natural literalism is quite different from "conscious literalism," a modern form of literalism that has become aware of problems posed by a literal reading of the Bible but insists upon it nevertheless.[10] Whereas natural literalism is effortless, conscious literalism is effortful. It requires "faith," understood as believing things hard to believe. But natural literalism does not insist upon literal interpretation. Rather, it takes it for granted, and it does not require "faith" to do so.

Fundamentalists and many evangelicals are conscious literalists. But their way of seeing the Bible stands in considerable continuity with the natural literalism of past centuries. Seeing the Bible through the lenses of natural literalism leads readers to the following conclusions about the Bible's origin, authority, and interpretation—conclusions that are similar to those of conscious literalism:

1. *Origin.* The Bible is a divine product. Such is the natural or immediate meaning of how the Bible has been spoken about by Christians through the centuries. The Bible is the Word of God, inspired by the Holy Spirit; it is sacred scripture. The Bible is thus not a human product, but comes from God in a way no other book does.

2. *Authority.* The Bible is therefore true and authoritative. The truth and authority of the Bible are grounded in its origin. As a divine product, it has a divine guarantee to be true and must be taken seriously as the ultimate authority about what to believe and how to live.

3. *Interpretation.* The Bible is historically and factually true. In a state of natural literalism, it is taken for granted that what the Bible says happened *really* happened. The only exceptions are manifestly metaphorical language, such as "mountains clapping their hands with joy." Natural literalists can recognize and appreciate metaphor. But when the Bible seems to be reporting something that happened, it happened. Moreover, believing in the factuality of the Bible takes no effort; in a state of natural literalism, there is no reason to believe otherwise.

Though most readers of this book will not see the Bible this way, the perspective is nevertheless familiar. Its familiarity flows in part from the conventional status it held until recently within Christianity. Most of our ancestors two or three generations back were natural literalists. For those of us who are older, perhaps even our parents were.

Many of us grew up immersed in this tradition. So it was for me. As a child growing up in a Lutheran church in the middle of the previous century, I heard the Bible spoken of as "the Word of God." It was thus obvious that I should take it seriously.

In Sunday school, we were expected to memorize the Ten Commandments. They were important because they were in the Bible and were thus God's laws. We sang "Jesus loves me, this I know"—and how did we know? Because "the Bible tells me so."

In common with most Protestants, we Lutherans thought of the Bible as the sole authority for faith and morals. Though I did not know the Latin phrase then, *sola scriptura*—"scripture alone"—was one of the battle cries of the Protestant Reformation. To the same melody as the great hymn of the Reformation, "A Mighty Fortress Is Our God," we sang:

> God's Word is our great heritage,
> And shall be ours forever;
> To spread its light from age to age
> Shall be our chief endeavor.
> Through life it guides our way,
> In death it is our stay;
> Lord grant, while worlds endure,
> We keep its teachings pure,
> Throughout all generations.

My family and congregation were not fundamentalists. Rather, we were natural literalists, though we favored what we might call *"soft* literalism." We did not, for example, insist upon reading the Genesis stories of creation literally. It was fine to see the six days of creation as six geological epochs. We did not have to deny the existence of dinosaurs or the fossil record.

But as "soft literalists," we took it for granted that the most important events in the Bible happened pretty much as they are reported. That at the time of the exodus the sea really did part to allow the ancient Hebrews to pass through. That Jesus really was born of a virgin, really did walk on the water, really did multiply loaves, and so forth. This is what I mean by "soft literalism": taking it for granted that the most central events reported in the Bible really happened.

This older way of seeing the Bible went with an older way of seeing Christianity. The reason for the connection is obvious: the Bible has been foundational for Christianity throughout the centuries. How one sees the Bible and how one sees Christianity go hand in hand.

An Older Way of Seeing Christianity

This older understanding of Christianity was conventional Christianity as recently as a century ago. It is still the common understanding among fundamentalist and many conservative Christians. I will describe it with six adjectives, explaining each briefly.

First, as already mentioned, this older way of seeing Christianity was *literalistic* (whether in harder or softer form).

Second, it was *doctrinal*. Being a Christian meant believing Christianity's central doctrinal teachings. In churches that used either the Apostles' Creed or the Nicene Creed regularly, you were a "real" Christian if you could say the creed without crossing your fingers or becoming silent during any of the phrases.

Third, it was quite *moralistic*. By this I mean two things. First, being a Christian meant trying to be good, and being good meant trying to live in accord with the ethical teachings of the Bible, understood as "God's law" (whether understood as a narrow and highly specific code of righteousness or, more broadly, as general principles such as the golden rule or loving one's neighbor as oneself).

The second aspect of moralism seen in the older way of looking at Christianity grew out of the fact that we are not very good at being good. This older way of being Christian was centered on the dynamic of sin, guilt, and forgiveness. Indeed, it is striking how central sin and forgiveness are to this older, conventional version of Christianity. Most Christian worship services include a confession of sin, and most celebrations of the eucharist (also known as the mass, the Lord's supper, or communion) have sin, sacrifice, and forgiveness at their center. Even quite liberal churches emphasize sin and forgiveness. I was struck by this at a recent week-long conference in a liberal Christian setting. Each morning's worship service began with a confession of sin. I thought to myself, "It's nine o'clock in the morning, and we've already been bad."

Fourth, this older way of seeing Christianity was *patriarchal*. It not only used predominantly masculine language for God and people, but also legitimated male-dominated hierarchies in church, society, and family.

Fifth, it was *exclusivistic*. In hard form, Christian exclusivism is the insistence that Jesus is the only way of salvation and Christianity the only true religion. There is also a softer form held by Christians who feel uncomfortable with this claim but fear that letting go of the traditional stance might be un-Christian.

Sixth and finally, this older way of seeing Christianity was *afterlife-oriented*. In the Christianity I learned as a child, the primary meaning of salvation was "going to heaven." Indeed, heaven was so central that if you had been able to convince me at age twelve or so that there was no afterlife, I would have had absolutely no idea why I should be a Christian. Heaven was what it was all about.

Cumulatively, to put this older understanding into a single sentence: "Be a Christian now for the sake of salvation later." To express the same notion in only slightly different words: "Believe in Christianity now for the sake of heaven later." And the emphasis was on "believing"—believing all of this to be true.

But this way of seeing the Bible and Christianity has come undone for the majority of people in Western culture. The natural literalism of my childhood could not endure, just as the natural literalism of most of our ancestors has largely disappeared. Conscious literalism, of course, remains. But for many of us, it is not an option.

It is important to note that this older vision is often seen as *traditional* Christianity by both Christians and non-Christians, and by both conservatives (who defend it) and liberals (who reject it). But this older way of seeing the Bible and Christianity is not "the Christian tradition." Rather, it is a historically conditioned way of seeing the tradition (including the Bible) that has been shaped by the circumstances of the past few centuries. Thus the issue is not whether to keep or abandon the Christian tradition, but a transition from one way of seeing it to another. The question concerns the lenses through which we see and read the Bible and the Christian tradition as a whole.

Seeing Again: Our Cultural Context

Why has this older way of seeing and reading the Bible ceased to be persuasive? Why do the older lenses no longer work? The primary reason: who we have become. By "we," I mean most of us in modern Western culture at the beginning of the twenty-first century. I will describe who we have become with four statements. Though not a comprehensive description of who we are, these statements name four factors that affect the way we see the Bible, Christianity, and religion more broadly.

Religious Pluralism
We are aware of religious pluralism. We are aware of the world's religions in a way that most people have not been for most of human history, even as recently as a century ago. We know about other religions to varying degrees and in a variety of ways: from college religion courses, or from our own reading, or from public television series such as those featuring Joseph Campbell and Huston Smith, or from personal acquaintance with people of

other traditions. This is simply part of our increasingly global awareness.

Thus many of us find the exclusivistic claims of the Christian tradition impossible to accept. This is so for both commonsense reasons and Christian theological reasons. Does it make sense that the creator of the whole universe would be known in only one religious tradition, which (fortunately) just happens to be our own?

Moreover, such a claim is difficult to reconcile with the centrality of grace in the Christian tradition. If one must be a Christian in order to be in right relationship with God, then there is a requirement. By definition, then, even though we may use the language of grace, we are no longer talking about grace.

Historical and Cultural Relativity

We are aware of historical and cultural relativity. In only slightly different words, we know about historical and cultural conditioning. We are aware that how people think is pervasively shaped by the time and place in which they live, as well as by social and economic class.

This applies not only to people in earlier times and other places, but also to us. Our concepts, images, language, knowledge, beliefs—even our thought processes themselves—are all profoundly shaped by culture. They are all conditioned by and relative to the time and place in which they originated. We are thus suspicious that any collection of teachings can be absolute truth or the only truth, just as we are suspicious of attempts to exempt anything from this category (such as the Bible or the religious teachings of our own tradition).

Modernity

We are modern people. By this I mean simply that we live in that period of Western cultural history known as "modernity." Modernity is the cultural mind-set that began with the Enlightenment of the seventeenth century and continues into the present. Modernity is a complex phenomenon, of course, with both impressive achievements and important limitations. For our purposes, I will mention two of its most central features, both closely connected to each other.

First, modernity is characterized by scientific ways of knowing. Indeed, the birth of modern science is the birth of modernity. With modern science came a new epistemology (or theory of how we know): unlike people of earlier eras, we know something to be true today through experimentation and verification.

Second, modernity is marked by what is sometimes called "the modern worldview" or "the Newtonian worldview." A worldview is an image of reality—an understanding of what is real and what is possible. The modern worldview is based on scientific ways of knowing: what is real is that which can be known through the methods of science. Epistemology (how we know) has become ontology (what is real).

The modern worldview yields a material understanding of reality. What is real is the space-time world of matter and energy. Reality is made up of tiny bits and pieces of "stuff," all of them interacting with each other in accord with "natural laws." The result is a picture of the universe as a closed system of cause and effect. Although this worldview has already been superseded in theoretical physics, it continues to operate powerfully in our minds.

Modernity has produced much of great value. Its most obvious accomplishments are in the sciences, technology, and medicine. But its achievements extend beyond those realms into systems of government, human rights, the study of the past, the empathetic awareness of other cultures, and on and on. I am very appreciative of modernity, even as I now mention two of its deeply destructive effects upon religion in general and Christianity and the Bible in particular.

The first of these effects: modernity has made us skeptical about spiritual reality. Modernity's material understanding of reality has made the reality of God problematic for many of us. It is no accident that "death of God" theology emerged in the modern period. It is the logical outcome of absolutizing the modern worldview.

Second, modernity has led us to be preoccupied with factuality—with scientifically verifiable and historically reliable facts. Indeed, modern Western culture is the only culture in human history that has identified truth with factuality. We are "fact fundamentalists": if a statement isn't scientifically or historically factual, it isn't true.[11]

Within the church, both biblical fundamentalists and Christian liberals are often fact fundamentalists. For the former, the Bible must be factually true in order to be true at all (hence they emphasize the literal and historical factuality of biblical texts). The latter have tended to follow a different strategy, seeking to rescue a few facts from the fire. But fundamentalists and liberals alike have agreed: facts are what matter.

The modern preoccupation with factuality has had a pervasive and distorting effect on how we see the Bible and Christianity. During most of the nineteenth and twentieth centuries, many Christians and much of Christian theology were caught between the two sterile choices of literalism (in harder or softer form) and reductionism. The first sought to defend the factual accuracy and uniqueness of the Bible and Christianity. The second tended to reduce the Bible and Christianity to what made sense within the modern worldview. Both are thoroughly modern positions.

A further result: Christianity in the modern period became preoccupied with the dynamic of believing or not believing. For many people, believing "iffy" claims to be true became the central meaning of Christian faith. It is an odd notion—as if what God most wants from us is believing highly problematic statements to be factually true. And if one can't believe them, then one doesn't have faith and isn't a Christian.

The thoroughly modern character of this notion of faith can be seen by comparing what faith meant in the Christian Middle Ages. During those centuries, basically everybody in Christian culture thought the Bible to be true. They had no reason to think otherwise; the Bible's stories from creation through the end of the world were part of the conventional wisdom of the time. Accepting them did not require "faith." Faith had to do with one's relationship to God, not with whether one thought the Bible to be true.[12]

Postmodernity

We live on the boundary of postmodernity. We are not simply modern people; in addition, we are living in the borderland of a new period of cultural history. The central and defining features of that new period have not yet become clear, so we do not know what to call it yet. Hence we simply call it *postmodernity:* it is what comes next.

Like modernity, postmodernity is a large and complex phenomenon. Moreover, some postmodern movements strike me as dead ends. Thus I will not attempt a comprehensive description or definition of postmodernity but will simply highlight three characteristics of primary importance for our purposes.

First, postmodernity is marked by the realization that modernity itself is a culturally conditioned, relative historical construction. The modern worldview is not the final word about reality any more than previous worldviews have been. Postmodernity knows that someday the Newtonian worldview will seem as quaint and archaic as the Ptolemaic worldview, a development that has already occurred among theoretical physicists.

Second, postmodernity is marked by a turn to experience. In a time when traditional religious teachings have become suspect, we tend to trust that which can be known in our own experience. This turn to experience is seen in the remarkable resurgence of interest in spirituality within mainline churches and beyond. Spirituality is the experiential dimension of religion.

Third, postmodernity is marked by a movement beyond fact fundamentalism to the realization that stories can be true without being literally and factually true. This development is reflected in much of contemporary theology's emphasis on metaphorical theology. An obvious point that has often been forgotten during the period of modernity: metaphors and metaphorical narratives can be profoundly true even if they are not literally or factually true.

This realization is central for the way of seeing and reading the Bible that I will be suggesting in this book.

Given who we have become, one of the imperative needs of our time is a re-visioning of the Bible and Christianity. I deliberately hyphenate the word "re-vision" in order to distinguish what I mean from a common meaning of "revision" (without a hyphen). We often use the latter word to describe the improvement of something that has been poorly done—for example, a manuscript or a term paper. But that is not what I mean.

Rather, to re-vision means "to see again." The emphasis upon "seeing again" also reminds us that the older form of Christianity is not "traditional Christianity" but was an earlier way of seeing the Bible and the Christian tradition. What is needed in our time is a way of seeing the Bible that takes seriously the important and legitimate ways in which we differ from our ancestors.

The way of seeing and reading the Bible that I describe in the rest of this book leads to a way of being Christian that has very little to do with believing. Instead, what will emerge is a relational and sacramental understanding of the Christian life. Being Christian, I will argue, is not about believing in the Bible or about believing in Christianity. Rather, it is about a deepening relationship with the God to whom the Bible points, lived within the Christian tradition as a sacrament of the sacred.

NOTES

1. The point is made in a remark I have heard attributed secondhand to Peter Gomes, author of a recent best-selling book on the Bible, *The Good Book* (New York: William Morrow, 1996). Because I am uncertain of Gomes's exact words, I do not use quotation marks, but the gist of the statement is this: Has the Bible become a hindrance to the proclamation of the gospel?
2. Mainline Protestant denominations include most of the older Protestant churches: the United Church of Christ, the Episcopal Church, the United Methodist Church, the Presbyterian Church USA, the Evangelical Lutheran Church in America (the largest Lutheran body), the Christian Church (Disciples), American Baptists, Quakers, and some others. On the Bible, the Catholic Church has more in common with mainline Protestant churches than with fundamentalist and conservative-evangelical churches.
3. For an important essay on variations within conservative attitudes toward

the Bible, see Gabriel Fackre, "Evangelical Hermeneutics: Commonality and Diversity," *Interpretation* 43 (1989), pp. 117–29.
4. See L. William Countryman, *Biblical Authority or Biblical Tyranny?* (Harrisburg, PA: Trinity Press International, 1994), pp. ix–x: "These Christians imagine that the nature of biblical authority is perfectly clear; they often speak of Scripture as inerrant. In fact, however, they have tacitly abandoned the authority of Scripture in favor of a conservative Protestant theology shaped largely in the nineteenth century. This fundamentalist theology they buttress with strings of quotations to give it a biblical flavor, but it predetermines their reading of Scripture so thoroughly that one cannot speak of the Bible as having any independent voice in their churches." Countryman's book as a whole is strongly recommended.
5. I do not mean that the number of mainline Christians is increasing. As virtually everybody knows, membership in mainline churches has declined sharply over the last forty years. Among the reasons: when there was a cultural expectation that everybody would belong to a church, mainline denominations did very well, for they provided a safe and culturally respectable way of being Christian. Once the cultural expectation disappeared (as it did in the final third of the twentieth century), membership in those denominations declined. But among those in mainline churches, the appetite for modern biblical scholarship is remarkable.
6. Attributed to Jerry Falwell by George M. Marsden, *Understanding Fundamentalism and Evangelicalism* (Grand Rapids, MI: Eerdmans, 1991), p. 1. Marsden himself expands the definition slightly: "[A]n American fundamentalist is an evangelical who is militant in opposition to liberal theology in the churches or to changes in cultural values and mores." Marsden affirms that "fundamentalists are a subtype of evangelicals." For American fundamentalism and its relation to evangelicalism, see also Marsden's *Fundamentalism and American Culture* (Oxford: Oxford Univ. Press, 1980). Both books strike me as particularly illuminating and fair.
7. See the important new study of Christian, Jewish, and Muslim fundamentalism (all understood as reactions to modern culture) by Karen Armstrong, *The Battle for God* (New York: Knopf, 2000).
8. See the books by Marsden cited in note 6. The origin of a movement explicitly known as "Fundamentalism" is usually traced to the publication between 1910 and 1915 of twelve paperback volumes known as "The Fundamentals."
9. See the very helpful and interesting article on "Scriptural Authority" in *The Anchor Bible Dictionary*, ed. David Noel Freedman (New York: Doubleday, 1992), vol. 5, pp. 1017–56. The article is written by a number of authors.

On page 1034, Donald K. McKim notes that the second- and third-generation Reformers affirmed "plenary inspiration," the notion that the Bible was directly inspired by God, ". . . in essence a 'dictation' theory of inspiration." Roughly a hundred years after Luther, the Lutheran Johann Quenstedt (1617–88) wrote that the books of the Bible ". . . in their original text are the infallible truth and are free from every error. . . . [E]ach and every thing presented to us in Scripture is absolutely true whether it pertains to doctrine, ethics, history, chronology, topography," and so forth.

On page 1035, Henning Graf Reventlow notes that this was a significant change from Luther: "[W]hereas for Luther the Bible becomes the living word of God in being preached and heard, in the orthodox systems Scripture in its written form is identified with revelation."

10. For natural literalism and the distinction between it and conscious literalism, see Paul Tillich, *Dynamics of Faith* (New York: Harper & Row, 1957), chap. 3, esp. pp. 51–53.

11. I owe this very useful phrase to Huston Smith, "Jesus and the World's Religions" in *Jesus at 2000*, ed. Marcus Borg (Boulder: Westview, 1997), pp. 116–17. In his *Forgotten Truth* (San Francisco: HarperSanFrancisco, 1976, 1992), especially the first chapter, Smith speaks of modernity as marked by scientism, which he carefully distinguishes from science. Scientism affirms that only that which can be known by science is real. To which I would add that modernity is also marked by historicism: historicism affirms that only that which is historically factual matters. Both perspectives are serious mistakes.

12. For this and other meanings of faith, see my *The God We Never Knew* (San Francisco: HarperSanFrancisco, 1997), pp. 168–71.

2

Reading Lenses:
The Bible and God

Christians have always affirmed a close relationship between the Bible and God, just as other religions affirm a close connection between the sacred and their holy scriptures. In this chapter, I begin to describe a way of seeing and reading the Bible again by focusing on how we might see the relationship between the Bible and God. Four topics are most central: the Bible as a human response to God, the Bible as sacred scripture, the Bible as sacrament of the sacred, and the Bible as the Word of God.

The Bible as Human Response to God

Foundational to reading the Bible is a decision about how to see its origin. Does it come from God, or is it a human product? Are we to see and read what it says as a divine product or as a human product?

Through the lenses of natural literalism and its modern descendants, the Bible is seen as a divine product (as already emphasized).

The inspiration of scripture is understood to mean that God guided the writing of the Bible, directly or indirectly. What scripture says, then, ultimately comes from God.

The alternative, of course, is to see the Bible as a human product—the product of two ancient communities. This is the lens through which I see scripture. The Hebrew Bible (the Christian Old Testament) is the product of ancient Israel. The New Testament is the product of the early Christian movement. What the Bible says is the words of those communities, not God's words.

To see the Bible as a human product does not in any way deny the reality of God. Indeed, one of the central premises of this book is that God is real and can be experienced.[1] I have put that as simply as I know how. At the risk of repetition, I mean that God (or "the sacred" or "Spirit," terms that I use synonymously) is a reality known in human experience, and not simply a human creation or projection. Of course, whatever we *say* about the sacred is a human creation. We cannot talk about God (or anything else) except with the words, symbols, stories, concepts, and categories known to us, for they are the only language we have. Nevertheless, we also have *experiences* of "the holy," "the numinous," "the sacred." These experiences go beyond our language, shatter it, and relativize it. I am convinced that the Bible, like sacred literature generally, originates in such experiences. I am also convinced that the Bible (like everything else expressed in words) is a human construction.

There is a third way of seeing the relationship between God and the writing of the Bible: there is no relationship, for there is no God. For this position, the Bible is of course a human product, but it has no religious significance beyond what it tells us about what these ancient people mistakenly thought. This is not how I see scripture.

I see the Bible as a human response to God. Rather than seeing God as scripture's ultimate author, I see the Bible as the response of these two ancient communities to their experience of God. As such, it contains their stories of God, their perceptions of God's character and will, their prayers to and praise of God, their perceptions of the human condition and the paths of deliverance, their religious and ethical practices, and their understanding of what faithfulness to God involves. As the product of these two communities, the Bible thus tells us about how *they* saw things, not about how *God* sees things.

The Difference Our Perspective on the Bible Makes

The justifications for seeing the Bible as a human product are compelling, and the case has been made by many writers.[2] Most basically, it seems to me that a close and careful reading of the Bible makes it impossible to think that what it says comes directly or indirectly from God. So, rather than making the case that the Bible is a human product, I will offer five illustrations of the difference that these two ways of seeing and reading the Bible make.

The first illustration is a story. I sometimes listen to Christian radio. One night I was listening to a call-in show about the Bible and ethical questions. In response to a listener's phone call, the host said, "Let's see what God says about that," and then quoted a passage from the Bible (one that happened to be from Paul). I was a bit stunned by the host's leap from God to scripture, even as I immediately understood it. After all, the host saw what the Bible says as coming from God. But the difference between seeing the Bible as a divine product and seeing it as a human product is apparent in this illustration: Does a passage from Paul tell us what *God* says or how *Paul* saw things?

My second illustration concerns the Genesis stories of creation. If we see the Bible as a divine product, then these are *God's* stories of creation. As God's stories, they cannot be wrong. If we go very far down this road, we may find ourselves attracted to scientific creationism (the attempt to show that a certain kind of "science" supports a literal reading of Genesis). We may even become involved in conflicts about whether Genesis should be taught alongside evolution in biology courses in public schools.

But if we see the Bible as a human product, then we read the opening chapters of Genesis not as God's account of creation but as ancient Israel's stories of creation. Like most ancient cultures, Israel had such stories. If we ask, "What are the chances that ancient Israel's stories of creation contain scientifically accurate information?" the answer would be, "About zero." And if they did, it would be sheer coincidence. Having said that, though, let me add that I think Israel's creation stories are profoundly true—but true as metaphorical or symbolic narratives, not as literally factual accounts.[3]

My third illustration concerns the laws of the Bible. If we think of the Bible as a divine product, then the laws of the Bible are God's laws. To illustrate with a contemporary Christian controversy, the single law in the Hebrew Bible prohibiting homosexual behavior between men is found in Leviticus: "You shall not lie with a male as with a woman; it is an abomination." The penalty (death) is found two chapters later.[4]

If we see the Bible as a divine product, then this is one of God's laws. The ethical question then becomes, "How can one justify setting aside one of the laws of God?" This is, of course, how fundamentalist and many conservative Christians see the issue.

But if we see the Bible as a human product, then the laws of the Hebrew Bible are ancient Israel's laws, and the prohibition of homosexual behavior tells us that such behavior was considered unacceptable in ancient Israel. The ethical question then becomes, "What would be the justification for continuing to see homosexual behavior as ancient Israel did?"

The question becomes even more acute when we realize that this law is embedded in a collection of laws that, among other things, prohibit planting two kinds of seed in the same field and wearing garments made of two kinds of cloth.[5] We do not worry about these matters; most of us wear clothing made of blends without giving it a second thought. We readily recognize some of these prohibitions as the laws of an ancient culture that we are not bound to follow. Why, then, should we single out some as "the laws of God"?

My fourth illustration is a strange little story in Exodus involving Moses, Zipporah (his wife), and their son.[6] They are on their way back to Egypt, in obedience to God's commissioning of Moses as the liberator of Israel. We are told, "On the way, at a place where they spent the night, the LORD met him and tried to kill him." Zipporah then circumcises their son and touches Moses' feet with the foreskin. The result: God lets him alone; the divine intent to kill Moses vanishes.

If we see the Bible as a divine product, the question becomes, "Why would God want to kill Moses—especially since Moses has been chosen by God and is doing what God has commanded him to do?" The question is impossible to answer. It suggests a disturbingly capricious and malevolent God. Appealing to the familiar "God's ways are not our ways" seems like a dodge, not an adequate response.

But if we see the Bible as a human product, we realize that this is a story told by ancient Israel. The question then becomes, "Why would Israel tell this story?" The answer may still not be clear (presumably it has something to do with the importance of circumcision), but at least we are not left with the dilemma of seeing it as a true story about God.

Because the previous three illustrations have been taken from the Hebrew Bible, I conclude with one from the New Testament. The passage is from I Timothy, a letter attributed to Paul but almost certainly not written by him:[7]

> Women should dress themselves modestly and decently in suitable clothing, not with their hair braided, or with gold, pearls, or expensive clothes, but with good works, as is proper for women who profess reverence for God. Let a woman learn in silence with full submission. I permit no woman to teach or to have authority over a man; she is to keep silent. For Adam was formed first, then Eve; and Adam was not deceived, but the woman was deceived and became a transgressor. Yet she will be saved through childbearing, provided they continue in faith and love and holiness, with modesty.[8]

This is an extraordinary passage. Not only are women not to teach or have authority over men, but they are not to braid their hair or wear pearls or gold or expensive clothes. Furthermore, they are held responsible for the origin of sin in the world: it was the woman who was deceived, not the man. The "good news" is that women can be saved—through childbearing.

If the Bible is seen as a divine product, then these are God's restrictions on the behavior and roles of women. Indeed, for those Protestant churches that continue to prohibit the ordination of women, this is the way the passage is seen (even though the other restrictions are commonly ignored).[9] For them, the ordination of women is against "God's Word."

However, if the Bible is seen as a human product, then this passage tells us about how an early Christian author—a man— saw things. As just mentioned, Paul almost certainly did not write these words. The author is commonly seen as a second- or third-generation follower of Paul writing in his name. But it is equally possible that the author is not a follower of Paul, but a "corrector" seeking to negate the remarkable gender egalitarianism of the early Christian movement. When the Bible is seen as a human product, the contrast between this text and other texts in the New Testament requires that we recognize more than one voice in early Christianity speaking about the role of women and that we seek to discern which voice to honor.

Thus much is at stake in whether we see the Bible as a human or a divine product. When we are not completely clear and candid about the Bible being a human and not a divine product, we create the possibility of enormous confusion.

Why Our Perspective Needs to Be Either-Or

To anticipate a possible objection: Why see the question as an either-or choice? Why not see the Bible as *both* divine and human? In my experience, affirming that it is both only compounds the confusion.

When the Bible is seen as both divine and human, we have two options. One is to say that it is *all* divine and *all* human.

That may sound good, but it leaves us with the dilemma of treating all of scripture as divine revelation. More typically in my experience, affirming that the Bible is both divine and human leads to the attempt to separate the divine parts from the human parts—as if some of it comes from God and some is a human product. The parts that come from God are then given authority, and the others are not. But the parts that we think come from God are normally the parts we see as important, and thus we simply confer divine authority on what matters to us, whether we be conservatives or liberals.

To use an example: most Christians who think of the Bible as both divine and human would say that the Ten Commandments are among the parts that come from God. They seem important in a way that the prohibition against wearing garments made of two kinds of cloth does not.

But a moment's reflection suggests that the Ten Commandments are also a human product. They are written from a male point of view: for example, they prohibit coveting your neighbor's wife but say nothing about coveting your neighbor's husband.[10] Moreover, the commandments against stealing, adultery, murder, bearing false witness, and so forth are simply rules that make it possible for humans to live together in community. Divine genius is not required to come up with rules like these. The point is not that the Ten Commandments are unimportant. Rather, the point is that their human origin is apparent.

Thus the lens I am advocating does not see the Bible as a whole as divine in origin, or some parts as divine and some as human. It is *all* a human product, though generated in response to God. As such, it contains ancient Israel's perceptions and misperceptions of what life with God involves, just as it contains the early Christian movement's perceptions and misperceptions.

Thus it is we who must discern how to read and interpret, how to hear and value, its various voices. The Bible does not come with footnotes that say, "This passage reflects the will of God; the next passage does not," or "This passage is valid for all time; the previous passage is not." So also the Bible does not come with footnotes that say, "This passage is to be read literally; that passage is not." Reading the stories of creation or the stories of Jesus' birth literally involves an interpretive decision (namely, a decision to read them literally) equally as much as does the decision to read them metaphorically.

Thus any and every claim about what a passage of scripture means involves interpretation. There is no such thing as a noninterpretive reading of the Bible, unless our reading consists simply of making sounds in the air. As we read the Bible, then, we should ask not, "What is God saying?" but "What is the ancient author or community saying?"[11]

The Bible as Sacred Scripture

Though the Bible is a human product, it is also sacred scripture for three religious traditions. The Hebrew Bible is sacred for Judaism, the Hebrew Bible and the New Testament are sacred for Christianity, and both are sacred for Islam (though neither is given the same holy status as the Koran).

Sacred Status
What does it mean to refer to the Bible as "sacred scripture"?[12] I begin by noting that the books of the Bible were not sacred when they were written. Paul, for example, would have been amazed to know that his letters to his communities were to become sacred scripture. Rather, the various parts of the Bible became sacred through a process that took several centuries.

The process whereby the Bible became sacred is known as "canonization." So far as we know (and we do not know much), the canonization process did not involve official councils that met and made decisions. Rather, it was gradual, happening in stages. The first five books of the Hebrew Bible (the Law, also known as the Torah or the Pentateuch) were apparently regarded as sacred by about 400 BCE. The second part of the Hebrew Bible (the Prophets) had achieved sacred status by about 200 BCE. The third part (the Writings) became canonical by about 100 CE. The canon of the Hebrew Bible was then complete.

For the twenty-seven books of the New Testament, the process took about three centuries. Though most of the documents now in the New Testament were written by the year 100, the first list that mentions all twenty-seven of them as having special status is from the year 367.

The awareness that the Bible became sacred scripture over a period of centuries has implications for our understanding of its origin, status, and authority. To speak of the Bible as sacred addresses not its origin but its status within a religious community. Any document is sacred only because it is sacred *for a particular community.* To mistake status for origin leads to the kind of confusion I described in the previous section of this chapter.

For Christians, the status of the Bible as sacred scripture means that it is the most important collection of writings we know. These are the primary writings that define who we are in relation to God and who we are as a community and as individuals. This is the book that has shaped us and will continue to shape us.

Because of the importance of this point, I will make it in another way. In common with many scholars of religion, I see each of the world's religions as a "cultural-linguistic world." Two things are meant by this somewhat abstract phrase. First, each religion emerges within a particular culture and uses language and symbols from that culture (even if it also subverts or challenges the central values and understandings of that culture). Thus religions are born within an existing cultural-linguistic world.

Second, if the new religion survives over time, it becomes a cultural-linguistic world in its own right. As such, it provides a world in which its followers live. Its stories and practices, its teachings and rituals, become the lenses through which its members see reality and their own lives. It becomes the primary basis of identity and vision.

Within this framework of understanding, the Bible as sacred scripture is the foundation of the Christian cultural-linguistic world. The Bible is the "constitution" of the Christian world, not in the sense of being a collection of laws but in the sense of being its foundation.

The Authority of the Bible

To see the Bible as sacred in status and not origin also leads to a different way of seeing the authority of the Bible. The older, conventional way of seeing the Bible grounded scripture's authority in its origin: the Bible was sacred because it came from God. The result was a monarchical model of biblical authority. Like an ancient monarch, the Bible stands over us, telling us what to believe and do. But seeing the Bible as sacred in its status leads to a different model of biblical authority. Rather than being an authority standing above us, the Bible is the ground of the world in which Christians live.

The result: the monarchical model of biblical authority is replaced by a dialogical model of biblical authority. In other words, the biblical canon names the primary collection of ancient documents with which Christians are to be in a continuing dialogue. This continuing conversation is definitive and constitutive of Christian identity. If the dialogue ceases or becomes faint, then we cease to be Christian and become something else. Thus the authority of the Bible is its status as our primary ancient conversational partner.

Yet because the Bible is a human product as well as sacred scripture, the continuing dialogue needs to be a critical conversation. There are parts of the Bible that we will decide need not or should not be honored, either because we discern that they were relevant to ancient times but not to our own, or because we discern that they were never the will of God.[13]

But critical dialogue with the Bible implies not simply that we make discerning judgments about the texts. It also means that we allow the texts to shape and judge us. As we read the Bible, we are not only to bring our critical intelligence with us, but also to listen. I often tell my students that reading well involves listening well—seeking to hear what the text is saying to us and not simply absorbing the text into what we already think.

To be Christian means to live within the world created by the Bible. We are to listen to it well and let its central stories shape our vision of God, our identity, and our sense of what faithfulness to God means. It is to shape our imagination, that part of our psyches in which our foundational images of reality and life reside. We are to be a community shaped by scripture. The purpose of our continuing dialogue with the Bible as sacred scripture is nothing less than that.[14]

The Bible as Sacrament of the Sacred

Thus one major function of the Bible is the shaping of Christian vision and identity. The Bible has another primary function as well, and it is a further aspect of the relationship between the Bible and God. Namely, the Bible is a sacrament of the sacred.

In the Christian tradition, the word "sacrament" often refers to one of the specific sacraments: for Protestants, the two sacraments of baptism and the eucharist; for Catholics, those two plus five more. Central to the definition of "sacrament" in this particular sense is that something that is sacramental is "a means of grace."

The word "sacrament" also has a broader meaning. In the study of religion, a sacrament is commonly defined as a mediator of the sacred, a vehicle by which God becomes present, a means through which the Spirit is experienced. This meaning thus includes the two (or seven) Christian Sacraments even as it is broader. Virtually anything can become sacramental: nature, music, prayer, birth, death, sexuality, poetry, persons, pilgrimage, even participation in sports, and so forth. Things are sacramental when they become occasions for the experience of God, moments when the Spirit becomes present, times when the sacred becomes an experiential reality.

The Bible often functions in this sacramental way in the lives of Christians. It did so, for example, in the conversion experiences of many of the central figures of Christian history. Augustine's conversion experience happened when he heard a child singing, "Take up and read," which led him to read a passage in Paul's letter to the Romans that changed his life. Martin Luther's breakthrough from anxious striving to the experience of grace, as well as the movement of the Spirit in John Wesley's heart, happened through immersion in scripture. In each case, they experienced the Bible as a means whereby the Spirit addressed them in the present.

The sacramental use of the Bible is also among the spiritual practices of both Jews and Christians. Meditation upon the Torah is an ancient Jewish practice. In the Christian tradition, a spiritual practice designed by Ignatius of Loyola involves meditating upon the images of a biblical text until they become animated by the Spirit. Another practice, *lectio divina*, involves entering a contemplative state and listening while a passage of scripture is read aloud a number of times with periods of silence between each reading. In these examples, the purpose of the practice is not to read or hear the Bible for information or content. Rather, the purpose is to listen for the Spirit of God speaking through the words of the biblical text.

For many Christians the Bible sometimes becomes sacramental in private devotional reading. As with the practices mentioned above, the purpose of devotional reading is not acquisition of content. Rather, it is openness to the experience of God addressing the reader through a phrase or verse, openness to a sense of the Spirit present within. In such moments the Bible becomes sacramental, a means of grace and mediator of the sacred. God "speaks" through the words of the biblical text.

To see the Bible as a sacrament of the sacred also connects us back to the Bible as a human product. The bread and wine of the Christian sacrament of the eucharist are manifestly human products. Somebody made the bread and somebody made the wine. We do not think of the bread and wine as "perfect" (whatever that might mean). Rather, to use a common eucharistic phrase, we affirm that "in, with, and under" these manifestly human products of bread and wine, Christ becomes present to us. So also "in, with, and under" the human words of the Bible, the Spirit of God addresses us.

In the worship services of many denominations, including my own, the following words are spoken after the reading of a passage from the Bible: "The Word of the Lord." With my emphasis on the Bible as a human product, I sometimes joke that we should say instead, "Some thoughts from ancient Israel," or "Some thoughts from the early Christian movement." But when I am being serious rather than flippant, I find the words used in the New Zealand Anglican Book of Common Prayer exactly right: "Hear what the Spirit is saying to the church." The Spirit of God speaks through the human words of these ancient documents: the Bible is a sacrament of the sacred.

The Bible as the Word of God

The sacramental function of scripture leads to a final point about the relationship between God and the Bible: the Bible as "the Word of God." As already mentioned, speaking of the Bible as "the Word of God" has often led Christians to see the Bible as coming from God. By now it is obvious that the lenses I am prescribing for reading the Bible do not see it that way.

What then does it mean to call the Bible "the Word of God"? It is important to emphasize that the Christian tradition throughout its history has spoken of the Bible as the *Word* of God (capital *W* and singular), not as the *words* of God (lowercase *w* and plural). If it had used the latter phrase, then one might reasonably claim that believing the words of the Bible to be God's words is intrinsic to being Christian.

But the use of a capital *W* and the singular suggests a different meaning. Namely, "Word" is being used in a metaphorical and nonliteral sense. As with metaphors generally, this one resonates with more than one nuance of meaning. A word is a means of communication, involving both speaking and hearing. A word is a means of disclosure; we disclose or reveal ourselves through words. Words bridge the distance between ourselves and others: we commune and become intimate through words.

To call the Bible the Word of God is to see it in all of these ways, and no doubt more. The Bible is a means of divine self-disclosure. The traditional theological phrase for this is "the Bible as the revelation of God." In the Bible, as the foundation of the Christian cultural-linguistic world, Christians find the disclosure of God—not because the Bible is the words of God but because the Bible contains the primary stories and traditions that disclose the character and will of God.

Seeing the Bible as the Word of God also underlines its sacramental function: the Bible's words sometimes become a mediator of the sacred whereby the Spirit addresses us in the present. In short, calling the Bible the Word of God refers not to its origin but to its status and function.

Concluding Metaphors for Seeing the Bible

In the modern period, Christians have often emphasized believing in the Bible. I conclude this chapter with three metaphors, all suggesting a very different way of seeing the relationship between Christians and the Bible.

A Finger Pointing to the Moon

The first metaphor comes from the Buddhist tradition. Buddhists often speak of the teaching of the Buddha as "a finger pointing to the moon." The metaphor helps guard against the mistake of thinking that being a Buddhist means believing in Buddhist teaching—that is, believing in the finger. As the metaphor implies, one is to see (and pay attention to) that to which the finger points.

To apply the metaphor to the Bible, the Bible is like a finger pointing to the moon. Christians sometimes make the mistake of thinking that being Christian is about believing in the finger rather than seeing the Christian life as a relationship to that to which the finger points.

The Bible as Lens

Until now, I have been speaking about the lenses through which we see the Bible. Now I am applying the lens metaphor to the Bible itself: the Bible is a lens. I owe this use of the metaphor to a student who a few years ago took my introductory-level course on the Bible. About two weeks into the term, he said to me, "I think I'm beginning to get it. You're saying that the Bible is like a lens through which we see God, but some people think it's important to believe in the lens."

His simple statement has stayed with me. The point, of course, is the same as the finger metaphor: there is a crucial difference between believing in the lens and using the lens as a way of seeing that which is beyond the lens.

The Bible as Sacrament

For my final metaphor, I return to the Bible as sacrament. Now, though, I extend the metaphor so that it includes the Christian tradition as a whole: the Bible as well as Christian creeds, liturgies, rituals, practices, hymns, music, art, and so forth. When one sees Christianity as a sacrament of the sacred, being Christian is not about believing in Christianity. That would be like believing in the bread and wine of the eucharist rather than letting the bread and wine do their sacramental work of mediating the presence of Christ. It would be like believing in the finger or the lens.

Rather, being Christian is about a relationship to the God who is mediated by the Christian tradition as sacrament. To be Christian is to live within the Christian tradition as a sacrament and let it do its transforming work within and among us.

NOTES

1. I cannot demonstrate this, of course, though I think I can make a persuasive case against those who think they can demonstrate God's nonreality. My study of religious experience in many cultures over many centuries and my acquaintance with contemporary religious experience have led me to the conviction that God is real and can be experienced, and that such experiences occur across cultures and religious traditions. See chapter 2 of my *The God We Never Knew* (San Francisco: HarperSanFrancisco, 1997).

2. Among recent books, see Paul J. Achtemeier, *Inspiration and Authority: The Nature and Function of Christian Scripture* (Peabody, MA: Hendrickson, 1999); John Shelby Spong, *Rescuing the Bible from Fundamentalism* (San Francisco: HarperSanFrancisco, 1991), esp. pp. 1–36; L. William Countryman, *Biblical Authority or Biblical Tyranny?* (Harrisburg, PA: Trinity Press International, 1994), pp. 1–15.

3. See chap. 4.

4. Lev. 18.22 and 20.13.

5. Lev. 19.19.

6. Exod. 4.24–26

7. I Tim. 2.9–15. Virtually all mainline biblical scholars see I and II Timothy and Titus (known together as "the pastoral epistles") as relatively late documents written around the beginning of the second century, some forty years or more after the death of Paul. In antiquity, it was acceptable practice to write in the name of a revered figure of the past.

8. The shift in pronouns in the last verse is puzzling. "She" obviously refers to woman/women; "they" could refer to women, or it could refer to the children born of "childbearing."

9. The Catholic prohibition of ordaining women as priests has a different basis.

10. Exod. 20.17 and Deut. 5.21.

11. Important clarification: I am not saying that the meaning of a biblical text is confined or restricted to what the ancient author or community said. As I will say in the next chapter, a metaphorical reading of the Bible yields meanings beyond the ancient historical intention of the text.

12. For a superb treatment of the meaning of "scripture," see Wilfred Cantwell Smith, *What Is Scripture?* (Minneapolis: Fortress, 1993). Smith argues that scripture is "a human activity," a phrase with several meanings: the writings that become scripture are produced by humans, are then declared to be scripture by a community, and then function to shape the lives of the people who regard them as scripture. See also the helpful book by John P. Burgess, *Why Scripture Matters* (Louisville: Westminster John Knox, 1998).

13. I do not wish to provide a comprehensive list, but an example of each may be helpful. (1) Paul's counsel about whether it is permissible to eat meat left over from pagan sacrifices was relevant to his time, though not very much if at all to our time. (2) I cannot believe that it was ever God's will that the women and children of one's enemies in war should be slaughtered, to use an example from the Hebrew Bible; or that it is God's will that the majority of the earth's population be destroyed at the second coming of Christ, to use an example from the New Testament.

14. This is how the Bible functioned in earlier periods of Christian history. See the comment by Rowan A. Greer in *The Anchor Bible Dictionary*, ed. David Noel Freedman (New York: Doubleday, 1992), vol. 5, p. 1028: During the period of the early church, "Scriptural authority was not so much a matter of propositions or of the application of principles to cases as a question of the way in which the lore of the church's past persuasively shaped the corporate lives of Christians."

3

Reading Lenses:
History and Metaphor

In this chapter, I move from ways of seeing the Bible to the more specific topic of reading the Bible. In radical shorthand, I call the method I will develop a "historical-metaphorical approach." It presupposes the central claims about the Bible made in the previous chapter: its origin as a human response to God, its status for Christians as sacred scripture, and its functions as foundation of the Christian world and sacrament of the sacred.

The Historical-Metaphorical Approach

Both adjectives in the phrase "historical-metaphorical approach" are crucially important. As shorthand, they are large umbrellas. I will compactly define each before describing them at greater length.

By "historical approach," I mean all the methods that are relevant to discerning the ancient historical meanings of biblical texts. The chief concern of the historical approach is the past-tense question, "What *did* this text mean *in the ancient historical setting in which it was written?*" By "metaphorical approach," I mean most broadly a nonliteral way of reading biblical texts. A metaphorical reading does not confine itself to the literal, factual, and historical meanings of a text. It moves beyond to the question, "What does this story mean as a *story*, independent of its historical factuality?"

The Historical Approach

The historical approach focuses on the historical illumination of a text in its ancient context. As a large umbrella category, this approach covers all the methods of historical criticism that have been developed by biblical scholars over the last few centuries. The word "criticism" is perhaps unfortunate, simply because in popular usage it often has the negative meaning of fault-finding (as when we say, "Oh, don't be so critical"). But in the phrase "historical criticism," "criticism" means "discernment"—in other words, making discerning judgments about historical matters.

What It Is The historical approach includes the traditional methods of source criticism, form criticism, redaction criticism, and canonical criticism.[1] It also includes more recent interdisciplinary methods of historical study. Sometimes called "social-scientific criticism," these involve the use of models and insights derived from studies of preindustrial agrarian societies, honor-shame societies, cultural anthropology, and so forth. These interdisciplinary methods are especially helpful for constructing the ancient context in which biblical texts were spoken or written. They help us to understand the very different cultural worlds in which the Bible originated.

The focus of a historical approach is twofold: the *historical meaning* of a text in its *historical context*. The context in which words are spoken or written, or deeds are done, pervasively shapes their meaning. The word "context" suggests as much: the Latin prefix *con* means "with." Thus con-text is that which goes with a text.

Why It Matters Though devotional use of the Bible can be quite independent of the historical approach, the latter is indispensable for genuinely hearing the Bible as a collection of documents from the past. It recognizes that the Bible as a whole and its individual texts are historical artifacts: things made in the past. To say the obvious, they are artifacts from the *distant* past. The Hebrew Bible was written from approximately the middle of the tenth century BCE to the middle of the second century BCE.[2] The New Testament was written from approximately 50 CE to the early or middle 100s CE.

Historical study takes seriously the vast historical and cultural distance between us and the biblical past. It recognizes the truth of the opening lines of the novel *The Go-Between:* "The past is a foreign country. They do things differently there."[3] It seeks to understand the Bible as a collection of ancient documents produced in worlds very different from our own.

The historical study of the Bible is one of the glories of modern scholarship. It has been immensely illuminating. Without it, much of the Bible would remain simply opaque. Setting biblical passages in their ancient context makes them come alive. It enables us to see meanings in these ancient texts that would otherwise be hidden from our sight. It unearths meanings that otherwise would remain buried in the past. Moreover, it allows us to hear the strangeness of these texts that come to us from worlds strange to us. Thus it helps us to avoid reading the Bible simply with our current agendas in mind and frees the Bible to speak with its own voices.

Limitations Yet the historical approach has its limitations. Some of these are due to the way it has been practiced in the modern period. When wedded to the modern worldview, with its skepticism about spiritual reality and its preoccupation with factuality, it sometimes leads to a "flattening" of the texts. That biblical texts may be saying something about God, or about genuine experiences of God, or about events that go beyond the boundaries of what is deemed possible by the modern worldview—these alternatives are often not addressed.

Moreover, much of modern biblical scholarship is highly technical and specialized, scholars often disagree with each other, and little seems certain. The result is that many people who went to seminary or graduate school in biblical studies motivated by a strong sense of Christian vocation and love for the Bible have experienced modern biblical scholarship as taking the Bible away from them. Some, clergy and scholars alike, have not recovered. For some, the Bible remains in shreds. Others launch broadside attacks on historical criticism, lambasting it as bankrupt.[4] But even those who attack it (unless they are fundamentalists) cannot do without it.

There is one further limitation, and it is intrinsic. Namely, historical criticism treats only the ancient meaning of the text. Its focus, as mentioned in the introduction to this chapter, is the past-tense question, "What did this text mean in and for the ancient community that produced it?" Unless supplemented by another approach, historical criticism leaves the text imprisoned in the past.

The Metaphorical Approach

The metaphorical approach enables us to see and affirm meanings that go beyond the particularity of what the texts meant in their ancient setting. Like the historical approach, it is a large umbrella, encompassing a range of disciplines. What everything beneath the umbrella has in common is a way of reading the Bible that moves beyond the historical meanings of texts.

What It Is I am using the words "metaphor" and "metaphorical" in a broad rather than a narrow sense. In its narrow meaning, "metaphor" refers to a very specific kind of comparative language and is distinguished from its close cousin "simile": a simile explicitly uses the word "like" as it makes a comparison, whereas a metaphor does not. For example, "My love is *like* a red, red rose" is a simile. "My love *is* a red, red rose" is a metaphor. In this chapter and book, I use "metaphor" and "metaphorical" in a much broader sense, however.

Metaphorical language is intrinsically nonliteral. It simultaneously affirms and negates: x is y, and x is not y. The statement "My love is a red, red rose" affirms that my beloved is a rose even as it negates it. My beloved is *not* a rose, unless I am literally in love with a flower. Rather, there is something about my beloved that is *like* a rose.

This realization leads to a second characteristic of metaphorical language: it has more than one nuance or resonance of meaning. In terms of its Greek roots, "metaphor" means "to carry with," and what metaphor carries or bears is resonances or associations of meaning. The use of the plural is deliberate: a metaphor cannot be reduced to a single meaning. (If it *could,* one might just as well express that meaning in nonmetaphorical language.) To return to the rose example again, to say, "My love is a red, red rose" calls up more than one association. The metaphor may point to my beloved's beauty, to her pleasant smell, to her being in full bloom; it may also point to ephemerality and finitude (since, like a rose, my beloved will wither and die); it may even point to difficulties, for there are thorns among the roses. In short, metaphorical language is intrinsically multivalent, with a plurality of associations.

"Metaphor" also means "to see as": to see something as something else. Metaphor is linguistic art or verbal art. If you can bear the rose example one more time, I *see* my beloved *as* a rose. Or, to use a biblical example, we can *see* the story of the exodus *as* a metaphorical narrative of the divine-human relationship, depicting both the human predicament and the means of deliverance.

A metaphorical approach to the Bible thus emphasizes metaphors and their associations. It emphasizes *seeing,* not *believing.* The point is not to believe in a metaphor, but to see in light of it.

Finally, metaphors can be profoundly true, even though they are not literally true. Metaphor is poetry plus, not factuality minus.[5] That is, metaphor is not less than fact, but more. Some things are best expressed in metaphorical language; others can be expressed only in metaphorical language.

A metaphorical approach to the Bible is central to a number of types of modern interpretation. These types include narrative theology, which focuses on the meaning of stories as stories, and some forms of literary criticism, in which the focus is on how the texts function as literature independent of their original historical meanings.

Archetypal criticism, a third type of metaphorical approach, involves the study of archetypal symbols and stories, which are typically transcultural. Archetypal criticism most obviously leads to a psychological reading of biblical texts. But it moves beyond the psychological as well, for such stories and symbols sometimes also connect to social realities.[6]

A metaphorical approach also includes some ancient types of interpretation. The writers of the New Testament frequently used texts from the Hebrew Bible in a nonliteral way. The practice continued in the "spiritual" or "allegorical" reading of scripture that was widespread in Christianity from the second century through the Middle Ages. During these centuries, Christian theologians often spoke of four levels of interpretation of biblical texts: the literal, the allegorical, the anagogical, and the tropological.[7] The details of these levels do not matter for my present purpose, which is simply to indicate the scope and antiquity of metaphorical interpretation.

Justification The justification for a metaphorical approach is at least twofold. First, some of the biblical narratives are manifestly metaphorical and thus require a metaphorical interpretation. This realization is not modern, but ancient. In the 200s, an early Christian theologian and biblical scholar named Origen distinguished between the "spiritual" and "bodily" meanings of the Bible. By "spiritual meanings," he meant approximately what I mean by metaphorical. By "bodily meanings," he meant literal-factual meanings. Using these distinctions, Origen argued that while the Bible as a whole is to be read in a spiritual sense, some parts are *not* to be read in a bodily sense.[8]

But even when a biblical narrative is not manifestly metaphorical, there is justification for reading it with a metaphorical approach. The reason is that the Bible is a "religious classic."[9] A classic is a piece of literature that has endured through time and has been (and continues to be) read and reread in new settings. By definition, a classic has a surplus of meaning. Its meaning is not confined to the intention of its author or to its original setting.

Limitations The primary limitation of a metaphorical approach is the danger that the imagination will roam too freely, producing uncontrolled, fanciful interpretations that have little or nothing to do with the actual text.

A classic example is Augustine's interpretation of the familiar parable of the Good Samaritan in the gospel of Luke.[10] As Jesus tells the story, a man traveling from Jerusalem to Jericho is attacked and beaten by robbers and left lying on the road half-dead. Two temple officials (a priest and a Levite) come along and pass by on the other side of the road. Then a Samaritan, a member of a despised group, comes along, attends to the wounded man's injuries, puts him on a donkey, and takes him to an inn. For Jesus, it is a story of what it means to be compassionate.

Augustine read the story quite differently. I mention here only a few of the meanings he found. The man traveling from Jerusalem to Jericho is Adam. The thieves who attack him are the devil and his angels. They beat Adam by persuading him to sin and strip him of his immortality. The priest and Levite who pass by are representatives of the old dispensation, which cannot provide salvation. The Samaritan who comes to his aid is Jesus. The oil with which he anoints Adam's wounds is the comfort of good hope. The animal upon which Adam is put is the flesh of the incarnation. The inn to which Adam is taken is the church, and the innkeeper is St. Paul. Thus, on Augustine's reading, the parable becomes an allegory of the Christian story of salvation from the fall of Adam through Jesus to Paul.

It is ingenious, and too clever by half. The problem, of course, is that this reading has nothing to do with the text. Neither Jesus nor the author of Luke can be imagined to have meant anything like this. Not only is it completely fanciful, but it obscures the meaning of the parable and thus in a sense destroys the text.

So the metaphorical approach needs controls: one cannot claim a metaphorical reading that has no conceivable connection to the text. The controls should be "soft," however, since one of the main functions of the metaphorical approach is to keep a text from being confined to the past.

The needed controls are provided in part by the historical approach and in part by the discernment of the community to which the interpretation is offered. Several factors enter into the discernment of the community: their sense of the meaning of the Bible as a whole, their understanding of the Christian story as a whole, and their sense of "fittingness." If an interpretation makes sense to nobody other than the individual who offers it, it is unlikely to have any meaningful significance.

In short, the historical and metaphorical approaches to reading the Bible need each other. The historical needs the metaphorical so that the text is not imprisoned in the past. The metaphorical needs the historical so that it does not become subjective fancy.

In the rest of this chapter, I have two purposes. The first is to suggest that the Bible is a combination of history and metaphor and therefore requires this approach. The second is to illustrate the kind of reading that results from this approach.

The Bible as History and Metaphor

The Bible is a combination of history and metaphor. To say the same thing only slightly differently, the Bible is a combination of historical memories and metaphorical narratives.

The meaning of "history remembered" or "historical memories" is obvious. Some events reported in the Bible really happened, and the ancient communities of Israel and the early Christian movement preserved the memory of their having happened. Indeed, the biblical story is grounded in the history of these two communities.

The meaning of "metaphorical narratives" requires more explanation. In the Bible, such narratives fall into two categories. The first encompasses narratives in which an event that happened (or may have happened) is given a metaphorical meaning. The second covers purely metaphorical narratives.

Narratives That Metaphorize History

The first type of metaphorical narrative is a story that combines both history and metaphor; it results in what we might call "history metaphorized." A historical event lies behind the story, but the way the story is told gives the narrative a metaphorical meaning as well. For example, I think there are good historical grounds for saying that Jesus really did restore sight to some blind people. One or more of the stories reporting such an event probably reflect historical memory. But the way these stories are told gives them a metaphorical meaning as well.

The way the author of Mark's gospel tells the stories of two blind men to whom Jesus gave sight provides an illuminating example. The two stories frame the great central section of that gospel—a section that describes Jesus' final journey to Jerusalem, contains three solemn sayings about his impending death and resurrection, and speaks of discipleship as following Jesus on this journey.[11]

At the beginning of this section, Mark places the story of the blind man of Bethsaida. Jesus restores his sight in two stages. After the first, the blind man sees people, but not clearly: "They look like trees, walking." After Jesus lays his hands on him a second time, the blind man sees "everything clearly."[12]

At the end of the section is the story of a blind beggar named Bartimaeus. He cries out to Jesus, "Have compassion on me!" Jesus asks, "What do you want me to do for you?" In superbly evocative language, Bartimaeus expresses his deepest desire: "Let me see again." Then, we are told, "Bartimaeus regained his sight and followed Jesus on the way."[13]

By placing these stories where he does, the author of Mark gives them a metaphorical meaning, even as one or both of them

may reflect history remembered. Namely, gaining one's sight—
seeing again—is seeing the way of Jesus. That way, that path, involves journeying with him from Galilee to Jerusalem, the place
of death and resurrection, of endings and beginnings. To see
that is to have one's eyes opened.

Thus the way Mark uses these stories results in history metaphorized. Moreover, the section as a whole provides yet another
example of history remembered and metaphorized. History
remembered: Jesus really did make a final journey to Jerusalem.
History metaphorized: the way the story of that journey is
told turns it into a metaphorical narrative about the path of discipleship.

Purely Metaphorical Narratives

The second type of metaphorical narrative consists of stories that
are *purely* metaphorical. No particular historical event lies behind
them. Rather, the stories as a whole are metaphorical or symbolic. Examples of this category from the Hebrew Bible are Israel's stories of creation and human beginnings (the subject of
the next chapter), the story of Jonah and the huge fish that swal-
lowed him, and the story of the sun standing still in the time of
Joshua. Examples from the New Testament include some of the
early Christian movement's stories about Jesus—his birth, walking on water, multiplying loaves and fish, changing water into
wine, and so forth.

The decision about whether to see a story as a purely
metaphorical narrative involves two factors. The first centers on
elements within the story itself. Does the story *look* as if it is reporting something that happened, or are there signs within the
story suggesting that it is to be read symbolically? Israel's stories
of the world's beginnings contain many such signals, and the
stories about Jesus just mentioned make use of rich symbolic
motifs drawn from the Hebrew Bible.

The second factor involves a judgment about what I call
"the limits of the spectacular." I deliberately speak of "the
spectacular" rather than "miracles." The common modern un-

derstanding of miracles, accepted by both those who affirm and those who deny them, presupposes an understanding of the universe as a closed system of natural laws. Miracles are understood as supernatural interventions by a God "out there" into an otherwise completely predictable system of natural cause and effect. Because I do not accept that way of thinking about God's relation to the universe, I avoid the term "miracles." "The spectacular," on the other hand, simply refers to events that go beyond what we commonly think to be possible.

Thus the question whether there are "limits to the spectacular" asks, "Are there some things that never happen anywhere?" As we think about that question, it is important not to draw the limits too narrowly, as the worldview of modernity does. More things are possible, and more things happen, than the modern worldview allows.

For example, I think that Jesus really did perform paranormal healings and that they cannot simply be explained in psychosomatic terms. I am even willing to consider that spectacular phenomena such as levitation perhaps happen. But do virgin births, multiplying loaves and fish, and changing water into wine ever happen anywhere? If I became persuaded that they do, then I would entertain the possibility that the stories about Jesus reporting such events also contain history remembered. But what I cannot do as a historian is to say that Jesus could do such things even though nobody else has ever been able to. Thus I regard these as purely metaphorical narratives.

The recognition that the Bible contains both history and metaphor has an immediate implication: the ancient communities that produced the Bible often metaphorized their history. Indeed, this is the way they invested their stories with meaning. But we, especially in the modern period, have often historicized their metaphors. To make the same point only slightly differently: they often mythologized their history (again, for the sake of expressing meaning), while we have tended to literalize their mythology. And when one literalizes metaphor or myth, the result is nonsense. On the other hand, when one recognizes a metaphorical narrative as such, the result is a powerful story. This leads directly to the next point.

The Bible as Stories about the Divine-Human Relationship

Though the Bible contains more than stories, a surprisingly large amount of it consists of narratives. There are hundreds of individual stories, as well as what I have elsewhere called "macro-stories," stories that shape the Bible as a whole.[14] Moreover, to a large extent, these stories—both individual and macro—are about the divine-human relationship. The Hebrew Bible is ancient Israel's story (and stories) of her relationship with God. The New Testament is the early Christian movement's story (and stories) of her relationship with God as disclosed in Jesus.

Importantly, these stories are not just about the divine-human relationship in the past. They are also about the divine-human relationship in the present. The way the exodus story is used in the Jewish celebration of Passover each year illustrates this claim. In the liturgy accompanying the Passover meal, the following words (slightly paraphrased) are spoken:

> It was not just our fathers and our mothers who were
>   Pharaoh's slaves in Egypt, but we, all of us gathered here
>   tonight, were Pharaoh's slaves in Egypt. And it was not just
>   our fathers and mothers who were led out of Egypt by the
>   great and mighty hand of God, but we, all of us gathered
>   here tonight, were led out of Egypt by the great and mighty
>   hand of God.

What does it mean to say that "we" (and not just our ancient ancestors) were slaves in Egypt and that "we" were led out of the land of slavery by God? It does not mean that we were there in the loins of our ancestors, as if our genes or DNA were present. Rather, the exodus story is understood to be true in *every* generation. It portrays bondage as a perennial human problem and proclaims God's will that we be liberated from bondage. The story of Israel's bondage in Egypt and her liberation by God is thus a perennially true story about the divine-human relationship. It is about us and God.

Reading the Bible in a State of Postcritical Naivete

Given the above, a major need for contemporary readers of the Bible is to move from precritical naivete through critical thinking to postcritical naivete. Though these phrases sound like intellectual jargon, they are very illuminating. They identify ways of reading and hearing the Bible that we can recognize in our own experience.[15]

Precritical naivete is an early childhood state in which we take it for granted that whatever the significant authority figures in our lives tell us to be true is indeed true. In this state (if we grow up in a Christian setting), we simply hear the stories of the Bible as true stories.

To illustrate, I recall the way I heard the Christmas stories when I was a child. I assumed that the birth of Jesus really happened the way Matthew and Luke and our Christmas pageants portrayed it. Without difficulty, I took it for granted that Mary really was a virgin; that she and Joseph really did travel from Nazareth to Bethlehem, where Jesus was born in a stable; that angels really sang in the night sky to the shepherds; that wisemen guided by a special star really came to Bethlehem bearing gifts; and so forth.

It did not occur to me to wonder, "Now, how much of this is historically factual, and how much is metaphorical narrative?" I simply heard the familiar stories as true. Moreover, it took no effort to do so. It did not require faith. I had no reason to think that things were otherwise than the stories reported.[16]

Critical thinking begins in late childhood and early adolescence. One does not need to be an intellectual or go to college or university for this kind of thinking to develop. Rather, it is a natural stage of human development; everybody enters it.[17] In this stage, consciously or quite unconsciously, we sift through what we learned as children to see how much of it we should keep. Is there really a tooth fairy? Are babies brought by storks (if children are ever told that anymore)? Did creation really take only six days? Were Adam and Eve real people?

In modern Western culture, as mentioned in chapter 1, critical thinking is very much concerned with factuality and is thus deeply corrosive of religion in general and Christianity and the Bible in particular. As critical thinkers in that culture, most of us no longer hear the biblical stories as true stories—or at the least their truth has become suspect. Now it takes *faith* to believe them, and faith becomes believing things that one would normally reject.

Postcritical naivete is the ability to hear the biblical stories once again as true stories, even as one knows that they may not be factually true and that their truth does not depend upon their factuality.

This way of hearing sacred stories is widespread in premodern cultures. In Arabia, traditional storytellers begin their stories with "This was, and this was not." In Georgia (the country, not the state), similar words are spoken to introduce a traditional story: "There was, there was, and yet there was not."[18] A favorite of mine is the way a Native American storyteller begins telling his tribe's story of creation: "Now I don't know if it happened this way or not, but I know this story is true." If you can get your mind around that statement, then you know what postcritical naivete is.

Importantly, postcritical naivete is not a return to precritical naivete. It brings critical thinking with it. It does not reject the insights of historical criticism but integrates them into a larger whole.

Let me return to the Christmas stories to illustrate this. Postcritical naivete is the ability to hear the Christmas stories once again as true stories, even though one knows with reasonable certainty that the primary elements of the story are not historically factual. Critical thinking in the form of historical criticism sees the story of the virginal conception of Jesus as a continuation of the theme of special births from the Hebrew Bible. It is aware that the story of the special star and the wisemen bringing gifts is not history but rather is almost certainly Matthew's literary creation based on Isaiah 60. It knows that Jesus was most likely born in Nazareth and not Bethlehem, and so forth.

In the state of postcritical naivete, one knows that the truth of the birth stories lies in their meanings as metaphorical narratives. Using both biblical and archetypal religious imagery, the birth stories speak about the significance of Jesus and about the divine-human relationship.[19]

Though the movement from precritical naivete into critical thinking is inevitable, there is nothing inevitable about moving into the state of postcritical naivete. One can get stuck in the state of critical thinking all of one's life, as a significant number of people in the modern period do. The initial movement into critical thinking is often experienced as liberating, but if one remains in this state decade after decade, it becomes a very arid and barren place in which to live, like T. S. Eliot's "wasteland."

We need to be *led* into the state of postcritical naivete. It does not happen automatically. This is one of the major tasks in our time as we learn how to read the Bible using a historical and metaphorical approach.

In the rest of this book, we will explore what it means to read the Bible as a combination of history and metaphor. Using the tools of historical criticism, we will seek to illuminate the ancient meanings of biblical texts by setting those passages in their historical context. We will also explore the meanings that arise out of taking seriously the fact that the Bible is a religious classic whose texts have a surplus of meaning that goes beyond the particular meanings of the texts in their ancient contexts. We will see what it means to read the Bible as a true story (and as a collection of true stories) about the divine-human relationship.

NOTES

1. Source criticism is the attempt to discern earlier sources of some biblical books. Form criticism is the study of oral forms of tradition and their setting in the ancient communities that produced the Bible. Redaction criticism focuses on the intentions of the author(s) (redactor[s]) who put the document into its final form. Canonical criticism seeks the meaning of passages within the context of the canon as a whole.

2. Many scholars date the earliest portions (found in the Pentateuch) to the 900s BCE and date the latest portion (the book of Daniel) to about 165 BCE. The earliest New Testament document is probably Paul's first letter to his community in Thessalonica, written around 50 CE, and the latest is II Peter, written perhaps as late as 125 or 150 CE.

3. Leslie P. Hartley, *The Go-Between*. (New York: Stein and Day, 1953).

4. I explicitly exempt Walter Wink from this category, even though he wrote a now-famous book that begins with the sentence "Historical biblical criticism is bankrupt." *The Bible in Human Transformation* (Philadelphia: Fortress, 1973), p.1. As Wink's subsequent work makes clear, he is a skilled practitioner of historical criticism.

5. "Metaphor is poetry plus, not factuality minus" builds on a Swedish proverb cited by Wilfred Cantwell Smith and attributed to Krister Stendahl in Smith's *What Is Scripture?* (Minneapolis: Fortress, 1993), p. 277, n.2. The original proverb is "Theology is poetry plus, not science minus."

6. An example of the relationship between archetype and society: the ancient cosmic combat myth is an archetypal narrative that tells the story of a world that has fallen under the rule of a brutal oppressive lord, the advent of a hero who defeats the evil power, and the restoration of the rule of the good lord. As I will suggest later in this book, this is a major structural element in the book of Revelation: the conflict between the lordship of Caesar and the lordship of Christ is portrayed in these terms.

7. Robert M. Grant and David Tracy, *A Short History of the Interpretation of the Bible,* second ed. (Philadelphia: Fortress, 1984), pp. 85–86.

8. Origen, *De Principiis* IV.1, in *The Ante-Nicene Fathers,* ed by Alexander Roberts and James Donaldson (Grand Rapids: Eerdmans, 1979, reprint of the 1885 edition), pp. 360–73.

9. David Tracy, *The Analogical Imagination* (New York: Crossroad, 1987) pp. 99–229.

10. Luke 10.29–37. Augustine's interpretation is found in his *Quaestiones Evangeliorum* II.19, paraphrased from C. H. Dodd, *The Parables of the Kingdom,* rev. ed. (New York: Scribner, 1961). Dodd uses this as an example of how *not* to interpret a parable.

11. Mark 8.27–10.45.

12. Mark 8.22–26. So also, in the following text, as Mark tells the story, the disciples and Peter see who Jesus is in two stages (Mark 8.27–30). (1) Jesus asks the disciples, "Who do people say that I am?" and they respond with various reports. (2) Jesus then asks them, "Who do you say that I am?" and

Peter responds with, "You are the Christ" (Christ = messiah). As with the blind man of Bethsaida, their "seeing" who Jesus is involves two stages.

13. Mark 10.46–52.

14. See my *Meeting Jesus Again for the First Time* (San Francisco: HarperSanFrancisco, 1994), chap. 6.

15. I have treated this topic in previous books—briefly in *Meeting Jesus Again for the First Time,* pp. 6, 17, 24; more extensively in *The Meaning of Jesus: Two Visions* (San Francisco: HarperSanFrancisco, 1998), co-authored with N. T. Wright, pp. 247–49. I treat it again here because of its importance for this book.

16. Precritical naivete is thus very similar to the natural literalism that I described in chap. 1.

17. It can be resisted. Fundamentalism is the refusal to apply critical thinking to the Bible. As a form of conscious literalism (see chap. 1), fundamentalism sees the corrosive effect of modern critical thinking on the Bible and insistently rejects it.

18. See George Papashvily, *The Yes and No Stories* (New York: Harper & Brothers, 1946).

19. For a fuller exposition of this way of reading the birth stories, see *The Meaning of Jesus: Two Visions,* chap. 12, pp. 179 86.

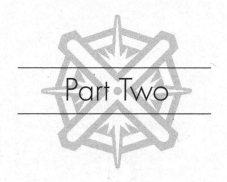

Part Two

THE HEBREW BIBLE

4

Reading the Creation
Stories Again

We begin with the Hebrew Bible, commonly known among Christians as "the Old Testament."[1] As in most recent scholarship, I will use the term "Hebrew Bible" instead of "Old Testament," for two reasons. The first is respect for Judaism. For Jews, the Hebrew Bible is *the* Bible, not "the Old Testament."

The second reason pertains to Christians. For many Christian readers, the adjective "old" implies outmoded or superceded, as if the "New" Testament were intended to replace the "Old" Testament. Commonly accompanying this usage is the notion that the "Old" Testament speaks of a God of law and judgment, whereas the "New" Testament speaks of a God of grace and love. Though this stereotype is widespread among Christians, it is simply wrong: both visions of God appear in both testaments. The notion that the New Testament (and its God) replaces the Old Testament (and its God) was rejected by early Christianity in the second century.[2] Despite a continuing Christian tendency to relegate the "Old" Testament to second place, it is for Christians just as much "Bible," just as sacred scripture, as is the New Testament. When Christians do not see this, we not only reject much of our heritage but impoverish our understanding of Jesus, the New Testament, and Christianity itself.

Within the Jewish tradition, the Hebrew Bible has three main divisions. In English, they are called "the Law," "the Prophets," and "the Writings." In Hebrew, they are, respectively, *Torah, Neviim, and Kethuvim*. The first letters of each of the Hebrew terms form the acronym *Tanak*, a common Jewish term for the Hebrew Bible as a whole.

The Torah is the first and foundational division of the Hebrew Bible. It consists of five books: Genesis, Exodus, Leviticus, Numbers, and Deuteronomy. Though the books themselves do not say anything about their authorship, both the Jewish and Christian traditions have attributed them to Moses. Thus they are sometimes spoken of as "the five books of Moses." And though the most common English designation for this group of books is "the Law," the Torah contains much more than what is commonly meant by the word "law." The word "torah" itself means more; it can be translated as "instruction" or "teaching." The Torah does indeed include the laws of Israel, but it also contains the stories of her origins. It is "instruction" and "teaching" about the people's story and identity, as well as the foundation of their laws. In other words, it combines narrative and legal traditions.

The Torah is also commonly called "the Pentateuch" (as we saw earlier), a Greek word meaning "the five scrolls." In fact, this is probably the most commonly used term for these five books.

The Pentateuch begins with Israel's stories of creation, to which we now turn.

Israel's Stories of the World's Beginnings

Ancient Israel's stories of the world's beginnings in the first eleven chapters of Genesis are among the best-known parts of the Bible. Almost everybody in Western culture has heard of them:

- The creation of the world in six days
- Adam and Eve in the Garden of Eden, their temptation by a talking serpent, and their expulsion from Eden
- Their sons Cain and Abel, and Cain's murder of Abel
- The great ages of early people, with Methuselah topping the list at 969 years
- The giants born from the sexual union of "the sons of God" with "the daughters of men"
- Noah's ark and the great flood
- The building of the Tower of Babel, its destruction by God, and the fragmentation of humankind into different language groups

Major battles about the factual truth of these stories have marked Western culture in the modern period. Prior to the birth of modernity in the Enlightenment of the seventeenth and eighteenth centuries, however, the factual truth of Genesis was accepted in the Jewish and Christian worlds without controversy, even though its stories were not always read literally.[3] There was little or no reason to question their factuality. Theology and science alike took it for granted that the universe was relatively young and that the earth and its continents, mountains, oceans, and varieties of life were created in very much the same form in which we now find them. Common estimates of the time of creation ranged from 6000 BCE to 4000 BCE.

Around 1650, the age of the earth was calculated with great precision by an Anglican archbishop of Dublin named James Ussher. Using the genealogies in Genesis, Ussher concluded that creation occurred in the year 4004 BCE.[4] His calculation was made just in time to collide with the birth of modern science. Geology and paleontology soon began to point to an immeasurably older earth. The challenge to the factual reading of the Genesis stories of creation was intensified by Charles Darwin's argument for evolution in *On the Origin of Species,* published in 1859. Suddenly the issue was not simply the age of the earth but the development of present life forms from much earlier life forms through natural processes.

The nineteenth century was a time of intense conflict between science and the Bible. Some intellectuals and village atheists delighted in using science to debunk the Bible and Christianity. Among Christians, some adjusted quickly to the new scientific claims and integrated them into a nonliteral reading of Genesis.[5] Others felt that the truth of the Bible and Christianity were under attack.

The controversy continues to this day, though it involves a much smaller number of Christians. Advocates of scientific creationism still defend the factual accuracy of the six-day creation story.[6] Expeditions are launched every few years to Mt. Ararat in Turkey, in search of the remains of Noah's ark. Some still think of the Garden of Eden as a real place and seek to figure out its geographical location. (Most often it is pinpointed somewhere in the Middle East, though I recall seeing a pamphlet arguing that it was in Wisconsin.)

But contemporary biblical scholarship does not read these stories as historically factual accounts of the world's beginnings. Instead, it sees them as ancient Israel's stories of the world's beginnings and interprets them as profoundly true mythological stories. In this chapter, I will describe these stories as seen through the lens of contemporary scholarship. More specifically, I will offer a historical-metaphorical reading, focusing primarily on the creation stories in the first three chapters of Genesis.

First, though, I will describe how I heard these creation stories the first time.

Hearing the Creation Stories the First Time

As a child growing up in the church, I heard the stories in Genesis in a state of precritical naivete and thus heard them as true stories.[7] Though I cannot recall a time when I took the six days of creation literally, I am sure I did so in very early childhood. And I would have done so without effort, even as I apparently let go of hearing them literally without conflict. When I learned about dinosaurs and the immense age and size of the universe in elementary school, I did not experience a religious crisis.

But as I think back on those years, I realize that I continued to take Adam and Eve quite literally as the first two human beings and that letting go of them was more of an issue. In elementary school, I learned about early humanoids with names like Neanderthal, Cro-Magnon, and Peking.[8] But it was not until my teenage years that I was struck by the implications of the evidence of such creatures. When I entered the stage of critical thinking, I began to wonder if I was supposed to identify the earliest of these with Adam and Eve. But I thought of these early humanoids as hulking brutes, perhaps barely capable of language. They did not seem likely candidates for Adam and Eve, whose sons Cain and Abel had engaged in the complex tasks of farming and herding—and Cain had even built a city.

So I began to take seriously the likelihood that Adam and Eve had not been real people. But if that likelihood turned out to be true, what were we to make of the story of the first sin, commonly called "the fall," in the Garden of Eden? If "the fall" was not historical, how (I wondered) would this affect the Christian story of universal sin, our need for redemption, and Jesus' death as the necessary sacrifice? Something more seemed to be at stake in the historical factuality of Adam and Eve and "the fall" than was involved in lengthening the six days of creation to geological epochs. Resolving these questions was a major theological problem for me. As I wrestled with it, the foundations of my religious understanding began to shake. If the story of Adam and Eve was not "true" (as a modern teenager, I thought of truth as that which was factual), what happened to the truth of the Bible and Christianity as a whole?

I now see these chapters quite differently. Reading them through the lens of historical scholarship and with sensitivity to their meanings as metaphorical narratives has enabled me once again to see them as profoundly true stories. And because their purpose is not to provide a factually accurate account of the world's beginnings, it is beside the point to argue whether they are accurate or mistaken factual accounts. They are not God's stories of the world's beginnings; rather, they are ancient Israel's stories of the world's beginnings.

As we look at these stories now, we will ask two key questions: Why did ancient Israel tell these stories? And why did they tell them this way? A historical-metaphorical approach provides illuminating answers to both.

Historical Illumination

The first eleven chapters of Genesis need to be understood not only as the introduction to the Pentateuch, but also in the context of the Pentateuch as a whole.

They are ancient Israel's stories of her prehistory. By that I mean two things. First, they are Israel's account of humankind in the time before her own particular history, a history whose telling begins with the stories of Abraham and Sarah, the father and mother of Israel. Abraham and Sarah, then, are the first *historical* figures in the Bible.[9] Their names appear in a genealogy at the end of Genesis 11, and the story of their call to be the ancestors of Israel begins in Genesis 12. Everything before them is Israel's prehistory and functions as a prologue to the Pentateuch and Israel's story of her own ancestors.

Second, to call these early chapters of Genesis prehistory means that they are not to be read as historical accounts. Rather, as ancient Israel's stories about the remote beginnings before there was an Israel, they are to be read as a particular kind of metaphorical narrative—namely, as myths, about which I will soon say more. For now, I simply note that while myths are not literally true, they can nevertheless be profoundly true, rich in powerfully persuasive meanings.

There is one further point before we turn to the stories themselves. Namely, though we typically begin reading the Bible with the first chapters of Genesis, they are not where ancient Israel first began telling her story. The creation stories were written relatively late. Israel as a people came into existence with the exodus from Egypt in the thirteenth century BCE. At the earliest, Israel told a story of creation some three hundred years later. As we shall see in the next chapter, the story of the exodus, the covenant, and the gift of the promised land is Israel's primal narrative and foundational story. In short, Israel told the story of the exodus and God's creation of her as a people long before she told the story of God's creation of the world.

Two Stories of Creation

The first three chapters of Genesis contain two stories of creation, written about four hundred years apart. The first one, Genesis 1.1–2.3, was probably written in the 500s BCE. Commonly called the "priestly" or "P" story, it is part of a larger block of material extending through the Pentateuch and reflecting priestly and ritual concerns. The second one was written earlier. It begins in Genesis 2.4 and continues through the end of chapter 3. Perhaps written in the 900s BCE, it is commonly called the "Yahwist" or "J" creation story, because the author uses "Yahweh" as the name of God.[10] The Yahwist story is also part of a larger narrative account of Israel's origins that extends throughout much of the Pentateuch.[11] The two stories are quite different.

The P Story

The P story (and the Bible as a whole) begins with the earth as "a formless void." In the primeval darkness, the wind (or Spirit) of God moves over the primordial waters:

> In the beginning, when God created the heavens and the
> earth, the earth was a formless void and darkness covered
> the face of the deep, while a wind from God swept over the
> face of the waters.[12]

Then God creates the universe in six days. In a literary structure repeated for each day of creation, the story begins with the creation of light:

Then God said, "Let there be light," and there was light. And
God saw that the light was good; and God separated the
light from the darkness. God called the light Day, and the
darkness God called Night. And there was evening, and
there was morning, the first day.[13]

In rapid succession, the rest of the universe is created. On day
two, God creates the dome of the sky (the "firmament"), separating the primordial waters above the sky from those below. On
day three, God creates dry land, the seas, and vegetation. On day
four, lights are placed in the dome of the sky: sun, moon, and
stars.[14] On day five, God creates sea life and birds. Finally, on day
six, God creates land creatures, concluding with the simultane-
ous creation of man and woman: "Then God said, 'Let us make
humankind in our image, according to our likeness. . . . So God
created humankind in his image, in the image of God he created
them; male and female he created them.'"[15]

There are interesting correlations between what God creates on
each of the first three days and what God creates on each of the
second three days. A "domain" is created and then populated:

Day one: light   Day four: sun, moon, and stars
Day two: waters and the sky   Day five: sea life and birds
Day three: dry land   Day six: land creatures

Then, we are told, on the seventh day God rests, thereby
blessing and hallowing that day as the sabbath.

The J Story

The J creation story begins in Genesis 2.4. It focuses on the creation of humankind and barely treats the creation of the world.
It does not mention the creation of light, or firmament, or sun,
moon, and stars, or sea creatures. Rather, it begins with the creation of humankind, of *adham*, a Hebrew word meaning "humankind" and often translated "man." The creation of *adham* is
the climax of the very long sentence with which the story begins:

In the day that the LORD God made the earth and the heavens, when no plant of the field was yet in the earth and no
herb of the field had yet sprung up—for the LORD God had
not yet caused it to rain upon the earth, and there was no
one to till the ground; but a stream would rise from the
earth, and water the whole face of the ground—then the
LORD God formed *adham* from the dust of the ground, and
breathed into his nostrils the breath of life; and *adham* became a living being.[16]

The P story portrays humankind as the climax of creation by
having people created *last*, after everything else. The J story
gives humankind priority by having people created *first*, before
vegetation and animals. In the P story, humans as male and female are created simultaneously; in J, the creation of woman
comes later.

To provide *adham* with a place to live, God plants the Garden
of Eden and gives *adham* permission to eat of all of its trees, except one: "You may freely eat of every tree of the garden; but of
the tree of the knowledge of good and evil you shall not eat, for
in the day that you eat of it you shall surely die."[17]

Then God creates companions for *adham:* "Then the LORD
God said, 'It is not good that *adham* should be alone; I will
make him a helper as his partner.'" God creates every beast of
the field, and every bird of the air, and brings them to *adham*.
But none of them meets the need: "There was not found a
helper fit for *adham*." So God puts *adham* to sleep and forms
woman out of one of his ribs. No longer alone, *adham* exclaims,
"This at last is bone of my bones and flesh of my flesh."[18]

Into this paradise comes a talking snake. The serpent tempts
the primeval couple to eat from the forbidden tree, "the tree of
the knowledge of good and evil." He promises them that if they
do, they "will be like God, knowing good and evil." They accept
the serpent's invitation, and their lives change dramatically. Now
aware of their nakedness, they make loincloths out of fig leaves.
Of more serious consequence, they are afraid and hide themselves

from God. Punishment follows. The woman, now named Eve, is sentenced to pain in childbearing and subjugation to her husband. The man, now named Adam, is sentenced to the toil and sweat of raising food from an earth filled with thorns and thistles. Both are exiled from the Garden of Eden. The story concludes with Adam and Eve living "east of Eden," the garden's entrance guarded by an angel with a flaming sword. Life in paradise is over.[19]

To return to our two key questions: Why did the people of ancient Israel tell these stories, and why did they tell them this way? One answer sometimes given is that these stories functioned as primitive science: ancient Israel did not know how the world came into existence, and so she created these stories in order to explain how things came to be. But there is much more going on here than a prescientific explanation of origins. To state my central claim in advance, Israel told these stories to express her deepest convictions about God and the world, and about what is often called "human nature"—that is, what we are like, and what our lives "east of Eden" are like.

Before treating more fully the first of these key questions, I begin with the second question: Why did ancient Israel tell the stories *this way?*

Reading the P Story through a Historical Lens

Historical study helps us to understand why ancient Israel told these stories in the way that she did. As already noted, the P story was most likely written in the 500s BCE. To connect this to ancient Israel's history, the Jewish people went into exile in Babylon after the Babylonian Empire conquered their homeland and destroyed Jerusalem in 586 BCE. The exile lasted almost fifty years, until 539 BCE, when a small number of Jews returned to a Jerusalem in ruins and began the task of rebuilding a Jewish homeland under the domination of a new imperial power, Persia. Thus, the P story of creation was written during or shortly after the exile.

The Six-Day Creation

Because the Jews were sharply reduced in numbers during this period of history, distinctive practices as a means of sustaining their identity as a people became vitally important. Among these practices was the observance of the sabbath (the seventh day of the week) as a day of rest. Though sabbath observance predated the exile, it became even more important during and after the exile. So why does creation take six days in the P story? To make the point that even God observes the sabbath. Rather than being intended as a literal account of how long creation took, the six-day creation story was meant to reinforce the importance of the sabbath.

The Ancient Cosmology

The word "cosmology" refers to one's image or "map" of the cosmos or universe. In common with Babylonian and other ancient Middle Eastern cosmologies, the ancient Israelites thought of the earth as the center of the universe. Above the earth was the dome of the sky, called the "firmament" in many English translations. This understanding is reflected in the P story. On the second day of creation, God said, "Let there be a dome in the midst of the waters, and let it separate the waters from the waters. . . . And God called the dome Sky." On the fourth day, God created the sun, moon, and stars and "set them in the dome of the sky to give light upon the earth."[20]

What seems like a strange notion to us today actually coincides well with human experience. The sky *looks* like a dome over our heads. On it are mounted the sun, moon, and stars, and it rotates around us. Moreover, the notion that there is water above the dome of the sky also reflects experience: water comes from the sky as rain and snow. Thus, as the flood begins in the time of Noah, we are told, "The fountains of the great deep burst forth *and the windows of the firmament were opened.*"[21] Far from providing us with an understanding of the universe that can be reconciled with modern or postmodern science, the cosmology of the P creation story simply reflects the way ancient Israel thought things were. Israel told the story this way because she thought of the universe this way. Thus it is Israel's story of creation, not God's story of creation.

The Literary Form of the P Story

The P story of creation was likely adapted from an ancient Israelite liturgy or hymn of praise to God. Its use of repeating phrases suggests refrains such as are found in hymns and liturgies. Each of the following is repeated seven times:

"God said, 'Let there be . . .'"
"And it was so."
"And God saw that it was good."

"There was evening and there was morning . . ." is repeated after each day of creation. Moreover, the six days of creation suggest six stanzas. If a liturgy does lie behind the first chapter of Genesis, we should imagine it being sung or chanted, perhaps antiphonally with a cantor and one or more choirs.

The recognition that the P story is likely to have been a hymn or liturgy has an immediate implication: we do not expect hymns to provide accurate factual information. When Christians sing the hymn "Jesus shall reign where're the sun does its successive journeys run," we are not saying that we believe the sun goes around the earth. The language of hymns is the language of poetry, metaphor, and praise. Creation cannot be described, but it can be sung.[22]

Indeed, Genesis 1 has been described as a "doxology." The roots of that word mean "words of, or about, glory." A doxology is a hymn of praise, as the most familiar English doxology reminds us: "Praise God from whom all blessings flow, praise God all creatures here below." Thus the book of Genesis and the Bible as a whole begin with a hymn of praise to God as creator. It is difficult to imagine a more appropriate beginning.

The Proclamation of Israel's God as Creator

The origin of the P story in the time after the Babylonian conquest adds one more dimension of meaning. In antiquity, when a nation was decisively conquered by another nation, it was commonly thought that the god (or gods) of the victorious nation had defeated the god of the vanquished nation, exposing that god as inferior or perhaps as no god at all. To many—Babylonians and Jews alike—it looked during the exile as if the gods of imperial Babylon had triumphed over the God of Israel.

In this setting, the opening line and the central claim of the P creation story defiantly assert that the God of Israel is the creator of heaven and earth—of all that is. It proclaims the lordship of Israel's God over against the lordship of Babylon and its gods. The story affirms a "counter-world," an alternative world to the world of empire.[23] This affirmation is, as we shall see, a theme that runs throughout the Bible from beginning to end.

Reading the J Story through a Historical Lens

Just as the P story is illuminated by setting it in its historical context, so also is the J story of creation.

The Symbolic Meaning of Names

The author of the J story uses names in such a way as to suggest that they are symbolic. Adam is not a proper name in ancient Hebrew; no other person in the Bible is named Adam. Rather, Adam is the Hebrew *adham,* which (as already noted) is a common noun meaning "humankind." Indeed, the term involves a play on words: *adham* comes from the Hebrew word *adhamah,* which means "ground" or "dust." In other words, the first human is a "dust-creature." We are made of dust, made from the earth. Moreover, because this word means "humankind," its use suggests that the author is thinking not of a specific human but of Everyman (to borrow the name of the well-known medieval morality play). The author is telling the story not of a particular person but of "everyone."

So also the name Eve is not a proper name in Hebrew. It means "mother of all living." "Garden of Eden" also has a symbolic meaning: it means "garden of delights" (and, by extension, paradise). Living in a semiarid climate, the ancient Hebrews pictured paradise as a green and bountiful garden filled with streams of flowing water.

Connections to Israel's History

There are a number of suggestive parallels between the narrative flow of the J story and Israel's history. Like *adham*, ancient Israel was created in a dry land (through the covenant with God in the Sinai desert). Like *adham,* ancient Israel was given a green and pleasant land in which to live. As in the case of *adham,* a prohibition came with the covenant and gift of the land, with the threat of expulsion if the prohibition was violated. And, more speculatively, the tempter is a serpent, a common symbol of Canaanite fertility religion, which was the primary temptation to infidelity to God that Israel faced in the land. The J story may thus have a prophetic edge to it: if Israel abandons the covenant of faithfulness to Yahweh, she faces expulsion and exile from the land/garden that God had given to her.[24]

Reading the Creation Stories through a Metaphorical Lens

Now that we have seen some of the historical reasons why Israel told the creation stories as she did, we turn to a reading of these chapters as metaphorical narratives. A metaphorical (and thus nonliteral) approach to these stories is not new. In the third century, a Christian biblical scholar named Origen, commonly seen along with St. Augustine as one of the two most brilliant theologians of the early church, wrote:

What intelligent person can imagine that there was a first day, then a second and third day, evening and morning, without the sun, the moon, and the stars? [Sun, moon, and stars are created on the fourth day.] And that the first day—if it makes sense to call it such—existed even without a sky? [The sky is created on the second day.] Who is foolish enough to believe that, like a human gardener, God planted a garden in Eden in the East and placed in it a tree of life, visible and physical, so that by biting into its fruit one would obtain life? And that by eating from another tree, one would come to know good and evil? And when it is said that God walked in the garden in the evening and that Adam hid himself behind a tree, I cannot imagine that anyone will doubt that these details point symbolically to spiritual meanings by using a historical narrative which did not literally happen.[25]

The Creation Stories as Myths

As we begin to address the question of why Israel told these stories, it is important to realize that the Genesis stories of creation are *myths*. That term needs careful explanation, because it has been virtually ruined by its most common modern use. In popular language, "myth" is a dismissive term. To call something a myth is to dismiss it: one need not take it seriously. A myth is seen as a mistaken belief, a falsehood.

But the term means something very different in the study of religion. Myths are not explanations. Myths are not primitive science. Myths are not mistaken beliefs. Rather, myths are metaphorical narratives about the relation between this world and the sacred. Myths typically speak about the beginning and ending of the world, its origin and destiny, in relation to God. Myths use nonliteral language; in this sense, they do not narrate *facts*. But myths are necessary if we are to speak at all about the world's origin and destiny in God. We have no other language for such matters.

The difference between the common dismissive use of the word "myth" and its meaning in the study of religion is pointed to in the title of a book written by Mircea Eliade, one of the greatest scholars of religion in the twentieth century: *Myth and Reality*.[26] In the modern world, myth and reality are commonly seen as opposites: we speak of myth *or* reality. Eliade's point is the opposite: myth and reality go together, myth being the language for talking about what is ultimately real. For Eliade, myths are true, even though not *literally* true.

To cite another definition: "Myth is a form of poetry which transcends poetry in that it proclaims a truth."[27] To echo what I said about metaphor in the previous chapter, myth is poetry plus, not science minus.

In Christian thought, the Genesis stories of creation have been an exceedingly rich mine of mythological and theological meanings. They treat the great themes of God as creator, the God-world relationship, the nature of reality, human nature, and the character of human existence. As we explore these themes, we will use conceptual language to clarify the meanings of Israel's myths of the beginnings.

God as Creator

To the extent that there is a literal affirmation in ancient Israel's creation myths, it is simply this: God is the source of everything that is. As one of my seminary professors said several decades ago, "The only literal statement in Genesis 1 is 'God created the heavens and the earth.'"

Genesis speaks of creation as having happened "in the beginning." In subsequent Christian thought, there are two quite different ways of understanding this statement. The first sees creation as "historical origination." Namely, at a particular moment in the past, at the beginning of time, God created. The second sees the notion of creation as pointing to a relation of "ontological dependence." This perhaps unfamiliar phrase means that God is the source of everything that is *in every moment of time*.[28] For this view, affirming that God is creator is not primarily a statement about origination in the remote past; rather, it is a statement about the present dependence of the universe upon God. If God ceased to vibrate the universe (and us) into existence, it (and we) would cease to exist. In traditional Christian language, God as creator is also the sustainer of everything that is.

The latter way of thinking about creation seems more important. From a scientific point of view, we do not know whether there was a time when there was "nothing." The contemporary "big-bang theory" of the universe's origin, which speaks of a moment roughly fifteen billion years ago when the present universe began, is quite compatible with thinking of creation as historical origination. Indeed, some have seen the primordial "cosmic flash" of the big-bang theory as strikingly similar to the first act of creation on the first day of the Genesis story: "Let there be light." Twenty years ago, a scientist wryly observed about the big-bang theory:

> For the scientist who has lived by his faith in the power of reason, the story ends like a bad dream. He has scaled the mountains of ignorance; he is about to conquer the highest peak; as he pulls himself over the final rock, he is greeted by a band of theologians who have been sitting there for centuries.[29]

But it is also possible that there were universes before the present one. Indeed, it is possible that there have always been universes. Seeing the statement "God is the creator" as a claim about ontological dependence means that Christians and Christian theology can be religiously indifferent to the question of whether the universe had a beginning. To say "God is creator" affirms a relationship and process that continues into the present. It need not refer to a specific event at a particular time in the distant past.

This way of thinking about God as creator is compatible not only with the big-bang theory but also with whatever scientific theory might (and almost certainly will) replace it. Indeed, thinking about creation this way means that the affirmation of God as "maker of heaven and earth" is compatible with *any* scientific account of the universe's origins. At the level of ultimate origins, there need be no conflict between Genesis and science. The two do not directly compete.

The God-World Relationship

Just as there are two ways of thinking about creation, so there are two models for thinking about the God-world relationship— that is, the relation of God as creator to the universe.[30] The first is known as a "production" model. Namely, like an artisan or artist, God makes the universe as something separate from God's self. Once created, the universe exists separate from God, just as a house or a painting exists separate from the builder or artist who produced it. This model is associated with a particular concept of God. Known as "supernatural theism," this way of thinking about God conceptualizes God as "another being" separate from the universe.

The second way of thinking about the God-world relation has been called a "procreative" or "emanationist" model: God brings forth the universe from God's being. Because the universe comes out of God's being, it is in some sense "God-stuff." This model does not identify the universe with God, for God is *more* than the universe; rather, it sees the universe as being "of God" and "in God." (In other words, the model is panentheistic.)[31] To quote a passage from the New Testament, God is "the one in whom we [and everything] live and move and have our being."[32]

The differences between these two models for thinking about the God-world relation matter. The production model suggests that the universe is separate from God and that creation happened in some past moment. The procreative model affirms the presence of God within and beyond the universe and fits the notion that creation is an ongoing process, not simply a past event. Finally, whereas the production model and its association with supernatural theism emphasize God's separation from the world, the latter model leads to a much more intimate sense of the closeness of God to the world—indeed, of the presence of God in the world.

Obviously, the Genesis stories speak of creation using a production model. In Genesis 1, God speaks and the universe comes into being. In Genesis 2, God is like an artisan molding *adham* out of earth, like a gardener planting a garden, and so forth. In short, God is portrayed as creating a universe separate from God.

But because this is the language of myth and metaphor, the way we think about the creation stories need not be confined to a semiliteral reading. To cite an analogy, the Bible often speaks of God as a person-like being; this is the natural language of worship and devotion. But that does not mean we must think of God as a person-like being. In any case, whether our thoughts of creation follow a production model or a procreative model, the central truth-claim of the myth remains: God is the source of everything.

The Nature of Reality

Central to Genesis 1 is the refrain repeated after each day of creation: "And God saw that it was good." The pronouncement covers everything that exists. To use a Latin phrase from medieval theology, *Esse qua esse bonum est,* or "Being as being is good." This does not mean that everything that *happens* is good. But whatever *exists* is good.

The creation story is thus strikingly world-affirming. Indeed, the Jewish tradition as a whole has consistently been world-affirming, in spite of the horrendous sufferings that Jews have experienced. The affirmation is also central to Christian theology, although popular Christianity, with its emphasis on the afterlife, has sometimes seen the world (especially "the flesh") as highly problematic, something to keep at a distance, a place to get through on the way to one's heavenly home. But against all world-denying theologies and philosophies, Genesis affirms the world as the good creation of the good God. All that is is good.

Human Nature

Ancient Israel's stories of creation affirm two things about us. We are the climax of creation, created in the image of God and given dominion over the earth. Yet we are also "dust-creatures," people made of earth. As dust-creatures, we are finite and mortal. "You are dust, and to dust you will return" are the final words spoken by God to Adam in paradise.[33]

We do not know what ancient Israel meant by affirming that we are created "in the image of God." Perhaps the claim simply reflects the fact that the Genesis stories of creation are anthropocentric; that is, they are told from a human point of view and are human-centered, highlighting humans as the climax of creation. The stories are also theocentric, of course—that is, centered in God—but the divine creation they describe leads up to us: we are God's culminating act of creation. Thus whatever created "in the image of God" means, it is clear that ancient Israel thought there was something special about us.

The paradoxical juxtaposition of our special status and our smallness in relation to the universe is expressed in the familiar words of one of the creation psalms. In the first half of Psalm 8, the author addresses God and reflects on our insignificance:

> When I look at your heavens, the work of your fingers,
>   the moon and the stars that you have established:
> what are human beings that you are mindful of them,
>   mortals that you care for them?

Then the author affirms:

> Yet you have made them a little lower than the angels,
>   and crowned them with glory and honor.
> You have given them dominion over the works of your hand;
>   you have put all things under their feet.

The assessment is realistic. We are small, we are finite, we are mortal. And yet there is something different about us.

Though we have learned in the last half-century not to speak of an absolute difference between us and the nonhuman animals, we do have greater consciousness than any species we know of. In us, the universe has become conscious of itself. And to a degree that ancient Israel did not dream of, we have become dominant, with very mixed consequences for the earth and ourselves.[34] Yet we are creatures of dust, fated to return to dust. Moreover, according to Genesis, we are not simply mortal, but "fallen."

The Character of Human Existence

The term "the fall" does not occur in the Genesis story of creation. As a description of the events surrounding Adam and Eve's expulsion from paradise, it is largely a Christian label; Jews typically do not speak of "the fall."

Within the Christian tradition, "the fall" has commonly been understood to mean "the fall *into sin.*" It has also been associated with the notion of "original sin," which is not simply the *first* sin, but a sinfulness that is transmitted to every individual in every generation. This latter notion, which goes far beyond what the Bible says, is usually attributed to the brilliant but troubled theologian Augustine around 400 CE. So as we hear and read this story again, we should try to free ourselves of specifically Christian associations of "the fall."

Though the term "the fall" does not occur in the story itself, the story of Adam and Eve's accepting the temptation offered by the snake points to something having gone wrong. The consequences are vivid, evocative, and thorough. Adam and Eve find themselves living east of Eden in a world that must endure toil and sweat for one's bread and pain and suffering in childbirth. They are banished from paradise forever. The rest of the stories in the first eleven chapters of Genesis describe the deepening consequences. In the next generation, murder: Adam and Eve's son Cain kills his brother Abel. The violence deepens, until even the boundaries of the cosmos are violated: "the sons of God" are mating with "the daughters of men," with monstrous consequences. Things are so out of control that God sends a flood to destroy all life except for those on Noah's ark, so that creation can be renewed. But soon thereafter, the cycle begins again in the story of the tower of Babel: humans try to build a tower that reaches into the heavens. But God overturns their effort and humankind is fragmented into its "babble" of different languages.

Clearly the Hebrew storyteller is saying that something has gone wrong. Life began in paradise but is now lived outside the garden, in an exile of hard labor, suffering, pain, violence, and fragmentation. Though the world is beautiful, something is not right; we *do* live in a world of suffering and pain.

But what went wrong? What action, desire or deed, led to such pervasive consequences? The language of the storyteller is evocative, not precise. It does not clearly point to a particular reading. Thus, over the centuries, a variety of understandings of "what went wrong" have emerged. Each leads to a somewhat different understanding of "sin"—that primal act that plunged human beings into a world of suffering—and each expresses nuances of "what went wrong."

The Primal Act as Disobedience   The first understanding is the simplest, though not necessarily the most perceptive. The act responsible for Adam and Eve's expulsion from Eden was *disobedience*. God gave them a command, they disobeyed it, and that was that. The emphasis is on the disobedience itself, not on what the act of disobedience was. For this view in its most elementary form, it would have made no difference if God's prohibition had been, "Please don't eat the daisies." This view typically leads to seeing sin in general as a matter of disobedience: God gives us commands and rules and laws, and we break them. The human problem is disobeying God the law-giver.

The Primal Act as Hubris   A second understanding agrees that disobedience was involved but emphasizes *what* the act of disobedience involved. In particular, it focuses on the first half of the serpent's temptation: *"You will be like God,* knowing good and evil." The desire is to become Godlike, to tower above who we are, to be the center of creation. In the Christian theological tradition, this is known as *hubris,* a Greek word commonly translated "pride."

But in this context it means more than the everyday meaning of the word "pride," as in the sentence, "I was proud of myself when I did that." *Hubris* means exceeding one's proper limits; it means giving to one's self the place that belongs to God alone; it means making one's self the center. *Hubris* can take many forms, ranging from a world-conquering arrogance to a self-preoccupied malaise. What these forms have in common is a life centered in the self and its concerns. Sin—the human problem—is thus *hubris* understood as self-centeredness.

The Primal Act as Sloth A third understanding is almost the opposite of the pride discussed above. The word "sloth" does not mean "laziness" in this context. Rather, it means "leaving it to the snake"—letting something else author one's existence. It means uncritically accepting somebody else's ideas about how to live one's life. In this view, sin—the human problem—is heteronomy: living the agenda of others.[35]

The Primal Act as the Birth of Consciousness A fourth understanding also focuses on *what* the primal act was, but it emphasizes the second half of the serpent's temptation: "You will be like God, *knowing good and evil*." "Knowing good and evil" is understood broadly to mean having knowledge of opposites, a capability that is intrinsic to the birth of consciousness. Consciousness involves distinguishing one thing from another; above all, it involves the self-world distinction, the awareness that the world is "other" than one's self.

The birth of consciousness is something we all experience; all of us become aware of the self-world distinction very early in life. Thus we cannot avoid the primal act. Indeed, this understanding emphasizes not the disobedience and sinfulness of "the fall," but its inevitability. All of us begin life in the womb with an experiential sense of undifferentiated unity; we begin in paradise. But the very process of growing up and the birth of consciousness that is intrinsic to it propels us into a world of division, anxiety, and suffering. Living "east of Eden" is intrinsic to the experience of being human. We all go through "the fall" and live in a state of exile and estrangement; it cannot be avoided.[36]

These various understandings can also be combined. For example, the birth of consciousness typically leads to *hubris,* understood as being centered in one's self. Moreover, centering in one's self intensifies the sense of separation from the world, deepening the experience of exile. The process of socialization leads to sloth understood as heteronomy: we internalize and live in accord with the agendas of others, including parents, culture, and religion.

As already mentioned, it is impossible to say that the Hebrew storyteller intended one of these more than the other, or intended any or all of these. But the creation stories are an example par excellence of a religious classic: they are stories that have a surplus of meanings.

Moreover, whatever the storyteller's sense of what went wrong in paradise, the story's picture of the consequences is persuasive and compelling. Most of us most of the time live "east of Eden." What this means is vividly portrayed in the painting *The Expulsion of Adam and Eve* by the fifteenth-century Italian artist Masaccio. As the first couple is driven out of Eden, Adam's head is down, both hands covering his eyes; Eve's face is upturned, but her mouth is open in a howl of pain, her features full of grief and sorrow. At least some of the time, life outside of Eden is like that.

The Creation Stories and Postcritical Naivete

Given the richness of meaning that a historical-metaphorical reading of Genesis reveals, the creation stories strike me as profoundly true. Critical thinking leads to an understanding of why the details of Genesis are as they are and also makes clear that their truth is not to be understood in literal, factual terms. Rather, their truth is expressed in the nonconceptual language of myth and metaphor, and no particular reading can exhaust their meanings.

But I can hear the truth of their central claims. "This"—the universe and we—is not self-caused, but grounded in the sacred. "This" is utterly remarkable and wondrous, a Mystery beyond words that evokes wonder, awe, and praise. We begin our lives "in paradise," but we all experience expulsion into a world of exile, anxiety, self-preoccupation, bondage, and conflict. And yes, also a world of goodness and beauty: it is the creation of God. But it is a world in which something is awry.

The rest of the Bible is to a large extent the story (and stories) of this state of affairs: the human predicament and its solution. Our lives east of Eden are marked by exile, and we need to return and reconnect; by bondage, and we need liberation; by blindness and deafness, and we need to see and hear again; by fragmentation, and we need wholeness; by violence and conflict, and we need to learn justice and peace; by self- and other-centeredness, and we need to center in God. Such are the central claims of Israel's stories of human beginnings.

NOTES

1. The Hebrew Bible and the Protestant Old Testament are identical in content, though divided differently. In the former, there are twenty-four books; in the latter, thirty-nine books. The Catholic Old Testament includes another twelve books, commonly called "The Apocrypha" or "Deuterocanonical" books. Orthodox Christians (often called "Eastern Orthodox") include another four.

2. This rejection came about in what is known as the Marcionite controversy. Marcion was a second-century Roman Christian who rejected the Hebrew Bible as un-Christian and affirmed a very abbreviated portion of what later became the New Testament.

3. See quotation from the third-century Christian theologian Origen later in this chapter.

4. The dates he calculated still appear in the margins of some Bibles.

5. See George M. Marsden, *Fundamentalism and American Culture* (Oxford: Oxford Univ. Press, 1980), pp. 17–26; Ian G. Barbour, *Issues in Science and Religion* (New York: Harper & Row, 1966), pp. 96–104, and *Religion and Science* (San Francisco: HarperSanFrancisco, 1997), pp. 49–74.

6. For an analysis and critique of "scientific creationism" or "creation science," see Conrad Hyers, *The Meaning of Creation: Genesis and Modern Science* (Atlanta: Knox, 1984). His book as a whole is an excellent study of the creation stories, integrating modern biblical scholarship, science, and myth.

7. For a discussion of precritical naivete, see chap. 3.

8. And, of course, we now know of humanoids much older than the ones I heard of when I was a child.

9. To speak of them as historical figures does not imply that the stories about them are straightforward historical reports, or even that we have any accu-

rate historical information about them. Rather, it means that Israel located the story of Abraham and Sarah in a recognizable historical context.

10. Let me explain why J is the common abbreviation for the "Yahwist" source of the Pentateuch. The source theory of the Pentateuch originated in German biblical scholarship in the nineteenth century. The German language, which does not have the letter *Y*, uses the letter *J* for the sound made by the English *Y*. Thus in German the name of God is "Jahweh" and the abbreviation is J. But it is conventional in English to spell "Jahweh" as "Yahweh." Hence the odd result that the Yahwist source is the J source.

11. In this section I accept what has been the common scholarly understanding of the sources of the Pentateuch for over a century. Recently that understanding has come under review and revision by some Hebrew Bible scholars. Though P and its dating in the 500s are still widely accepted, there are serious questions about whether J should be thought of as an early connected narrative or as a mixture of traditions from many periods of Israel's history, with some of it as late in date as P. For a summary of the case made by several scholars for regarding much of J as late, see Joseph Blenkinsopp, *The Pentateuch* (New York: Doubleday, 1992). Some recent scholars continue to see J as early. See, for example, Terence Fretheim's commentary on Genesis in *The New Interpreter's Bible* (Nashville: Abingdon, 1994), vol. 1, pp. 319–674. Harold Bloom and David Rosenberg's *The Book of J* (New York: Grove Weidenfeld, 1990) is based on an early date for J (and somewhat provocatively and eccentrically argues that the author was likely a woman). If the debate among Hebrew Bible scholars concludes with a later date for J, my analysis would not be affected in any significant way, for my comments on J do not depend upon an early date.

12. Gen. 1.1–2.

13. Gen. 1.3–5.

14. The *sequence* of creative acts points to the impossibility of reconciling the Genesis stories of creation with modern scientific knowledge simply by extending the timeframe from days to geological epochs. Note that light is created on the first day and yet sun, moon, and stars are not created until the fourth day. Indeed, the creation of vegetation (day three) precedes the creation of sun, moon, and stars.

15. Gen. 1.26–27. The use of the plural pronouns "us" and "our" has often puzzled people: Who is God talking to? Though Christians have sometimes seen this as a reference to the Trinity, that is impossible in an ancient Hebrew story, roughly a thousand years earlier than the notion of the Trinity. Most scholars think that the passage makes use of the image of God as a king surrounded by a heavenly council, such as we find, for example, in I Kings 22.19–23.

16. Gen. 2.4–7. Note: whenever the word LORD appears all in capital letters, as it does here, it is a translation of "Yahweh," the Hebrew sacred name of God.

17. Gen. 2.17.

18. Gen. 2.18–23.

19. Gen. 3.1–24.

20. Gen. 1.6, 14–17.
21. Gen. 7.11.
22. For other hymns of creation in the Hebrew Bible, see Ps. 8, Ps. 104.
23. Walter Brueggemann, *Genesis* (Atlanta: Knox, 1982), pp. 24–27. His exposition of Gen. 1–3 is filled with brilliant insights (pp. 11–54).
24. If J is early, then the possibility of exile is a warning. If J is late, then exile has happened. And whether or not the J material is early, its integration into the P narrative occurs during or after Israel's actual experience of exile.
25. Origen, *De Principiis,* 4.1.16. Translation is mine; parenthetical material added. For an older English translation, see *The Ante-Nicene Fathers,* ed. by Alexander Roberts and James Donaldson (Grand Rapids: Eerdmans, 1979, reprint of 1885 edition) vol. 4, p. 365. Origen also says that the Bible contains "countless instances of a similar kind that were recorded as having occurred, but which did not literally take place." Even "the gospels themselves are filled with the same kind of narratives." Origen also strongly affirms that he sees much of the Bible as historical.
26. Mircea Eliade, *Myth and Reality* (New York: Harper & Row, 1963).
27. H. and H. A. Frankfurt, *The Intellectual Adventure of Ancient Man* (Chicago: Univ. of Chicago Press, 1946), p. 8. The quotation continues by affirming that myth is "a form of reasoning which transcends reasoning."
28. But not of everything that *happens.* The distinction between "everything that is" and "everything that happens" is important. To say that God is the source of every existing entity is not to say that God is the cause of everything that happens. This applies especially to human behavior, but also to "natural" occurrences such as weather, earthquakes, hurricanes, and so forth.
29. Robert Jastrow, *God and the Astronomers* (New York: Warner Books, 1980), pp. 105–6. The literature on the relationship between religion and science is vast. Among recent books that I especially recommend are Conrad Hyers, *The Meaning of Creation: Genesis and Modern Science* (see note 6 above); Barbara Brown Taylor, *The Luminous Web* (Harrisburg: Morehouse, 2000); Philip Clayton, *God and Contemporary Science* (Grand Rapids: Eerdmans, 1997); Ian G. Barbour, *Religion and Science* (San Francisco: HarperSanFrancisco, 1997).
30. For the two models, see Sallie McFague, *The Body of God* (Minneapolis: Fortress, 1993), pp. 151–57. See also her *Models of God* (Philadelphia: Fortress, 1987), pp. 109–16.
31. This view is not to be confused with *pantheism,* commonly understood to mean the identification of the universe with God. The roots of *panentheism* are very ancient. In the Jewish and Christian traditions, the roots go back to the Bible's affirmation of both the transcendence and the immanence of God. For my description of the differences between supernatural theism, pantheism, and panentheism, see *The God We Never Knew* (San Francisco: HarperSanFrancisco, 1997), chaps. 2–3. As an explicitly developed concept, panentheism is becoming more and more common among mainline Christian theologians. See, for example, Clayton, *God and Contemporary Science,* pp. 82–124.

32. Acts 17.28.
33. Gen. 3.19
34. Some historians of culture have argued that the modern domination and destruction of nature has its roots in the Bible as the sacred text of Western culture, especially the creation story with its affirmation of God-given human dominion in Gen. 1.28: "Be fruitful and multiply and fill the earth and subdue it; and have dominion over the fish of the sea and over the birds of the air and over every living thing that moves upon the earth." The indictment has some substance: the dominion text was often cited to legitimate modern Western "development" of the world. But it is probably not fair to the text itself. Walter Brueggemann comments that the dominance referred to in Gen. 1.28 "is that of a shepherd who cares for, tends, and feeds the animals" and notes that it pertains to "securing the well-being of every other creature and bringing the promise of each to full fruition" (*Genesis*, p. 32).
35. I owe this understanding to the title and content of Harvey Cox's *On Not Leaving It to the Snake* (New York: Macmillan, 1967). Paul Tillich, one of the two most important Protestant theologians of the twentieth century, makes the same point when he speaks of "heteronomy" as one of three ways of living one's life. "Heteronomy" means living in accord with the agenda of others (people, culture, the nation, and so forth). "Autonomy" means living with one's self as the center (and is thus hubris). "Theonomy" means living with God as one's center; it is the desirable state of affairs, and that from which we have "fallen" into either heteronomy or autonomy.
36. For an exposition of this understanding within the framework of Jungian psychology, see Edward F. Edinger, *Ego and Archetype* (New York: Penguin, 1973), esp. pp. 16–36.

5

Reading the
Pentateuch Again

Israel's story of the beginning of the world in Genesis 1–11 is followed immediately by her story of her own beginning. The story fills all five books of the Pentateuch. As in the creation story, God is the central reality and actor. The one who created heaven and earth now creates Israel.

Israel's story of her origins begins in Genesis 12 with God's call of her nomadic ancestors Abraham and Sarah and continues through three generations to their great-grandsons, the "fathers" of the twelve tribes of Israel, who are living in Egypt as Genesis ends. The subsequent four books of the Pentateuch narrate the story of Israel's birth as a people and a nation: the exodus from Egypt under the leadership of Moses, the covenant and giving of the law at Mt. Sinai, and the journey through the wilderness to the border of the promised land.

Embedded within the narrative of the Pentateuch are the 613 laws revealed by God to Moses on Mt. Sinai. The most famous of these are, of course, the Ten Commandments. But the laws of the Pentateuch address far more than those ten issues. They cover not only what we think of as ethical and ritual matters, but also matters of civil and criminal law. In a comprehensive sense, they functioned as both constitutional and statutory law for ancient Israel. By grounding them in her story of sacred origins, Israel gave them the status of sacred law.

The combination of sacred narrative and sacred law made the Pentateuch the foundation of ancient Israel's life. It not only told the story of Israel's creation but shaped the world in which she lived.

The Story Crystallized

A very compact version of Israel's story of origins is included in scripture as part of the ritual of offering the firstfruits of the harvest to God:

> A wandering Aramean was my ancestor.
> He went down into Egypt and lived there as an alien, few in number, and there he became a great nation, mighty and populous.
> When the Egyptians treated us harshly and afflicted us by imposing hard labor upon us, we cried to the LORD, the God of our ancestors.
> The LORD heard our voice and saw our affliction, our toil, and our oppression. The LORD brought us out of Egypt with a mighty hand and an outstretched arm, with a terrifying display of power, and with signs and wonders;
> And the LORD brought us into this place and gave us this land, a land flowing with milk and honey.[1]

A generation ago, many Hebrew Bible scholars saw this text as a unit of very early oral tradition much older than the first written account of Israel's story. The present generation of scholars is less certain about this; in fact, many now see it as a late summary. But whether early tradition or late summary, it crystallizes Israel's story as found in the Pentateuch as a whole.[2] Indeed, the

Pentateuch is an expanded version of this basic narrative, which includes the following:

- We began as nomads, wanderers upon the earth without a home.
- We fell into slavery to the lord of Egypt.
- God heard our groaning and liberated us from bondage.
- And God gave us a bountiful land in which to live.

Historical Illumination

The exodus from Egypt under the leadership of Moses probably happened in the thirteenth century BCE. The stories of Israel's nomadic ancestors Abraham and Sarah are set a few hundred years earlier. For many centuries, both Jews and Christians routinely spoke of the Pentateuch as "the five books of Moses" and took it for granted that Moses (aided by God) was the author. Thus the Pentateuch was seen as roughly contemporary with the events it describes.

But modern historical scholarship, beginning in the seventeenth century, has rejected the notion of Mosaic authorship for good reasons. Instead, it sees the earliest accounts of Israel's beginnings as having been written much later. As mentioned in the previous chapter, some scholars think that the earliest extended narrative in the Pentateuch may have been written as early as the 900s BCE (the J source). Other scholars think that the narratives were written significantly later. In any case, the completed narrative in its present form, with its combination of stories and laws, is quite late, written during or after the Jewish exile in Babylon in the 500s BCE and perhaps finalized as late as the time of Ezra in the 400s BCE.[3]

My primary concern in this chapter is with Israel's story of origins in its present form, and not with a reconstruction of the history that lies behind it. Nevertheless, when it seems illuminating to make some observations about the possible history behind the stories, I will do so. Paradoxically, the primary effect of such observations is to turn attention from historical reconstruction to a metaphorical reading of these narratives.

The Fathers and Mothers of Israel

The stories of Abraham and Sarah; Isaac and Rebekah; Jacob, Leah, and Rachel, and their twelve sons (the fathers of Israel's twelve tribes) are found in Genesis 12–50.

The Question of Historicity

I begin with a memory from my first seminary course on the Hebrew Bible some thirty-five years ago. I recall sitting at my desk in my dorm room in New York City listening to an FM radio station (a new experience for a young man from the remote northern Midwest) and doing the reading assignment for the next day's class.

By then, I had learned that the first part of Genesis was a mythical prologue to the Pentateuch and that Israel's history began with the stories of "the fathers of Israel"—"the patriarchs," as they were called in those days: Abraham, Isaac, Jacob, and his twelve sons. The time of Abraham was commonly said to be about the 1700s BCE.

The assignment consisted of conflicting essays about whether the patriarchs were historical or legendary figures. Did Abraham and Isaac and Jacob and his twelve sons really exist, or were they legendary personifications of tribal groups? It also included a short essay on when camels were domesticated. Its conclusion: whereas asses had been domesticated by the alleged time of Abraham, camels had not been.

The effect of the assignment was a strong feeling of vertigo. So, I thought, let me see if I've got this right. Our tradition began with Abraham—but he might never have existed. And if he did, he was an ass nomad, not a camel nomad. Somewhat irreverently (but not without fear and trembling), I wondered why, even if he did exist, I should take seriously what happened to him—an ass nomad from the 1700s BCE? What did he know about anything? The foundation of the tradition seemed to be crumbling.

I recovered from the vertigo of that evening, but I still do not have an opinion about the historicity of the stories of Abraham and Sarah and their immediate descendants. I have realized, though, that their historicity does not matter. What *does* matter is the two questions raised in the previous chapter: Why did Israel tell these stories? And why did she tell them this way?

Promise and Fulfillment

The theme of promise and fulfillment provides the overarching structure and narrative flow of the Pentateuch. The promise is found in the dramatic beginning of the story of Abraham and Sarah in Genesis 12.1–2. God calls the two of them to leave home and family and embark on a journey to a land they do not know: "Go from your country and your kindred and your father's house to the land that I will show you. I will make of you a great nation." The promise is twofold: the land of Canaan and a multitude of descendants.[4]

The rest of the Pentateuch is the story of the fulfillment of this promise. The Pentateuch ends several hundred years later with the descendants of Abraham at the Jordan River, ready to cross over to Canaan, the promised land.

The theme of promise and fulfillment is central not only to the Pentateuch as a whole, but to many of its individual stories. These stories often dramatize and intensify the theme of promise and fulfillment by adding a third element: a threat to the promise, a formidable obstacle to its fulfillment. As in a sacred melodrama, the ancestors find themselves in one predicament after another. Will God be able to fulfill the promise despite what look like hopeless circumstances?

The Barrenness of the Matriarchs

Of the many stories of threats to the promise that could be cited, I focus on a repeating theme about the mothers of Israel: the matriarchs are barren. Abraham and Sarah's role in the theme is well known. Though promised a multitude of descendants, Sarah is both barren and old. So the couple tries surrogate parenthood: Sarah gives her maidservant Hagar to Abraham, and Hagar bears his son Ishmael. But for the narrator of Genesis, this is not the fulfillment. It will not be brought about by human ingenuity.

Then, when Sarah is ninety and Abraham is ninety-nine— when humanly speaking it is *impossible*—Sarah conceives and gives birth to Isaac. The father and mother of Israel finally have a descendant. And, the narrator hardly needs to say, only because of God.[5]

Less well known is the repetition of this theme in the next two generations. Isaac, Abraham and Sarah's son, marries Rebekah, who like Sarah is barren. Through twenty years of marriage, they have no children. Then God answers Isaac's prayer, and Rebekah gives birth to Esau and Jacob.[6]

Jacob is now the child of promise. He falls in love with Rachel but is tricked into marrying her sister Leah as well. Leah (whom we are told he does not love) is marvelously fertile. But Rachel, whom he does love, is barren. After many years, we are told, God opens Rachel's womb and she gives birth to Joseph, who later saves his brothers—the ancestors of the twelve tribes of Israel—in a time of famine.[7]

What are we to make of this theme of the barrenness of the matriarchs? Why did the storytellers of Israel tell the story this way? By narrating these stories of threats to the promise, they intensified the theme of promise and fulfillment. The story as Israel tells it: even when it looks as if birth is impossible, when it seems that there is no hope, when we fear that we have no future, when the promises of God seem like pipe dreams—even then God finds a way to fulfill the promises made to our ancestors.

Joseph and His Brothers

The theme of promise and fulfillment (with the added drama of threat) is also central to the rich collection of stories that conclude the book of Genesis. Like a novella, Genesis 37–47 tells us about Joseph and his brothers, the sons of Jacob and the fathers of the twelve tribes of Israel. To condense these wonderfully written and often adventurous stories into a summary is a bit of a shame, but I do so now in order to show their connection to the theme of promise/threat/fulfillment.

Joseph, the favored son of Jacob and Rachel, is a dreamer and interpreter of dreams. His brothers become homicidally jealous of him. Having first planned to kill him, the brothers sell him into slavery instead, and then they tell their father that Joseph is dead.

Joseph ends up in Egypt as a servant. Through a series of adventures, he rises to the position of chief overseer, second in authority and power only to the pharaoh. He is placed in charge of organizing the storage of food in anticipation of a seven-year famine disclosed to him through the interpretation of dreams.

The famine strikes. Back home in the land of Canaan, hunger drives the family of Joseph to go to Egypt in search of food. They do not even suspect that Joseph might still be alive, much less imagine him as a person of power in Egypt. But they meet. Though Joseph recognizes them, they do not recognize him.

Finally Joseph tells them who he is: "I am your brother Joseph, whom you sold into Egypt." And then he says these extraordinary words:

> Do not be distressed [they might well have been afraid!], or
> angry with yourselves because you sold me here; for God
> sent me before you to preserve life. . . . God sent me before
> you to preserve for you a remnant on earth, and to keep
> alive for you many survivors. So it was not you who sent me
> here but God.[8]

This is an extraordinary claim: Joseph affirms, seeing things in retrospect, that even the event that ripped him from his homeland and family and sent him into slavery has been turned by God to a providential purpose.

In the Joseph stories, the threat to the promise was twofold. First, Joseph's brothers sold him into slavery; the one who was to be the savior of Israel in his time was betrayed by his brothers. Second, the famine left the ancestors of Israel desperate. But the narrator of Genesis turns the story into one of fulfillment in spite of these threats to the promise, and he does so in a strikingly provocative and evocative way. It is never the will of God that one sell one's brother into slavery; betrayal of that sort is always horrendous and wrong. Yet God can take even so great an atrocity and make it serve the providential purposes of God. God can be counted on to fulfill the promises made to Israel, the people of God.

The theme of promise and fulfillment connects closely to the theme of creation with which Genesis begins. Just as the world came into existence through God and is sustained by God, so the people of God come into existence through the call and promise of God and continue to exist only because of God's faithfulness. In the stories of the ancestors, God saves Israel from the abyss of nothingness again and again.

But the worst threat to the promise is yet to come. Genesis ends with Joseph's family—his father (Jacob), his brothers, and their households—settling in Egypt. There they prosper and live out their lives. Jacob dies, then Joseph and his brothers. Their descendants remain. Israel is now in Egypt.

The Exodus: Israel's Primal Narrative

We turn now to Israel's story of the exodus, shorthand for the rest of the core story that shapes the Pentateuch as a whole. The exodus story includes Israel's time of slavery in Egypt, the exodus itself, the covenant and laws given at Sinai, and the forty-year journey through the wilderness to the promised land.

In this story we encounter Israel's "primal narrative."9 The exodus story is primal in three meanings of the word. First, "primal" means "of greatest importance." Throughout Israel's history, the exodus story was the most important story she knew.

Second, "primal" means "originary" or "originating": the events narrated in this story gave birth to Israel; it is her story of origins par excellence. Third, "primal" means "archetypal": this story narrates the perennial struggle between the world of empire and the liberating will of God, between the lordship of Pharaoh and the lordship of God.[10]

Like biblical narratives generally, Israel's primal narrative combines historical memory with metaphorical narrative. Though the exodus story contains some history remembered, it is not what we think of as historical reporting; rather, it is history metaphorized.

As the storytellers of Israel narrate the exodus, they make use of remarkable literary artistry, dramatic hyperbole, and extraordinary numbers. Many of the scenes are exceptionally memorable, filled with both theological and psychological insights. The stories of the ten plagues and the crossing of the sea tell of stupendous miraculous interventions. According to the book of Exodus, the number of Israelites who left Egypt was six hundred thousand men *plus* women and children—presumably a total of two to three million.[11]

A couple generations of Americans have had their impressions of the exodus shaped by Cecil B. DeMille's 1950s epic movie *The Ten Commandments,* still shown each year near Easter on network television. Though the movie allows itself some Hollywood license, it basically takes the biblical story literally: God speaking to Moses through the burning bush, sending the ten plagues against Egypt, dividing the sea into two towering walls of water with a canyon of dry land between, writing the Ten Commandments on two tablets of stone with a flaming finger, and so forth. Like all literalizations of metaphorical narratives, it makes the story frankly incredible.

Nevertheless, the exodus is rooted in the historical experience of ancient Israel. The memory of having been Pharaoh's slaves in Egypt is indelibly printed on the pages of the Hebrew Bible and etched in the life of ancient Israel. It is delineated not only in the Pentateuch itself, but in the psalms and the writings of the prophets as well as in Israel's rituals and liturgies. But the exodus probably involved a few thousand people rather than a few million. And whatever historical events lie behind the stories of the plagues and the crossing of the sea, the texts are not simply reporting "what happened."

But for my present purposes, none of this matters. Rather, as in the first section of this chapter, my primary focus will be on the story in its present form, not on a historical reconstruction of what happened. Near the end of this chapter I will make a few more observations on the history behind the text, but for now we concentrate on the story itself. Throughout, my emphasis will be that *this is the way Israel told the story.*

Egypt and Bondage

The most severe threat to the promise made to the ancestors begins when a new pharaoh comes to power in Egypt. The first chapter of Exodus solemnly announces the change: "Now a new king arose over Egypt, who did not know Joseph."[12]

The result: Israel is enslaved by imperial power. Now in bondage to the lordship of Pharaoh, she is condemned to unremitting hard labor:

> The Egyptians became ruthless in imposing tasks on the Israelites, and made their lives bitter with hard service in mortar and brick and in every kind of field labor. They were ruthless in all the tasks they imposed upon them.[13]

And even worse: the imperial power in charge of the Israelites' world orders the killing of all male babies born to the Hebrews. Imperial oppression is now combined with genocide. Under the power of empire, Israel has no future.

Moses

Into this world, Moses is born. It is no accident that the Pentateuch has long been associated with Moses. His birth is narrated at the beginning of Exodus and his death in the final chapter of Deuteronomy, the last book of the Pentateuch. In between is the story of his life as the liberator, law-giver, and leader of Israel. Moses towers over the Pentateuch. Other than God, he is the central figure in Israel's primal narrative.

The story of Moses' infancy is well known.[14] Seeking to save the baby from the death sentence of Pharaoh, his mother hides him in a floating basket among the bulrushes along the bank of the Nile. There he is found by Pharaoh's daughter. She not only adopts him but unknowingly hires his mother as his nursemaid. The future liberator of Israel is then raised in the imperial household.

Now grown up, Moses one day sees an Egyptian beating a Hebrew slave. He intervenes, kills the Egyptian, hides the body in the sand, and flees Egypt. A fugitive from the empire, he finds refuge in Midian, marries a woman of that region, has a son, and becomes a shepherd.

Many years pass. In Egypt, the situation of the Hebrew slaves worsens:

> The Israelites groaned under their slavery and cried out. Out of the slavery their cry for help rose up to God. God heard their groaning, and God remembered the covenant with Abraham, Isaac and Jacob. God looked upon the Israelites, and God took notice of them.[15]

The twofold repetition of groaning, crying, and slavery underlines the desperation of the Israelites' plight. God hears their groaning, remembers the covenant, looks upon them, and takes notice of them.

Immediately thereafter God calls Moses to be the liberator of Israel. While tending his flock on Mt. Horeb, "the mountain of God," Moses has a numinous experience—an experience of the sacred—that changes his and Israel's life forever. It is the famous story of the burning bush:

The angel of the LORD appeared to him in a flame of fire out
of bush; he looked, and the bush was blazing, yet it was not
consumed.[16]

Moses sees a bush blazing with light, filled with the divine ra-
diance. This is the first of several direct experiences of God reported about Moses. Like Abraham and Jacob before him, he is
described as having firsthand experiences of the sacred.[17]
Then God speaks to him out of the bush and calls him to go
back to Egypt:

> I have observed the misery of my people who are in Egypt; I
> have heard their cry on account of their taskmasters. In-
> deed, I know their sufferings, and I have come down to de-
> liver them from the Egyptians. . . . So come, I will send you
> to Pharaoh to bring my people, the Israelites, out of
> Egypt.[18]

Moses is reluctant and resists. He asks, If I do this and the Israelites ask me about the name of the God who has sent me,
what shall I say? The answer God gives him still mystifies: "I am
who I am."[19] Moses finally agrees and, with his brother Aaron,
returns to Egypt.

Confrontation with Pharaoh: The Plagues
Moses and Aaron appear before Pharaoh and announce the divine imperative to the imperial power that rules their world:
"Thus says the LORD, the God of Israel, 'Let my people go.'" *Let
my people go*—an imperative, not a plea—is the repeated refrain
of the next several chapters. Pharaoh's response is haughty and
contemptuous: "Who is the LORD that I should let Israel go?"
Moreover, he increases the work burden of the Hebrew slaves,
saying, "You are lazy, lazy."[20]
Then begin a series of dramatic episodes in which God sends
plague after plague against the empire. The plagues afflict the
Egyptians, but not the Israelites.

- The Nile and all the other water in Egypt turn to blood.
- Frogs fill the land.
- Gnats afflict humans and animals alike.
- Flies ruin the land.
- All the livestock of the Egyptians die.
- Boils attack Egyptians and their animals.
- Hail kills all exposed Egyptians and animals and ruins half the crops.
- Locusts consume the rest of the crops.
- Thick darkness covers the land for three days.[21]

In the late nineteenth and early twentieth centuries (and still occasionally today), it was common for historical scholars to seek to correlate the plagues with natural phenomena known to occur in Egypt. But such correlations miss the point. By seeking to save the historicity of the plague stories with natural explanations, they eliminated the central claim made by the storytellers of Israel: *God did this*. It was *God* who sent the plagues and "brought us out of Egypt with a great and mighty hand."

But even after nine plagues, Pharaoh still refuses the imperative to "let my people go." And so the most devastating plague strikes: the death of the firstborn of all Egyptians, including Pharaoh's son. The Israelites are spared by smearing blood upon the doorposts and lintels of their dwellings so that God will "pass over" their houses. Thus, in the midst of the tenth plague, the festival of Passover is established.[22] But the empire is not spared.

The Liberation and the Sea
The death of all firstborns does it. Pharaoh finally relents and lets the Israelites leave Egypt. But almost immediately he changes his mind. His army pursues the fleeing slaves and catches up to them at the sea. With the water in front of the Israelites and the army of the empire behind them, the threat to God's promise is again acute: Israel faces extermination. Then occurs the event that has been remembered and celebrated in Jewish and Christian liturgies ever since: God causes the waters to fall back, the Israelites

cross, Pharaoh's army and chariots become mired in the mud, the sea returns, and they drown. God has rescued Israel.[23]

The deliverance of Israel at the sea is celebrated scripturally in a magnificent hymn of praise to God. Commonly called "the song of Moses" and filling almost all of Exodus 15, it obviously comes from a much later date. It praises God not only for the victory over the Egyptians but also for the conquest of Canaan. Its last lines refer to "the mountain" and "the place" and "the sanctuary" where God has chosen to dwell, apparently a reference to the temple in Jerusalem built by King Solomon on Mt. Zion in the 900s BCE.[24]

There may be a much more ancient hymn behind this one. Many scholars think that the song of Moses is based on the much shorter hymn at the end of the chapter, known as "the song of Miriam" (the sister of Moses).[25] Called a prophet in that hymn, Miriam takes a tambourine and leads the women in song and dance:

> Sing to the LORD, for God has triumphed graciously;
> Horse and rider God has thrown into the sea.

In the judgment of many scholars, this poetic couplet may be the oldest part of the Hebrew Bible.

From the sea, the liberated slaves continue their journey through the desert to Mt. Sinai, led and nourished by God. God guides them with a pillar of cloud by day and a column of fire by night. God quenches their thirst with water from a rock. God feeds them with manna, a breadlike substance that falls from the sky each morning, and with quails that cover the ground each evening.[26]

Sinai and the Covenant

What happens at Sinai occupies a major portion of the Pentateuch. It takes the narrator of Exodus eighteen chapters to tell the story of bondage in Egypt, the call of Moses, the confrontations with Pharaoh and the plagues, the departure from Egypt and the crossing of the sea, and the journey to Sinai. The events at Sinai take the remaining twenty-two chapters of Exodus, all of the twenty-seven chapters of Leviticus, and the first ten chapters of Numbers—fifty-nine chapters in all.

Theophany and Covenant
The Sinai events begin in Exodus 19 with a stupendous theophany (manifestation of God) or hierophany (manifestation of the sacred). Thunder and lightning erupt, and the sound of an ear-splitting trumpet can be heard as a thick cloud covers the sacred mountain. As God descends upon the mountain in fire, it quakes violently. Moses ascends the mountain and there, at the place where heaven and earth meet, goes to meet God. Moses' role as mediator of the covenant and giver of divine law has begun.

What happens at Sinai is that Israel becomes a people, a nation. Though the narrator of the Pentateuch has frequently used the words "Israelites" and "Israel" earlier in the story, it is here that Israel comes into existence. Here God offers the people a covenant:

> You have seen what I did to the Egyptians, and how I bore
> you on eagles' wings and brought you to myself. Now
> therefore, *if you obey my voice and keep my covenant,* you
> shall be my treasured possession out of all the peoples. In-
> deed, the whole earth is mine, but you shall be for me *a
> priestly kingdom and a holy nation.*[27]

With the offer and acceptance of the covenant with God, they become God's "treasured possession" and "a priestly kingdom and a holy nation."

The Giving of the Law
Most of the chapters covering what happens at Sinai consist of the laws given by God through Moses to Israel. They include the

Ten Commandments (in two slightly different forms), the Book
of the Covenant, and the rest of the laws of Exodus, Leviticus,
and Deuteronomy.[28] It is clear that these laws, drawn from many
different periods in Israel's history, have accumulated over a period of centuries.[29] But all are presented as God's revelation to
Moses on the sacred mountain, and all go back to a time of sacred beginnings.

As mentioned in the introduction to this chapter, they include
ethical and ritual laws as well as civil and criminal laws. Some of
them express broad ethical principles with a wide application,
such as "You shall love your neighbor as yourself." Many are
highly specific rules, dealing with issues such as what foods may
and may not be eaten, what the penalty is for cursing one's parents (death), what to do when an ox gores a person or another
ox, what to do after an emission of semen, and so forth.[30]

These laws also include some of the most radical socioeco-
nomic legislation in human history. For example, no interest is
to be charged on loans to fellow Israelites. Especially striking are
the regulations for the sabbath year and jubilee year. Every sabbath (seventh) year, all debts owed by Israelites to other Israelites are to be forgiven and all Hebrew slaves released.[31] Every
jubilee (fiftieth) year, all agricultural land is to be returned at no
cost to the original family of ownership.[32] These laws reflect Israel's origin in Egypt as a radically oppressed and marginalized
people. Their purpose was to prevent the emergence of a perma-
nently impoverished class within Israel.

Israel's Infidelity

There is yet one more theme to the Sinai story and the subsequent journey through the wilderness to the promised land—
namely, the threat to God's promise now coming from within
Israel itself. In several episodes, most famously in the story of the
golden calf that the Israelites erect while Moses is with God on
the mountain, Israel becomes unfaithful to God.[33] God the liberator of Israel then threatens to become the destroyer of Israel.
But Moses intercedes, God relents, and in another theophany re-

news the covenant with the people. In the middle of this episode, Moses again meets God on Sinai. We are told that God
passes before him and proclaims:

> The LORD, the LORD, a God compassionate and gracious,
>   slow to anger, and abounding in steadfast love and faithful-
>   ness, keeping steadfast love for the thousandth generation,
>   forgiving iniquity and transgression and sin, yet by no
>   means clearing the guilty, but visiting the iniquity of the
>   parents upon the children, to the third and fourth genera-
>   tion.[34]

This speech is one of the classic characterizations of God in
the Hebrew Bible.

From Sinai to the Promised Land

Because of their infidelity, the exodus generation is not allowed
to enter the land that God promised to the ancestors. Instead,
after they leave Sinai, they spend almost forty years in the wilderness.[35] As the book of Numbers ends, the descendants of the exodus generation are camped in the plains of Moab just east of
the Jordan River, the border of the promised land.

The Pentateuch then concludes with the book of Deuteronomy, structured as a series of speeches spoken by Moses to the
people of Israel just before they cross the Jordan.[36] "Deuteronomy" means "second law," a fitting title since much of the
book is a second giving or summary of the law. The final chapters of this book, rich in exceptional language, consist of Moses'
"farewell address" to the people he has led for forty years.

Deuteronomy 34 (the last chapter of the book) describes the
death of Moses, who at 120 years old climbs to the top of Mt.
Nebo on the east side of the Jordan. From its summit, God
shows him the whole of the promised land that he himself will
not enter. About the land displayed before Moses' eyes, God
says, "This is the land of which I swore to Abraham, to Isaac and
to Jacob, saying, 'I will give it to your descendants.'"[37] Then

Moses dies, just as the promise that arches over the Pentateuch is about to be fulfilled.

The narrator tells us that no one knows where Moses was buried. Jewish tradition suggests that God dug his grave and placed his body in it. The brief obituary that concludes Deuteronomy affirms, "Never since has there arisen a prophet in Israel like Moses." For the narrator of Deuteronomy and for the Jewish tradition ever since, Moses is the greatest of the prophets.

Central Meanings of Israel's Primal Narrative

I return briefly to the question of historicity—to the question of how much of the exodus story and subsequent events "really happened." I do so because of what is at stake in the question. It is not simply that "the modern mind" has difficulty with the most spectacular elements in these stories and needs reassurance that they need not be taken literally. Rather, it is that how we address the question of historicity affects (and is affected by) how we see God and the ways that God interacts with the world.

To use the story of the crossing of the sea as an example: something happened at the sea. But it was not the sea dividing into parallel walls of water with a canyon of dry land in between. To imagine that God acted to bring about that in the past violates the principle of "divine consistency."[38] Divine consistency affirms that God acts now in the same way that God acted in the past. Some might—some *do*—argue with this claim. But the notion that God acted in fundamentally different ways in the past compared to how God acts now presents insurmountable difficulties. Why would God change how God acts? What possible reason can be imagined? If God intervened in such dramatic ways then, why not now?

The issue for me is not whether paranormal events that have no reasonable reductionistic explanation happen now. They do. And the issue is not whether there are movements of human liberation empowered by God now. There are. Rather, the issue is whether God has ever acted anywhere, anytime, as portrayed in the stories of the plagues and the crossing of the sea. To say that God did so act in Moses' day is to leave inexplicable the noninterventions in situations of intense human suffering in the centuries ever since.

It also risks making the story of the exodus irrelevant to subsequent generations. The narrative of the Israelites' rescue from Egypt would then become a story of what God did once upon a time *but no more*—a story about how God "jump-started" Israel but then became mysteriously inactive.

Instead, as Israel's primal narrative, the exodus account is a paradigmatic story of God's character and will. I turn now to some of its meanings as Israel's primal narrative and paradigmatic story.

The exodus story was Israel's decisive and constitutive "identity story." In the words of Walter Brueggemann, the best-known Hebrew Bible scholar in North America today, it is

> that most simple, elemental, and non-negotiable story line which lies at the heart of biblical faith. . . . It is an affirmation in story form which asserts, "This is the most important story we know, and we have come to believe it is decisively about us."[39]

For the ancient Israelites, and for Jews ever since, this was the most important story they knew. It was the primary story shaping their understanding of the divine-human relationship, their identity, their life together as a community, and their vision of the character of God.

Within this story, Egypt and Pharaoh are a type—an archetype—of a widespread way of organizing human society. In the exodus story, Egypt is of course Egypt. The ancestors of Israel were in bondage to the pharaohs of Egypt in the thirteenth century BCE. But Egypt is also a perfect type of "the ancient domination system" or "the preindustrial agrarian empire."

A common form of society in the time from the emergence of early agrarian empires in the 3000s BCE through the Middle Ages of the current era, these societies had two primary social classes. The urban ruling elites—elites holding the reins of power, wealth, and status—consisted of the traditional aristocracy, with the monarchy at its center. With their extended families, these elites comprised about one to two percent of the population. The other primary social class, typically making up slightly over ninety percent of the population, was composed of rural peasants (mostly agricultural workers, but also fishers, artisans, and so forth).[40]

The key economic fact necessary to an understanding of the central dynamic of these societies is this: roughly two-thirds of the annual production of wealth (mostly from agriculture, and thus produced by peasants) ended up in the hands of the ruling elites. The means whereby they acquired their wealth were primarily twofold: taxation on agricultural production, and direct ownership of agricultural land (with peasants working as sharecroppers, day-laborers, or slaves). The consequences for peasant existence were dire: unremitting labor, borderline nourishment, high infant mortality rates, and radically lower life expectancies.

To describe such societies with three phrases, they were marked by *economic exploitation* (just described), *political oppression* (ordinary people had no voice in the structuring of society), and *religious legitimation* (the religion of the elites affirmed that the structures of society were ordained by God).[41]

This is the world of Egypt and the world of empire—the world that Moses knew. Israel's "primal narrative" is the story of radical protest against and liberation from such a world, and it affirms that radical criticism of and liberation from such societies is the will of God. Moreover, the radical economic legislation of the Pentateuch was designed to prevent such a world from reemerging. Indeed, early Israel (for roughly the first two hundred years after gaining the promised land) was a remarkably egalitarian society, one with universal land ownership and no monarchy. The message of the Pentateuch was that God's people were to leave the world of Egypt and empire behind.

Thus Israel's primal narrative is profoundly political in the broadest sense of the word. Politics is about the shape and shaping of society. The exodus story is about the creation of a world marked by freedom, social justice, and *shalom,* a rich Hebrew word meaning "well-being, peace, and wholeness." It contrasts an "exodus worldview" with a "monarchical worldview."

Yet it is not *simply* political. At the center of Israel's primal narrative is God. God is the central reality of the story, and God's covenant with Israel begins, "I am the LORD your God, who brought you out of the land of Egypt, out of the house of slavery. You shall have no other gods before me."[42] The exodus story is not about social justice without God; equally, it is not about God without social justice.

Ancient Israel's primal narrative thus brings together two areas of life that we tend to separate: religious passion and social justice, God and this-worldly liberation. Even the obituary of Moses at the end of Deuteronomy unites these two contrasts. It not only refers to Moses' central role in the exodus but also describes him as one whom God "knew face to face":

> Never since has there arisen a prophet in Israel like Moses, whom the LORD knew face to face. He was unequaled for all the signs and wonders that the LORD sent him to perform in the land of Egypt, against Pharaoh and all his servants and the entire land, and for all the mighty deeds and all the terrifying displays of power that Moses performed in the sight of all Israel.[43]

Moses knew God; and Moses was the liberator of Israel. In Moses, as in the story of the exodus as a whole, the experience of God and the liberation from empire are brought together, in opposition to the monarchical worldview.

Finally, the story of the exodus is framed by the theme of the Pentateuch as a whole: promise and fulfillment. Both the exodus story and the theme of promise and fulfillment were strikingly relevant to the situation of the Jewish people in the exilic and postexilic periods—the years when the Pentateuch was composed in its final and present form.

They had been conquered, greatly reduced in numbers, and exiled by one imperial power; now they lived under another imperial power. The promise of God that they would be "a great nation" seemed profoundly threatened, as did their very existence. In this setting, they remembered and celebrated the promise given to their ancestors, the stories of Israel's liberation from a previous imperial power, and the gift of a new land and a new life.

Indeed, the theme of promise and fulfillment is strikingly relevant to people in *all* times. In spite of threats to the promise and seemingly insurmountable obstacles, when birth and rebirth seem impossible, when pharaohs and the powers of empires seem to rule the world, God's faithfulness can be counted on.

NOTES

1. Deut. 26.5–9.
2. Another compact summary also cited by a previous generation of scholars as early tradition is found in Deut. 6.20–24. Here the context is the instruction of children: "When your children ask you in time to come, 'What is the meaning of the decrees and the statutes and the ordinances that the LORD our God has commanded you?' Then you shall say to your children, 'We were Pharaoh's slaves in Egypt, but the LORD brought us out of Egypt with a mighty hand. The LORD displayed before our eyes great and awesome signs and wonders against Egypt, against Pharaoh and all his household. God brought us out from there in order to bring us in, to give us the land that God promised on oath to our ancestors. Then the LORD commanded us to observe all these statutes, to fear the LORD our God, for our lasting good.'"
3. See the story of the public reading of "the book of the law of Moses" by Ezra in Neh. 8–9. Obviously some stories in the Pentateuch were being told centuries earlier. The eighth-century prophets of Israel and Judah refer to the exodus and the ancestors. See, for example, Amos 2.10, 3.1, 9.7; and Mic. 6.4.
4. The promise is repeated and amplified in subsequent chapters. In Gen. 15.5, God promises Abraham descendants as numerous as the stars of the heavens; in 17.1–8, God promises to Abraham and his offspring an everlasting covenant and "all the land of Canaan." (Canaan is the name of the geographical area that eventually became Israel.)
5. Abraham and Sarah's inability to have a child is a major theme in Gen. 12–21.
6. Gen. 25.19–26.
7. Gen. 29.21–30.24.
8. Gen. 45.4–5, 7–8.

9. I owe the phrase "primal narrative" to Walter Brueggemann, *The Bible Makes Sense* (Atlanta: Knox, 1977), esp. chap. 3. He emphasizes meaning one: "of first importance."

10. The connection between "primal" and "archetypal" is suggested by the roots of the latter. *Arche* means "beginning," and *tupos* means "impression" (as in an impression made by a seal in wax, or by a piece of type on a sheet of paper). "Archetype" thus means something imprinted "from the beginning" that recurs again and again; an archetype imprints itself again and again.

11. Exod. 12.37. That this number is impossibly large is suggested by a number of factors. This may have been more than the population of Egypt at the time. Moreover, such a large group could not possibly have spent an extended period of time in the wilderness (which was mostly desert). Finally, it is probably more than the population of Israel some three hundred years later in the 900s BCE, during the time of the united kingdom under David and Solomon. Rather than reflecting historical fact, the number is the product of the storyteller's dramatic license.

12. Exod. 1.8.

13. Exod. 1.13–14.

14. The next several paragraphs (up through the call of Moses) are based on Exod. 2–3.

15. Exod. 2.23–25.

16. Exod. 3.2.

17. Abraham had visions (Gen. 15.1–17, 17.1–22, 18.1–15); Jacob saw a flaming ladder connecting heaven and earth and exclaimed, "Truly this is the gate of heaven" (Gen. 28.10–17).

18. Exod. 3.7–8, 10.

19. Exod. 3.14. What does this response mean? Formally, the statement is a tautology in which the second half repeats the first half without supplying any further information. But does that mean the answer says nothing? Or does it mean that God is ineffable, beyond all words? Or, as some scholars suggest, should the phrase be translated "I will be present as I will be present," thus affirming both divine presence and divine freedom?

20. Exod. 5.1, 17.

21. The first nine plagues are narrated in 7.14–10.29. They reflect the dramatization of storytelling. For example, although the fifth plague kills *all* the livestock of Egypt, there are still livestock alive to be killed in the subsequent plagues of boils and hail. We are also repeatedly told that God hardened Pharaoh's heart. On the one hand, this is an explanation of why Pharaoh is not impressed enough by the plagues to let Israel go. On the other hand, it also affirms that even Pharaoh is under the control of Israel's God. But presumably God never hardens anybody's heart. The plagues are also referred to in Ps. 78.42–51. There seven are listed: water turned to blood, flies, frogs, caterpillars and locusts, hail and frost, plague (on humans or animals?), and death of the firstborn. Not mentioned are gnats, boils, and thick darkness. Given the difference in genres (a psalm instead of a narrative), not much weight should be given to the variances. It is interesting, though, that the two lists make use of the common biblical numbers ten and seven.

22. The tenth plague is described in 11.1–9 and 12.29–32. The regulations for Passover are given in 12.1–28.

23. Exod. 14. The identity of the body of water is unknown. Though older translations refer to it as the Red Sea, the Hebrew phrase means "the sea of reeds," possibly referring to a shallow and marshy area near the shore of a body of water. Moreover, the story refers both to a strong wind driving the sea back all night long, as might happen to the shallow end of a body of water, and to the sea dividing in the middle. See 14.21–22.

24. This seems the most natural meaning of the language. Some scholars have suggested that the reference is not to the temple as God's dwelling place and sanctuary but to the "holy land" as a whole as God's dwelling place. In any case, the hymn reflects a time considerably later than the events it describes.

25. Miriam is named in Exodus as Aaron's sister. In Num. 26.59, she is also spoken of as Moses' sister. In Mic. 6.4, she, Moses, and Aaron are referred to as the three leaders of the exodus.

26. The journey to Sinai and God's provision of guidance, food, and drink in the desert are described in Exod. 16–18. In Num. 11.31–32, we are told that the quails covered the ground to a depth of two cubits (about three feet).

27. Exod. 19.4–6.

28. The Ten Commandments are found in Exod. 20.1–17 and Deut. 5.6–21. The Book of the Covenant is found in Exod. 20.22–23.33.

29. Many of them also have parallels in other ancient Near Eastern law codes. See Joseph Blenkinsopp, *The Pentateuch* (New York: Doubleday, 1992), pp. 200–204.

30. Respectively: Lev. 19.18, Exod. 21.17, Lev. 11.1–47, Exod. 21.28–36, Lev. 15.16–18.

31. Deut. 15.1–18.

32. Lev. 25. A bit of background: When the Israelites settled the land of Canaan, every family was given a plot of agricultural land. Over time, families that ran into difficulties sometimes lost their land because of debt. In the jubilee year, land was to be restored to the original family of ownership. So radical is this law of the Pentateuch that it may never have been observed (with a possible exception in the 400s BCE during the time of Nehemiah).

33. The story of the golden calf and its sequel is found in Exod. 32–34.

34. Exod. 34.6–7.

35. Num. 10.11 reports their departure, and the rest of the book speaks of their years in the wilderness.

36. The book of Deuteronomy is commonly dated to the 600s BCE. It (or a portion of it) is often identified with a book "discovered" in the temple in Jerusalem in the year 621 BCE, which then served as the basis of reforms of Israel's life and worship under King Josiah (see II Kings 22–23).

37. Deut. 34.4.

38. I owe this useful phrase to John Dominic Crossan. I cannot recall whether he has used it in one of his books, but I have heard him use it in lectures.

39. Brueggemann, *The Bible Makes Sense,* pp. 45–46. His commentary on Exodus in *The New Interpreter's Bible* (Nashville: Abingdon, 1994), pp. 675–981, is superb.

40. Another five percent are called "retainers," basically a service class attached to the elites and consisting of the army, government officials, high-ranking servants, scribes, the upper level of the priesthood, and so forth. I have taken this terminology and the information on the typical shape of such societies primarily from Gerhard Lenski, *Power and Privilege: A Theory of Social Stratification* (New York: McGraw-Hill, 1966). I have summarized this type of society elsewhere. See, for example, *The God We Never Knew*, pp. 134–36.

41. I owe the first two phrases to Walter Brueggemann, *The Prophetic Imagination* (Philadelphia: Fortress, 1978), chap. 1. He uses them to describe life under Pharaoh in the world of Egypt and often refers to this way of structuring society as "royal consciousness."

42. Exod. 20.2–3.

43. Deut. 34.10–12.

6

Reading the
Prophets Again

The classical prophets of ancient Israel are among the most remarkable people who have ever lived. Such is the indelible impression made by their words. Their language is memorable, poetic, and powerful. Their passion and courage are exceptional. Their message combines radical criticism of the way things are with urgent advocacy of another way of being. They disturb our sense of normalcy in several ways— socially, personally, and spiritually. And, in their own words, they speak for God.

Introduction

We move from the Pentateuch, or the Law, to the second major portion of the Hebrew Bible: the Prophets. The books contained in the Prophets are divided into two groups, "the former prophets" and "the latter prophets." The *former* prophets are a collection of historical books beginning with Joshua and including Judges, I and II Samuel, and I and II Kings. They narrate the history of Israel from the time of the occupation of the promised land until the fall of Jerusalem to the Babylonians in 586 BCE.

The *latter* prophets are those books named after the classical prophets. These persuasive messengers of God are themselves commonly divided into two groups, "the major prophets" and "the minor prophets." The designations do not refer to the prophets' relative importance; rather, they indicate the length of the books that bear the prophets' names. The three major prophets are Isaiah (sixty-six chapters), Jeremiah (fifty-two chapters), and Ezekiel (forty-eight chapters). The books of the twelve minor prophets range in length from Hosea and Zechariah (fourteen chapters each) to Obadiah (one chapter, the shortest book in the Hebrew Bible). Several are only two or three chapters long.[1]

We not only move now from the Pentateuch to the Prophets, but we also move forward in time about five hundred years, leaving behind the exodus of the thirteenth century BCE. For about two centuries after the Israelites settled the promised land, they lived as a "tribal confederacy" with no centralized government. Then, in about the year 1000 BCE, the tribal confederacy was replaced by a monarchy. The first king was the ill-fated Saul, followed by King David, who unified the new kingdom and made Jerusalem its capital. David's son King Solomon built the temple on Mt. Zion in Jerusalem and extended the kingdom to the greatest size it was to attain.

When Solomon died around 922 BCE, the united kingdom split into two parts: the northern kingdom of Israel and the southern kingdom of Judah. The northern kingdom lasted until 722 BCE, when it was conquered and destroyed by the Assyrian Empire and basically disappeared from history. The southern kingdom was conquered and destroyed by the Babylonian Empire in 586 BCE, and some of the survivors were exiled to Babylon. The exile lasted about fifty years, ending in 539 BCE, when the exiles were permitted to return to Judah and begin rebuilding their ruined country.

The classical prophets belong to the time of the divided kingdoms, their destruction, the exile, and the return. The earliest of these prophets (Amos) began speaking about 750 BCE, some thirty years before the destruction of the northern kingdom. The latest spoke in the century or two following the return from exile. Though they had predecessors (Samuel in the eleventh century, Nathan in the tenth, Elijah and Elisha in the ninth), I will focus primarily on the classical prophets.

Hearing the Prophets the First Time

I have heard the voices of the prophets in three quite different ways in my own religious journey as a Christian. My first impression of the prophets was formed when I was a child growing up in the church. In common with many Christians of my generation (and before), I heard the prophets spoken of primarily as predict-tors of the messiah, who was, of course, Jesus; they had been sent by God to foretell Jesus' coming. Moreover, given that they predicted events hundreds of years in the future (from their point of time), it was obvious that they had to be inspired by God.

I heard the New Testament itself, especially Matthew's gospel, speak about the prophets this way.[2] From the first chapter onward, Matthew uses a "prediction-fulfillment" formula. After he narrates the story of an angel telling Joseph in a dream that Mary is pregnant by the Holy Spirit, he quotes a passage from the eighth-century prophet Isaiah:

> All this took place to fulfill what had been spoken by the Lord through the prophet: Behold, a virgin shall conceive and bear a son, and they shall call him Emmanuel, which means "God with us."[3]

So the virgin birth had been predicted.

In his first two chapters, Matthew uses the prediction-fulfillment formula five times, all in connection with Jesus' birth and infancy. I cite two more examples. After Jesus is born in Bethlehem, Matthew writes, "It has been written by the prophet" and then quotes words derived primarily from Micah:

> And you, O Bethlehem, in the land of Judah, are by no means
> least among the rulers of Judah; for from you shall come a
> ruler who is to shepherd my people Israel.[4]

I took Matthew's claim for granted as a child: the birthplace of
Jesus had been predicted centuries earlier.

Matthew also tells us that Mary, Joseph, and the baby Jesus
flee to Egypt to escape the murderous plot of King Herod. (Like
Pharaoh centuries before, Herod had ordered the death of all
male babies.) After Herod dies, they return from Egypt, and
Matthew writes:

> This was to fulfill what had been spoken by the Lord through
> the prophet: "Out of Egypt have I called my son."

The quoted passage is from the prophet Hosea.[5] Used in con-
junction with Matthew's narrative, it gives the strong impression
that even Jesus' time in Egypt and his return from Egypt had
been predicted.

In Matthew as a whole, the prediction-fulfillment formula is
used thirteen times. And though the other authors of the New
Testament do not use the pattern so explicitly, many of them
correlate events in the life of Jesus with passages from the Hebrew Bible, especially in the passion narratives, which tell the
story of his death. Hearing the Bible in a state of precritical
naivete, I reached a conclusion that was inevitable: the prophets
were supernaturally inspired predictors of Jesus.

This reading of the prophets was reinforced by a copy of *Halley's Bible Handbook* that was in our home. First published in
1924, it soon became a best-seller. As I recall the edition I knew
as a child, there was a two-page layout of over one hundred predictions of the messiah in the Old Testament and their fulfillment in Jesus in the New Testament.[6]

The handbook's claim: "By the time we reach the end of the
Old Testament, the entire story of Christ has been pre-written
and pre-figured."

Then the handbook asks a question to which its answer is obvious:

> How can this amazing composite of Jesus' life and work, put
> together by different writers of different centuries, ages before Jesus came, be explained on any other basis than that
> ONE SUPERHUMAN MIND supervised the writing? The miracle
> of the ages.[7]

Thus the prophets predicted Jesus. Moreover, their predictions not only proved that Jesus was the messiah; they also proved the truth and supernatural origin of the Bible.

Seeing the prophets as predictors of the future was reinforced by the most common meaning of the words "prophet" and "prophecy" in our culture. For both Christians and non-Christians, the words most often refer to a supernatural (that is, more than natural) knowledge of the future. Some people within each group believe that prophecy is possible; others do not. But both groups agree that this is what prophecy is.

In short, the way I heard the prophets the first time is that they certainly predicted the first coming of Jesus and may have predicted his second coming. This way of seeing and reading the prophets is still around. *Halley's* is still in print, the best-selling Bible handbook in American history, and now in its twenty-fifth edition. In person or by letter, I continue to be asked by Christians who are puzzled about the historical study of Jesus, "What about the argument from prophecy?"

I no longer see the prophets as predictors of Jesus. Instead, there is another (and quite obvious) explanation of the correspondences between the New Testament and passages from the Hebrew Bible. Namely, the correspondences are there because the authors of the New Testament were all Jewish (with one possible exception) and knew the Hebrew Bible (whether in Hebrew or Greek) very well. Thus, as they told the story of Jesus and reflected about his significance, they often echoed language from Jewish scripture. Doing so was completely natural and legitimate.

The prophets were part of their sacred tradition, and they sought to show continuity between Jesus and the tradition out of which he and they came.

In short, the correspondences are not the product of prediction and fulfillment, but of prophecy historicized. In other words, the New Testament authors used passages from the Hebrew Bible to generate historical narrative. They did this in at least two different ways:

- Sometimes they used prophetic passages as a way of commenting about something that had happened. For example, the gospel writers often used phrases or passages from the Hebrew Bible to comment about the significance of Jesus' crucifixion (an actual historical event).[8]
- Other times they embellished their stories of Jesus with details drawn from texts of the Hebrew Bible.

As the New Testament authors historicized prophecy in these ways, they often took a passage out of its ancient context and gave it a meaning very different from what the prophet had intended. I illustrate with three passages already cited from Matthew.

Matthew uses Isaiah 7.14 as a prediction of the virginal conception of Jesus. But that earlier text did not originally refer to a virgin birth or to an event in the distant future. Rather, as the full context of Isaiah 7.10–17 makes clear, Isaiah was speaking to King Ahaz of the southern kingdom of Judah in the eighth century BCE. It was a time of crisis: Judah was threatened by a military invasion. Within that historical context, Isaiah tells King Ahaz that God will give him a sign—namely, a young woman already pregnant will give her child the symbolic name Immanuel. (Immanuel is not a proper name, but a phrase meaning "God with us.") Isaiah then tells Ahaz that before this child is old enough to know the difference between right and wrong, the crisis will be over. In its eighth-century context, the passage promises deliverance to Ahaz and Judah: they will be safe.

Matthew's use of Hosea 11.1 in his story of Mary, Joseph, and

Jesus returning from Egypt illustrates the same point. Matthew quotes only the second half of Hosea's verse: ". . . out of Egypt I called my son." But the full verse makes it clear that the prophet is referring backward in time to the exodus, not forward: "When Israel was a child, I loved him, and out of Egypt I called my son." Not only does the passage refer to the exodus, but it is Israel (and not Jesus) who is called God's son.

Finally, the story of Jesus' birth in Bethlehem may be an example of prophecy having generated historical narrative. The majority of mainline scholars think that Jesus was probably born in Nazareth, not in Bethlehem.[9] Why, then, do both Matthew and Luke have him born in Bethlehem? Probably because of the tradition that the messiah was to be "the son of David"— namely, a descendant of King David, Israel's greatest king. As the home of David, Bethlehem was "David's city." Indeed, the passage from Micah quoted by Matthew expresses this connection: the future and ideal king—a king like David—will be born in Bethlehem, the city of David. Thus the story of Jesus' birth in Bethlehem may not reflect history but instead express the early Christian movement's conviction that Jesus was the messiah, son of David, and ideal king.

But I am getting ahead of my story. I did not learn what I have just reported until later. Nevertheless, setting aside the notion that the prophets' primary purpose was to predict Jesus centuries ahead of time is an essential step in seeing and reading them again.

Hearing the Prophets the Second Time

I began to hear the prophets a second time in college, during a political philosophy course. Included in the course was the prophet Amos.[10] I learned that Amos and the other prophets of Israel did not write books (as if they were recording their predictions for the future), but were masters of oral speech. For the most part, they spoke short, memorable oracles and addressed people in their own time. And I learned that the words they spoke were disturbing.

The Prophetic Passion for Social Justice

Amos was downright electrifying. I was stunned by the rhetorical elegance and content of his "inaugural address" in the first two chapters of the book bearing his name. Speaking to the northern kingdom in the eighth century BCE, he indicts by name the kingdoms on its borders who were Israel's traditional enemies: Damascus, Gaza, Tyre, Edom, Ammon, and Moab.

The oracles against each of the neighboring kingdoms begin with the solemn words, "Thus says the LORD: For three transgressions and for four, I will not revoke the punishment." He indicts them for barbaric cruelty in warfare: they have exiled entire communities, pursued with the sword with no pity, and ripped open pregnant women, all for the sake of enlarging their borders. It is as if Amos were pinning up verbal atrocity posters. He announces God's judgment on each kingdom: they will be conquered and sent into exile. Then he indicts Judah, the southern kingdom, also an enemy of Israel.

The rhetorical strategy is brilliant. By indicting and pronouncing God's judgment against Israel's enemies, he draws his audience to his side. Then he turns the screw and indicts Israel itself in the name of Israel's God. Now the crimes are not cruelty in warfare but social injustice within the society:

> Thus says the LORD:
> For three transgressions of Israel and for four,
>   I will not revoke the punishment.
> Because they sell those who have done no wrong for silver
>   and the needy for a pair of sandals.
> They trample the heads of the poor into the dust of the earth,
>   and push the afflicted out of the way.[11]

In Amos, I heard for the first time the prophetic passion for social justice. Repeatedly and not only in his inaugural address, he indicts the wealthy for their exploitation of the poor:

> You oppress the poor and crush the needy.
> You trample on the poor and take from them taxes of grain.

You trample on the needy, and bring to ruin the poor of the
    land.[12]

He paints vivid and damning pictures of people who live lives
of luxury and yet are indifferent to the misery in their midst:

Woe to you who lie on beds of ivory and lounge on your
    couches,
eating lambs from the flock and calves from the stall;
who sing idle songs to the sound of the harp, and like David
    improvise
on instruments of music,
who drink wines from bowls, and anoint themselves with the finest
    oils, but are not grieved over the ruin of Joseph [the poor].
Therefore, you shall now be the first to go into exile.[13]

With words as sharp as a well-honed machete, Amos indicts
Israel's worship of God. In the name of God, he says that God
despises "solemn assemblies":

I hate, I despise your festivals, and I take no delight in your
    solemn assemblies.
Even though you offer me your burnt offerings and grain of-
    ferings,
        I will not accept them;
        and the offerings of your fatted animals, I will not look
    upon.
Take away from me the noise of your songs;
        I will not listen to the melody of your harps.

What then does God want? Amos continues:

But let justice roll down like waters, and righteousness like an
    ever-flowing stream.[14]

Amos also speaks about the judgment of God. But it is not the
final judgment or last judgment at which individuals will face

heaven or hell. Rather, it is God's judgment *within history:* societies filled with rampant injustice face destruction.

All of this was brand-new to me when I was introduced to it in college. Amos was passionate about social justice. Indeed, for him, sin was primarily injustice. Amos spoke of God's judgment not in the distant future—whether at the end of time or when an individual dies—but within history. I had had no idea that the prophets were like this, or that there were passages in the Bible like this. For the first time, I saw and heard the Bible without the domesticating lenses of my childhood faith. For me, the encounter with Amos marked the beginning of a new stage in my perception of the Bible, of Christianity, and of the world.

The Indictment-Threat Oracle

I went to seminary in part because of Amos. There, what I learned about the prophets underlined the impression I had gotten from Amos. I learned that the most common form of prophetic speech was the indictment-threat oracle. The form has two major elements, and sometimes a third.

- *The indictment:* an accusation or a list of offenses.
- *The threat* (or sentence): what will happen because of the offenses.
- *The summons to the accused:* the naming of the offenders. This third element, though sometimes explicit, is often implicit. When explicit, it is most often the first element in an indictment-threat oracle.

Seeing the form was (and remains) very illuminating. An awareness of the most common pattern of prophetic speech helps in reading the prophets because the pattern discloses what they most centrally were doing. In effect, they were prosecuting a covenant lawsuit on behalf of God against Israel.

I illustrate the indictment-threat oracle with two examples. The first is from Micah, who spoke in the southern kingdom in the eighth century. Jerusalem was that kingdom's capital, Zion was the mountain on which the temple stood, and "the house" in the last line of the oracle refers to the temple.

> *The summons to the accused:* Hear this, you rulers of the house
>   of Jacob and chiefs of the house of Israel.
> *The indictment:* You abhor justice and pervert all equity. You
>   build Zion with blood and Jerusalem with wrong. Its rulers
>   give judgment for a bribe, its priests teach for a price, its
>   prophets give oracles for money; yet they lean upon the
>   LORD and say, "Surely the LORD is with us! No harm shall
>   come upon us."
> *The threat:* Therefore because of you Zion shall be plowed as a
>   field; Jerusalem shall become a heap of ruins, and the
>   mountain of the house a wooded height.[15]

The indictment names injustice, and the threat speaks of Jerusalem and the temple in ruins.

A second example is from Amos. To clarify the first line, Bashan was an area known for its fine cattle. As the indictment makes clear, the phrase "cows of Bashan" refers to the wives of the wealthy men of Samaria, the capital of the northern kingdom.

> *The summons to the accused:* Hear this word, you cows of
>   Bashan who are on Mount Samaria.
> *The indictment:* You oppress the poor, you crush the needy,
>   you say to your husbands, "Bring something to drink."
> *The threat:* The Lord God has sworn by his holiness: The time is
>   surely coming upon you when they shall take you away with
>   hooks, even the last of you with fishhooks. Through breaches
>   in the wall, you shall leave, each one straight ahead.[16]

The indictment is once again against the oppression of the poor. The threat envisions the city of Samaria after a military conquest, its walls breached during the siege, and the survivors marched off by the conquerors as "booty."

The Dramatic Power of Prophetic Acts

In seminary I also learned about "prophetic acts." Sometimes the prophets performed attention-getting symbolic actions in order to dramatize their message. These included the symbolic naming of children. Hosea, for example, named two of his children *Lo-ruhamah* and *Lo-ammi*, Hebrew phrases that mean "not pitied" and "not my people."[17] The names are a threat: the days are coming, Hosea says, when Israel will be "not pitied" and "not my [God's] people."

Isaiah named two of his children *Maher-shalal-hash-baz* and *Shear-jashub*.[18] The first is a Hebrew phrase meaning "the spoil speeds, the prey hastes," and is a promise of deliverance to Judah: the two kingdoms threatening it will soon be prey and spoils of war for Assyria. The second is a Hebrew phrase meaning "a remnant will return." Though it has an element of promise, it is also a threat: that there will be *only* a remnant speaks of destruction.

More dramatic are public acts that amount to street theater. Isaiah, for example, walked naked and barefoot through the streets of Jerusalem for three years to symbolize that Judah should not enter a military alliance with Egypt against Assyria, for Assyria would conquer Egypt and carry them off naked and barefoot as prisoners of war.[19]

Jeremiah also performed several prophetic acts. In the presence of some of the leaders of Jerusalem, he shattered a clay jug, accompanying that gesture with the words, "Thus says the LORD, 'So will I break this people and this city.'"[20] On another occasion, Jeremiah is told by God to wear a wooden yoke on his neck in order to symbolize that Jerusalem and Judah are to wear the yoke of Babylon and not join a military alliance of small kingdoms against Babylon. His act set up one of the classic scenes in Hebrew prophecy, a confrontation between two prophets proclaiming opposite messages. A prophet named Hananiah challenged Jeremiah, broke the wooden yoke Jeremiah was wearing, and proclaimed, "Thus says the LORD: This is how I will break the yoke of King Nebuchadnezzar of Babylon." Soon thereafter

Jeremiah announced in the name of God words to this effect: You have broken a wooden yoke, but God has forged an iron yoke that you will wear.[21] For the people of the time, it must have been bewildering to see two prophets, both speaking in the name of God, making opposing pronouncements.

Ezekiel was the star of prophetic street theater. Shortly before the Babylonian conquest and destruction of Jerusalem, he is told by God to make a model of Jerusalem surrounded by a siege wall, camps, and battering rams. In a public place, he is to lie on his left side for 390 days, then on his right side for 40 days, to symbolize the number of years that Israel and Judah are to spend in exile. During all this time, he is to eat starvation rations such as would be available in a city under a prolonged siege, and he is to bake his bread using human dung as fuel. All of this would symbolize what was soon to happen to Jerusalem.

The way I heard the prophets the second time captivated me. I was struck by their passion for social justice, their antiestablishment message, and their warnings of the consequences facing a society that did not take peace and justice seriously. Their combination of prophetic critique and street theater was perfect for the times: it was the late 1960s. Especially to an idealistic college student, the prophets seemed like powerful allies in the movements against racism, poverty, and the Vietnam War.

Hearing the Prophets the Third Time

But I was to hear the prophets a third time. It was not that my second hearing was wrong; that hearing was simply incomplete. Since then, how I hear the prophets has been added to in three important ways.

The Prophets and God

I now see that God was utterly central to the prophets. More specifically, I have become convinced that experiences of the sacred were the source of their sense of mission, their passion for justice, and their courage to challenge the established power of domination systems.

To explain what I mean, I return for a moment to how I heard the prophets the second time. That hearing was not only "perfect" for the social activism of the 1960s; it also fit where I was personally in my religious life. During that same period of time, I had become increasingly uncertain about the reality of God. By my late twenties, my adolescent doubts about God had deepened to the extent that I was virtually a "closet atheist."[22] In any case, I was a "practical atheist" or "functional atheist"—namely, a person who lived as if there were no God.[23] And yet the Bible and Christianity remained very important to me.

Thus the prophets were especially attractive. Because their focus was on *this* world, not on another world, they seemed to provide a way of taking seriously a major strand of the biblical tradition independent of whether God was real. I heard them as deeply political and only incidentally religious; I heard them as passionate about justice *in this world* and about the destiny and fate of societies *within history*. Even if God was not real, these were crucially important matters.

Of course, I was aware that the prophets believed in God; that was obvious from their words. After all, most people in their time did. But I took it for granted that the prophets' convictions about God were inherited from tradition, not generated by experience.

Though I knew that most of the prophets' books included visions and "call stories" in which they reported having been commissioned by God, I gave little weight to such stories. I saw them as legitimations of the prophets' mission and message. I imagined that such stories were necessary as responses to those who challenged their radical criticism by asking, "What is your authority for what you are saying?" They would say, as Amos did, "The LORD took me from following the flock, and the LORD said to me, 'Go, prophesy to my people Israel.'"[24] I even wondered whether the visions and call stories were literary creations by followers of the prophets, the people who had collected the prophetic words into books.[25]

In short, I did not imagine that God was an experiential reality for the prophets. I did not think of the prophets as having experiences of the sacred. The reason: I did not think that such experiences happened. I knew about believing in God; but I did not imagine that people could *know* God.

But now I am convinced that experiences of the sacred do happen, that the prophets had such experiences, and that such experiences were foundational for what they were, said, and did. This claim does not flow out of a more detailed study of the prophets in particular, but from my conviction that such experiences have happened throughout the history and cultures of humankind from antiquity into the present.

If one grants that experiences of the sacred do happen, it seems obvious that the prophets had such experiences.[26] Though I recognize that the accounts of their visions, ecstatic states, and calls serve a literary function, I no longer see them as *simply* literary creations. Though I am not sure that we ever have an exact transcript of prophetic ecstatic experience, I am convinced that the prophets had such experiences.

Taking such experiences seriously accounts for much of what we see in the prophets. It takes their words seriously. They regularly say, "Thus says the LORD," and they speak in the first person on behalf of God. I do not think the words they use come from God. The prophet is "a person and not a microphone," as Abraham Heschel put it.[27] In other words, the prophet is not simply an amplifier for a divine voice but speaks out of his own personality and experience. But the words of the prophets suggest that they were speaking from their knowledge *of* God—not from their knowledge *about* God, but from their *knowing* God.

Their experiences of the sacred account for their courage. They were often in trouble. By command of the king, Amos was ordered to leave the kingdom.[28] Jeremiah was beaten, put in stocks, threatened with death, forced into hiding, imprisoned, and lowered into a muddy cistern to starve and die.[29] The prophets all spoke unpopular messages that challenged the rich and powerful, and most (if not all) had to contend with the opposition of court prophets in the service of the monarchy. Their source of courage was God.

The prophets' experiences of the sacred also account for their affirmation of a God not identified with the social order, but "behind" and "beyond" it. Like the God who appeared to Moses in the burning bush, such a God subverts rather than legitimates the social order.

Finally, the prophets lived within the traditions of Israel, especially the exodus and covenant traditions. Thus they interpreted their experiences of God within the framework of exodus and covenant. As they looked at their contemporary society, they did not see the kind of community envisioned by the story of the exodus and the laws associated with it.

To put the combination together: the prophets had experiences of God; they lived within the traditions of Israel; and they were passionate about social justice. That the three are connected seems apparent.

This claim is also the central theme of Abraham Heschel's *The Prophets*. Heschel was one of the two most influential Jewish theologians of the twentieth century in the English-speaking world, and this book (like all of his books) is a marvel of insight and language. He emphasizes the same combination: the prophets were passionate about social justice, and they were people who *knew* God. He speaks of "their breathless impatience with injustice" and affirms that they experienced "moments that defy our understanding." These moments were moments of knowing God, and what they experienced in such moments of knowing was "a fellowship with the feelings of God, *a sympathy with the divine pathos*."[30]

The word "sympathy" here has a much richer meaning than it often does in modern usage, where it commonly means something like, "I feel sorry for you." Its roots point to the richer meaning: *pathos* means "strong feeling" (often suffering, but other strong emotions as well—anger, compassion, love, joy, etc.); the prefix *sym* means "with." Thus "sympathy" means "feeling with," or feeling the feelings of another. For Heschel, the phrase "sympathy with the divine pathos" means that the prophets felt the feelings of God. Their passion was thus God's passion; it came out of knowing God.

Thus I now see the prophets as more (but not less) than radical cultural critics with a passion for social justice. I now see them as God-intoxicated, as filled with the passion of God. And so I speak of them as God-intoxicated voices of radical social criticism and God-intoxicated advocates of an alternative social vision. Their dream is God's dream.

Prophets, Peasants, and Elites

The second major factor shaping how I now hear the prophets is a more precise understanding of the social system of the world that they addressed. That understanding has enabled me to see the target and content of prophetic criticism much more clearly.

At the heart of that fuller understanding is the model of preindustrial agrarian societies sketched in the previous chapter. These social systems (comprising economic, political, religious, and social structures) were controlled and shaped by elites of power and wealth to serve their own interests. So thorough was the elites' control that there was no way of countering their self-serving manipulation of the system.[31]

This type of society began to develop within Israel with the emergence of the monarchy around 1000 BCE. By the time of Solomon, Israel's third king, the major features of the ancient domination system were in place: a politics of oppression centered in monarchical authority; an economics of exploitation centered in the monarchy and aristocracy; and a religion of legitimation centered in the temple built by Solomon in Jerusalem.

Thus, by the time the classical prophets began to speak in the eighth century, Israel and Judah had become miniature versions of the ancient domination system that had enslaved their ancestors in Egypt. The victims (the majority of the population) were Israelites, of course, but now the elites at the top were also Israelites! Egypt had been established in Israel.[32]

Seeing this social system as the world addressed by the prophets has been greatly illuminating. Before I was aware of it,

I heard the prophetic indictments against "Israel" in an undifferentiated way, as if the people as a whole were being indicted for injustice. It sounded as if *everybody* was guilty. This puzzled me. I wondered if perhaps Israel and Judah were especially unjust societies, or if perhaps the standards of the prophets (and God) were so high as to be ultimately unrealistic.

That puzzlement has been replaced by considerable clarity. I now see that most of the prophetic indictments are directed against the elites who were responsible for creating and maintaining structures of domination and exploitation. A careful reading of the prophets discloses that often the elites are explicitly named or, alternatively, that the offenses named are elite offenses. The prophets indict the elites; they do not blame the victims and hold them responsible for the injustice of their society.

The elites are addressed not only (or even largely) because they had the power to change things, but because it is they who were primarily responsible for Israel's becoming a radically unjust domination system—one hardly different from Egypt. They had deformed Israel, changing her from the exodus vision of an alternative community living under the lordship of God to just another kingdom living under the lordship of a native pharaoh.

Thus the prophets are not saying that all or most Israelites were equally guilty of social injustice, as if the victims of the system were as responsible as the perpetrators. Rather, they indict the elites of power and wealth at the top of the system on behalf of the victims and in the name of God. These God-intoxicated figures were utterly convinced that what they saw happening in their midst could not be the will of the God who had liberated Israel from bondage in Egypt.

I also have realized that the conflict between domination systems and the will of God runs through the Hebrew Bible as a whole. According to the first book of Samuel, the conflict does not begin in the time of the prophets but goes back to the origin of the monarchy in Israel in the late eleventh century BCE. First Samuel contains two very different traditions about the emergence of kingship—one anti-monarchical, the other pro-monarchical.

According to the anti-monarchical tradition, the people ask Samuel to appoint a king over them.[33] Their request displeases both Samuel and God. Indeed, their desire for a king is said to be a rejection of God's kingship. Nevertheless, God grants their request, but with a stern and remarkably precise warning about what a king will do to them: he will take their sons as warriors; conscript them into labor battalions to work his fields and produce weapons; take their daughters to be perfumers, cooks, and bakers; take the best of their fields and vineyards and orchards and give them to his friends; take one-tenth of their grain and their flocks; take their male and female slaves and the best of their animals and put them to his work; and, God says to them, "You shall be his slaves."[34]

According to the second and pro-monarchical tradition, God's intervention established the monarchy with Saul as its first king. In a charming folktale that begins with some lost donkeys, God discloses to Samuel that a certain man (Saul) will come to him whom God has chosen to be king and that Samuel is to anoint him as such. A confirming sign from God follows.[35]

The pro-monarchical tradition surfaces again in II Samuel in the promise given by God to King David. David is told that God will establish an everlasting dynasty for him: the throne of his son's kingdom will last forever. Indeed, the king is no less than a son of God: "I will be a father to him, and he will be a son to me."[36] In this tradition, Israelite kingship is not only a gift of God but guaranteed by God to last forever. The social order— the domination system—is ordained by God.

The pro-monarchical tradition obviously reflects the vantage point and self-interest of the elites. Sometimes called "royal theology," it shows the way the world looks from the elite point of view. The anti-monarchical tradition reflects prophetic theology: the domination system is not the will of God, but a betrayal of God. It is a rejection of God's kingship.

Both points of view are in the Bible, going back to the time of the exodus. The central conflict of the exodus—between the domination system of the pharaoh and an alternative and much more egalitarian social vision grounded in the character of

God—is replicated in the conflict between royal theology and prophetic theology within Israel itself.

It is important to note that the conflict is not between law and prophets, as if it were "the law" versus "the prophets," as scholars of an earlier generation sometimes saw it. From that earlier point of view, the prophets were good and the law was bad. Rather, the conflict is between the law and prophets together against the royal theology of the domination system.

Prophetic Energizing: The Language of Hope

The third main feature of how I hear the prophets now is a greater appreciation for prophetic energizing. To explain: Walter Brueggemann names the two primary dimensions of prophetic activity as prophetic *criticizing* and prophetic *energizing*.[37] So far in this chapter, we have seen much of the former. Prophetic energizing sounds a different note: it uses language to generate hope, affirm identity, and create a new future.

The predestruction prophets—those who spoke before the destruction of Israel and Judah—were mostly engaged in prophetic criticism, indicting and warning the elites of what would soon happen unless they abandoned their privilege and sought justice. The postdestruction prophets, on the other hand—those who spoke during and after the exile—were primarily engaged in prophetic energizing. The distinction is relative, however, not absolute. The predestruction prophets also used the language of energizing, and the postdestruction prophets also used the language of criticizing. Nevertheless, in general the predestruction prophets spoke against the perpetrators of the native domination system on behalf of the victims. The postdestruction prophets spoke to the victims of a new imperial domination system that now ruled over the Jewish people.

In my second phase of hearing the prophets, most of my attention was drawn to prophetic criticizing, largely because of the time in our own society's history. Though I continue to regard that message as vitally important, I am now also very much struck by prophetic energizing.

Second Isaiah and the Experience of Exile We see the language of prophetic energizing used with great power and beauty in the second part of the book of Isaiah, commonly called "Second Isaiah" or "Deutero-Isaiah."[38] The first thirty-nine chapters of Isaiah are primarily from the predestruction prophet Isaiah, who spoke to Judah in the eighth century. Chapters forty through fifty-five contain the words of Second Isaiah, a Jewish prophet whose name is unknown and who spoke to the Jewish people in exile beginning around the year 539 BCE.

To appreciate the energizing power of Second Isaiah's language, it is illuminating to set it in the historical context of the Jewish experience of exile. The Babylonian conquest of Judah and Jerusalem in 586 BCE not only brought massive death and destruction, as attested by archaeological and literary evidence alike. It also caused widespread desperation and despair among the survivors, many of whom were exiled to Babylon.

The experience seared itself into the memory of the Jewish people and left its mark in the Hebrew Bible. A number of the psalms reflect the experience of exile. Psalm 137 is especially poignant. Recall that Zion is the mountain in Jerusalem where the now-destroyed temple once stood:

> By the rivers of Babylon, there we sat down and there we wept
> when we remembered Zion.
> On the willows there we hung up our harps.
> For there our captors asked us for songs,
> and our tormentors asked for mirth,
> saying "Sing us one of the songs of Zion."
> How could we sing the LORD's song in a foreign land?[39]

The book of Lamentations is a sustained expression of grief and pain. The author personifies Jerusalem as a woman and mourns her desolation:

> How lonely sits the city that once was full of people!
> How like a widow she has become,
> she that was great among the nations!

She that was a princess among the provinces has become a vas-
sal. She weeps bitterly in the night with tears on her cheeks;
    among all her lovers, she has no one to comfort her. . . .
All her people groan as they search for bread;
    they trade their treasures for food. . . .
Is it nothing to you, all you who pass by?
Look and see if there is any sorrow like my sorrow.[40]

Much of the book describes the lives of the survivors with precision and anguish. Its concluding chapter begins:

Remember, O LORD, what has befallen us;
    look and see our disgrace.
Our inheritance [the promised land] has been turned over to
strangers,
    our homes to aliens.
We have become orphans, fatherless; our mothers are like
widows.
We must pay for the water we drink;
    the wood we get must be bought.
With a yoke on our necks we are hard-driven;
    we are weary, we are given no rest. . . .
Women are raped in Zion,
    virgins in the towns of Judah.
Our princes are hung up by their hands;
    no respect is shown to the elders.
Young men are compelled to grind,
    and boys stagger under loads of wood.
The old men have left the city gate,
    the young men their music.
The joy of our hearts has ceased;
    our dancing has been turned to mourning. . . .
Mt. Zion lies desolate; jackals prowl over it.[41]

The last three verses of Lamentations express with great power
the hive of emotions felt in exile: the bitter pain of feeling aban-

doned, the desperate desire for restoration, the gnawing apprehension of having been forsaken and forgotten forever, the anxious fear that things will always be the same and never get better:

> Why have you forgotten us completely?
> Why have you forsaken us these many days?
> Restore us to yourselves, O LORD, that we may be restored;
>   renew our days as of old—
>   unless you have utterly rejected us,
>   and are angry with us beyond measure.

Second Isaiah and the Return from Exile In this historical setting, Second Isaiah spoke his message of prophetic energizing. He is the prophet of the return from exile.

The return from exile became politically possible when the Babylonian Empire was conquered by the Persian Empire in 539 BCE. Persian imperial policy permitted the return of exiled peoples to their homelands. But the return from exile could not be taken for granted.

The Jewish exiles were a weakened community—weakened in power, wealth, identity, and spirit. Most of them had been born in exile in Babylon. Only a few were still alive who remembered Jerusalem and Zion. For most, life in the promised land was a faint and secondhand memory. They had put down roots, even if the roots were in Babylon. Moreover, the journey would be long and difficult: about a thousand miles through a mostly empty semidesert landscape. It would be on foot. Undertake this journey? It was no small thing.

Second Isaiah's task is to announce and encourage, to proclaim and empower, the return from exile. His energizing language is among the most magnificent in the Bible. It is no accident that much of it is familiar to us from Handel's *Messiah*.

The primary content of his message is announced in a passage that probably reflects his call to be a prophet. The tone and content are very different from the predestruction prophets:

Comfort, O comfort my people, says your God. Speak ten-
derly to Jerusalem, and cry to her that she has served her
term, that her penalty is paid.[42]

Second Isaiah's message is that God is preparing the way of return. Using metaphors of a superhighway being built in the
desert, he declares to the exiles victimized by the domination
system of Babylon:

In the wilderness prepare the way of the LORD,
    make straight in the desert a highway for our
God.
Every valley shall be lifted up,
    and every mountain and hill be made low;
    the uneven ground shall become level,
    and the rough places plain.[43]

Second Isaiah recognizes the exiles' despairing sense of having
been forgotten by God and recites their lament:

Why do you say, O Jacob, and speak, O Israel,
"My way is hidden from the LORD, and my right is disre-
    garded by my God."[44]

He counters their despondency with energizing affirmations
of their identity. He reminds them of who they are in God's
sight: precious, honored, loved, remembered.

But now, thus says the LORD,
    the one who created you, O Jacob,
    the one who formed you, O Israel.
Do not be afraid, for I have redeemed you;
I have called you by name, and you are mine. . . .
You are precious in my sight, and honored,
    and I love you. . . .
Do not be afraid, for I am with you.[45]

He assures them that God will not forget even one of them, for they and their offspring are sons and daughters of God:

> I will bring your offspring from the east,
>   and from the west I will gather you;
> I will say to the north, "Give them up."
> And to the south, "Do not withhold;
>   bring my sons from far away
>   and my daughters from the end of the earth—
>   everyone who is called by name."[46]

The imagery of God as parent and Israel as God's sons and daughters continues in a passage that boldly compares God to a mother nursing her child. The gnawing fear of the exiles surfaces again: "The LORD has forsaken me, my Lord has forgotten me." In the name of God, Second Isaiah says:

> Can a woman forget her nursing child,
>   or show no compassion for the child of her womb?
> Even these may forget,
>   yet I will not forget you.[47]

He not only assures the exiles that they are remembered by God, but promises God's empowering presence on the difficult journey of return:

> Have you not known? Have you not heard?
> The LORD is an everlasting God,
>   the Creator of the ends of the earth.
> God does not faint or grow weary.
>
> God gives power to the faint,
>   and strengthens the powerless.
> Even youths will faint and be weary,
>   and the young will fall exhausted;

but those who wait for the LORD shall renew their
    strength,
        they shall mount up with wings like eagles,
they shall run and not be weary,
        they shall walk and not be faint.[48]

God is the shepherd of Israel:

God will feed the flock like a shepherd,
    gather the lambs, carry them,
    and gently lead those who are with young.[49]

To the community of exiles, newness seemed impossible. But
Second Isaiah announces that God is doing a new thing:

See, the former things have come to pass,
    and new things I now declare.[50]

The new thing is nothing less than a new exodus. In language
that recalls the exodus from Egypt:

I am the LORD, your Holy One, the Creator of Israel, your
    king.
Thus says the LORD,
        who makes a way in the sea,
        a path in the mighty waters,
        who brings out chariot and horse, army and warrior;
        they lie down, they cannot rise,
        they are extinguished,
        quenched like a wick.
Do not remember the former things,
        or consider the things of old.
I am about to do a new thing;
        now it springs forth, do you not perceive it?
I will make a way in the wilderness
        and rivers in the desert.[51]

The energizing language of Second Isaiah worked. The words that went forth from his mouth did not return empty, but accomplished that which God purposed:

> For you shall go out in joy,
>   and be led back in peace.
> The mountains and the hills before you
>   shall burst into song,
>   and all the trees of the field shall clap their hands.[52]

A significant number of the Jewish exiles returned to their homeland, though some remained in Babylon. Within a generation, the returning remnant had rebuilt the temple in Jerusalem—a temple that, because of the relatively impoverished status of the exiles, was much more modest in size and splendor than the earlier temple built by King Solomon (and destroyed by the Babylonians).

Though the exiles continued for several centuries to be under the political control of a series of foreign empires, they were back in the promised land. They were *home*.

The prophetic energizing we encounter in Second Isaiah came from the same place as the prophetic criticizing of the pre-destruction prophets. Second Isaiah must have known the energizing power of God in his own experience. Only so could he have energized and empowered his community to embark on the journey of return.

Concluding Reflections

Prophetic criticizing and energizing are most relevant to our time when we hear what the prophets were saying in *their* time, not when we divorce them from their time and imagine that they were predicting a distant future. Though their language is full of metaphor, as poetic language always is, we hear them most clearly when we hear them most historically.

In much of Christian history, their voices have not been clearly heard. They have usually been domesticated, most often by those choosing to see them as predictors of Jesus as the messiah. The domestication is to a large extent the product of Christendom, the wedding of Christianity with Western culture (a union that began with Constantine in the fourth century and ended only recently). During the centuries that Christianity slept with the dominant culture, it did not (and in a sense could not) see the prophets as voices of radical social protest against domination systems. And so the prophets were made "safe," either by ignoring them or by making them irrelevant.

In our time, the end of Christendom creates the possibility of hearing and reading the prophets again as God-intoxicated voices articulating "the dream of God."[53] God's dream is a world of justice and peace:

> The nations will beat their swords into plowshares,
>   and their spears into pruning hooks.
> Nation shall not lift up sword against nation,
>   neither shall they learn war anymore;
>   but they shall all sit under their own vines and their own
> fig trees,
>   and no one shall make them afraid.[54]

For more than one reason, communicating the prophetic passion for social justice is difficult in the church in North America today. Some of us continue to be blinded by the blinkers of prediction and fulfillment. We also resist hearing the prophets because they easily make us, as residents of an affluent society, uncomfortable. Yet another reason is that the word "justice" has multiple meanings in our culture, and the most common of them have little to do with the prophetic meaning of justice.

I became aware of this while teaching the prophets to undergraduates. I was puzzled that my students did not get very excited as I passionately exposited the prophets' passion for justice, even though *I* had found the prophets to be the most exciting part of my college years. My students dutifully took notes, but nothing remarkable seemed to be happening.

So I paused and asked them, "When I say the word 'justice,' what do you think of?" After some silence, a student said, "I think of the criminal justice system." I realized that his response made sense. After all, in the United States, the Department of Justice is concerned with *criminal* justice, and its head is spoken of as "the nation's chief law enforcement official." But if one hears the prophets' passion for justice as being about convicting and punishing criminals, one has not heard them at all.

Yet another common meaning of *justice* is "procedural justice." Procedural justice is concerned with "fair play," with ensuring that the "procedures" (laws and legal processes) are the same for everybody, and are enforced the same for everybody. Because the concern of that sort of justice is the individual and individual rights, it fits nicely within the core American cultural value of individualism. Rather than challenging the ethos of individualism, it supports it. Of course, procedural justice does matter, and matters greatly, especially in the areas of criminal justice and human rights. But it is still not what the prophets meant.

A third meaning of *justice* is "social justice." More comprehensive than criminal justice and procedural justice, social justice is concerned with the structures of society and their results. Because it is results-oriented, it discerns whether the structures of society—in other words, the social system as a whole—are just in their effects. Do they produce a large impoverished class or result in a more equitable distribution of resources? Do they benefit some at the expense of many or serve all equally? Do they produce conflict or peace? Do they destroy or nourish a future?

One can imagine a society with very good procedural justice being nonetheless filled with social injustice. For example, one can imagine Pharaoh's Egypt or the Third Reich having perfect procedural justice (they did not, of course, but one can imagine it) and laws that were impeccably enforced, and yet one cannot imagine concluding that these were *just* societies. Social justice is about more than the fair enforcement of laws and procedures. It is concerned with the justice of *social systems*. Its opposite is systemic injustice.

Social justice is the kind of justice that the prophets proclaim. The passion of their prophetic criticism challenges us. For the conflict between the dream of God and the domination systems of this world is persistent. It not only runs through the history of ancient Israel, but surfaces again in the time of Jesus—a conflict between the kingdom of God and the kingdoms of the Herods and Caesars of this world. And, to say the obvious, this conflict abides with us to this day. The structuring of societies by elites to serve their self-interest continues.[55]

The message of prophetic energizing also remains relevant today—relevant to the victims and exiles of the domination systems of our time. It proclaims that their identity, value, and worth are grounded not in culture but in God's regard. It affirms that God's character, will, and justice are different from the justice of oppressive social orders.

It is also relevant to those of us of Pharaoh's household who yearn for a different kind of society.[56] Newness is possible; the future does not have to replicate the past; the dream of God is alive.

More so than prophetic criticizing, prophetic energizing reminds us of the reality of God. After all, one can be passionate about social justice without God. But the prophets were passionate about *both* God and justice. They bring together the same two emphases we heard in the exodus story: the spiritual and the social, God and justice, the sacred and this world. At the center of the spiritual life, of life with God, is a twofold relationship: with God, and with the world of the everyday (including the way the world of the everyday is structured).

We see this with special clarity in Second Isaiah. In addition to the historical meaning his words had for Jewish exiles in the sixth century, he has also bequeathed to us the language of "exile" and "return" as powerful religious metaphors. "Exile," with all of its metaphorical resonances, is a rich metaphor for the human condition and how we often experience our lives. We feel much of what ancient Israel felt in exile: grief, anguish, longing, weakness, homelessness.

The solution for exiles is, of course, a journey of return, a way or path through the wilderness. Imaging the religious life as a "way" or "path" or "journey" is central not only in Second Isaiah, but also in Judaism and Christianity and in other religious traditions.

Both Judaism and Christianity are about a "way." Indeed, the word "repent," so central to the Christian tradition, has its roots in the Jewish story of the exile. To repent does not mean to feel really bad about sins; rather, it means to embark upon a path of return. The journey begins in exile, and the destination is a return to life in the presence of God.

The journey of return leads to the place where we began: to paradise and Jerusalem and Zion, all symbolizing the place of God's presence. Of course, we are never outside the presence of God, even when we do not believe that or know that. The "way," the "path," leads to the place where we *do* know that. The journey of return of which Second Isaiah speaks leads to life in the presence of God—to the one in whom we live and move and have our being.

NOTES

1. Two chapters long: Joel and Haggai; three chapters long: Nahum, Habakkuk, and Zephaniah.
2. For the sake of economy of language, I will refer to the author of Matthew's gospel as Matthew, even though we are quite certain that Matthew (one of the twelve disciples of Jesus) did not write it (just as we are quite certain that John did not write the gospel that bears his name). Indeed, we are not certain of the names of any of the authors of the gospels. It is reasonably likely that Mark and Luke wrote the gospels bearing their names, however, though there is no consensus about this.
3. Matt. 1.22–23, quoting Isa. 7.14. I note in passing that Matthew quotes the Greek version of the Old Testament (known as the Septuagint and often abbreviated LXX), not the Hebrew text; and that the Hebrew word in Isa. 7.14 does not mean "virgin" but "young woman." Of course, I did not know this when I was a child.
4. Matt. 2.5–6, quoting Mic. 5.2.
5. Matt. 2.13–15, quoting Hos. 11.1.
6. While writing this book, I tried to verify this by locating an edition of *Halley's Bible Handbook* from the 1940s, but the oldest edition I could find was the twenty-second, published in 1959 (Grand Rapids: Zondervan). In it,

fifty-six specific "foreshadowings and predictions" of Jesus as the messiah are cited from the Hebrew Bible; see pp. 354–66. See also pp. 386–87, citing events in the gospels "predicted" in the Hebrew Bible.

7. Quotations are taken from pp. 354 and 367 of the twenty-second edition (see previous note).

8. For examples, see my book co-authored with N.T. Wright, *The Meaning of Jesus: Two Visions* (San Francisco: HarperSanFrancisco, 1999), pp. 84–85.

9. For reasons for this conclusion, see John P. Meier, *A Marginal Jew: Rethinking the Historical Jesus,* vol. 1 (New York: Doubleday, 1991) pp. 214–16.

10. The class was taught by Rod Grubb, then a young professor at Concordia College in Moorhead, Minnesota. Grubb was a remarkable combination of intellectual, political science professor, Lutheran pastor, assistant football coach, and former football player. He later taught at St. Olaf College. I also took a Christian ethics course from him, and it is possible that I encountered Amos in that course and not in his political philosophy course.

11. Amos 2.6–7. His "inaugural address" (a modern designation, not one from the text) begins in 1.3 and ends in 2.8 or 2.16.

12. Amos 4.1, 5.11, 8.4.

13. Amos 6.4–7.

14. Amos 5.21–24.

15. Mic. 3.9–12.

16. Amos 4.1–3.

17. Hos. 1.6–8. The root of *Lo-ruhamah* is the Hebrew word for "compassion," related to the Hebrew word for "womb" and sometimes used in the Bible to speak of the central quality of God's character. Thus "not pitied" means "not compassioned" or "not treated with the compassion a mother feels toward the children of her womb." But because these phrases either do not work well in English or are impossibly long, "not pitied" is used.

18. Isa. 8.1–4, 7.3. Immanuel, another symbolic name associated with Isaiah, has already been mentioned.

19. Isa. 20. Public nakedness was shocking in that culture. Presumably Isaiah did not walk in this manner continually for three years, but occasionally over a three-year period.

20. Jer. 19; quoted verse is 19.10.

21. Jer. 27–28. Hananiah was probably a "court prophet" employed by the king.

22. I discuss this in more detail in my *The God We Never Knew* (San Francisco: HarperSanFrancisco, 1997), pp. 19–26.

23. It was not that I had become a wild and free-spirited libertine. If anything, I was too serious and too "good."

24. Amos 7.15.

25. The academic discipline of biblical scholarship that I was then learning did not take these stories seriously either. It was common for biblical scholars to distinguish the classical prophets from prophets outside of Israel by saying that ecstatic religious experience was not characteristic of or important to the former.

26. They include Isaiah's dramatic numinous experience of God in the temple (Isa. 6), Amos's visions (Amos 7.1–9, 9.1), Jeremiah's call and visions (Jer. 1.4–13, 4.23–26), and Ezekiel's visions, "possession" by the Spirit of God, and "traveling" in the Spirit (Ezek. 1–3).
27. Abraham Heschel, *The Prophets*, 2nd ed. (New York: Harper & Row, 1969), vol. 1, p. x.
28. Amos 7.10–17. This is one of the most dramatic confrontation scenes between a prophet and the domination system. The priest Amaziah delivers the king's command in 7.12–13.
29. Jer. 20.1–6, 26.1–24 (note that a prophet contemporary with Jeremiah is executed by the king), Jer. 36, 37.11–21, 38.1–13 (which also reports his rescue from the cistern).
30. Heschel, *The Prophets*, vol. 1, pp. 4, 10, 26 (italics in original).
31. In the ancient world, there were only two limits on economic exploitation of peasants by the elites: subsistence was not to become starvation, and desperation was not to become so great as to incite revolt. Otherwise, the elites had a free hand.
32. I owe this way of putting it to Walter Brueggemann, *Prophetic Imagination*, (Philadelphia: Fortress, 1978), chap. 2. Brueggemann also says that Solomon in effect had become a new pharaoh. Note that this is not a comment on Solomon's personal morality or immorality; it is a comment about the system that emerged under him.
33. I Sam. 8.4–22, 10.17–19.
34. I Sam. 8.11–18.
35. I Sam. 9.1–10.16.
36. II Sam. 7.1–17, esp. vv. 12–16. See also Ps. 2, one of the "royal psalms" (so named because it was most likely used as a liturgy for the coronation of a new king). The king, called "son of God" and "anointed one" (messiah), is promised that God will establish his throne forever.
37. Brueggemann, *The Prophetic Imagination*, chap. 1.
38. Isa. 40–55. "Deutero" is Greek for "second." In the Bible itself, there is of course no I Isaiah and II Isaiah (as there is a I Samuel and II Samuel).
39. Ps. 137.1–4. The last three verses of the psalm express the anger of exile, beseeching God to avenge the Israelites and blessing those who will smash the children of their enemies against a rock. The psalms were traditionally attributed to King David, just as the Pentateuch was attributed to Moses. However, the Psalms as a collection of hymns, prayers, and liturgies were written over many centuries, including the postexilic period. Other psalms that most likely reflect the experience of exile are 42–44, 74, 77, 80, 85, and 126.
40. Lam. 1.1–2, 11–12.
41. Lam. 5.1–5, 11–15, 18.
42. Isa. 40.1–2, the opening verses of Second Isaiah.
43. Isa. 40.3–4.
44. Isa. 40.27.
45. Isa. 43.1, 4–5.
46. Isa. 43.5–6.

47. Isa. 49.14–15.
48. Isa. 40.27–31.
49. Isa. 40.11.
50. Isa. 42.9.
51. Isa. 43.15–19.
52. Echoing Isa. 55.11, and quoting 55.12.
53. I owe this wonderful phrase to Verna Dozier, *The Dream of God* (Cambridge, MA: Cowley. 1991).
54. Mic. 4.3–4. The full oracle in Mic. 4.1–4 is almost exactly paralleled in Isa. 2.2–4, suggesting that it was widely known in prophetic circles.
55. In the contemporary United States, we see this in the naming of high taxes as a (and perhaps *the*) primary political issue. The anti-tax sentiment of our society is fueled and financed primarily by the wealthy. Can anybody seriously believe that the anti-tax movement serves the interest of the society as a whole, and not simply the narrow self-interest of the wealthy? Unfortunately, many do; elites know how to shape public opinion (and thus the system as a whole).
56. "Pharaoh's household" is a metaphor for those who derive benefits from the domination system without being primarily responsible for it or even in favor of it.

7

Reading Israel's Wisdom Again

In Israel's wisdom literature we encounter the dailiness of life in ancient Israel. The focus of this literature is more on the individual and the world of the everyday than what we encounter in the exodus and prophetic traditions. Its central concerns are the eminently practical questions, "How shall I live?" and "What is life about?"

Israel's wisdom is extraordinarily rich. It ranges from the practical and pithy wisdom sayings of the book of Proverbs through the melancholic reflections about life's mysteries in Ecclesiastes to the anguished and magnificent book of Job. It covers everything from sage advice about the raising of children to deeply reflective thought about the nature of reality and the meaning of life. Its voices are diverse and provocative.[1]

Introduction

Israel's wisdom books are found in the third and final division of the Hebrew Bible: the Writings. This is a miscellaneous collection dating primarily from the postexilic period. In addition to the wisdom books of Proverbs, Ecclesiastes, and Job, this section of the Bible includes the Psalms (Israel's prayer- and hymnbook), the apocalyptic book of Daniel, the stories of heroic Queen Esther and the good Gentile woman Ruth, the erotic love poetry of the Song of Songs (sometimes called the Song of Solomon or Canticles), and the historical books of I and II Chronicles, Ezra, and Nehemiah.

The wisdom books are difficult to date with precision, largely because they contain no references to historical events contemporary with them by which they might be dated. Indeed, in striking contrast to both the Law and the Prophets, they do not refer even to historical events from Israel's past. History, whether secular or sacred, is not one of their concerns.[2]

From ancient times, Israel's wisdom has been associated with King Solomon, who reigned in the tenth century BCE. Much of the book of Proverbs is attributed to him, the book of Ecclesiastes claims him as its author, and the apocryphal Wisdom of Solomon is named after him. But there is a scholarly consensus that these books do not come from the time of Solomon. Thus the connection to Solomon is traditional (as are the connections between the Pentateuch and Moses and between the Psalms and David) and without historical significance.

Wisdom literature finds us not in Solomon's day, then, but in the postexilic period that began in 539 BCE. Though the book of Proverbs as a collection of sayings no doubt contains some earlier material, in its present form it is a postexilic composition put together around 500 BCE. The book of Job is most commonly seen as an exilic or postexilic document, though a few scholars would date it in the seventh century BCE. The book of Ecclesiastes is the latest, commonly dated in the third century BCE.

During these centuries, the Jewish people continued to live under the political control of foreign empires: under the Persian Empire until its conquest by Alexander the Great in 333 BCE and then under the Hellenistic Empires descended from Alexander. Jewish political independence was not regained until the time of the Maccabees in 164 BCE.

At the beginning of this period, we should imagine the Jewish community in the land of Israel as very modest in size and mostly clustered around Jerusalem. The temple in Jerusalem was the political as well as religious center of the community. Because theirs was a province in a foreign empire, the Jewish people had no king, of course. Thus domestic political authority as well as national-religious identity gravitated to the temple and its high priest. Over time, a native aristocracy emerged around the temple, consisting mostly of families from whom a high priest had been chosen. The Jewish people were in the process of becoming a "temple state" and a "theocracy"—a society ruled by God through God's priests and scribal interpreters.

We also need to imagine a religious community seeking to consolidate its identity and preserve its traditions. During this period of exceptional activity, the Pentateuch was put into its present form (including both consolidation and some creation of legal traditions), the Prophets as a collection of books took shape, and most or all of the Writings were composed. It is an impressive literary and religious accomplishment for a small group of people.

Israel's wisdom traditions also include two books found in the Christian Apocrypha but not in the Hebrew Bible. The first is known by several names: Sirach, or the Wisdom of Ben Sira, or Ecclesiasticus.[3] This book was written quite late in the postexilic period, probably between 200 and 180 BCE, and its author was a Jewish wisdom teacher in Jerusalem named Jesus Ben Sira, or "Jesus son of Sirach." The Wisdom of Solomon, the second apocryphal wisdom book, was written even later, commonly dated to the first century BCE (and perhaps even to the early first century CE). Its author is unknown. As part of the Christian Apocrypha, these two books are seen as sacred scripture by Catholic, Orthodox, and Anglican Christians, but not by most Protestants. Though they contain very interesting material, we will focus on the three wisdom documents included in the Hebrew Bible: Proverbs, Ecclesiastes, and Job.

Israel's wisdom literature is very different in content, tone, and form from the Pentateuch and the Prophets. Its subject matter, as mentioned earlier, is more concerned with the individual. It looks at the individual *as embedded within family and kinship systems and society,* however, so it is not "individualistic" in the modern American sense of the term. But unlike the rest of the Hebrew Bible, it is not concerned with Israel's sacred story as a people or with the criticism and reshaping of the social order.

Its tone and form are also different. It does not claim to be the product of divine revelation but is grounded in observation of and reflection upon human experience. Unlike the laws of the Pentateuch, which are said to have come from God, and unlike the prophets, who claim to speak the "Word of the LORD" on God's behalf, Israel's wisdom does not claim to be revealed truth.

Instead, wisdom is insight based on experience. Sometimes, as in the short sayings of the book of Proverbs, wisdom is crystallized experience—compact insights about how to live generated by long experience of the world. As the product of the community's experience over centuries, Proverbs is thus to a large extent *"community* wisdom." Ecclesiastes and Job, on the other hand, are sustained reflections on experience from the vantage point of their particular authors. But all three books are based on observation of life: they say, in effect, This is what life is like.

As we explore these books, we will not only taste the riches of Israel's wisdom tradition, but also become aware of an intense and probing dialogue—even a conflict—within it. Is life as simple as knowing the right things to do and doing them? Does everything work out if you live right? And if life is *not* so simple but much more mysterious, what does that say about the nature of God, the purpose of life, and how we are to live?

Proverbs

The book of Proverbs has thirty-one chapters and falls into two main parts. The first part (made up of the first nine chapters) is a series of "wisdom poems" that might be labeled "in praise of wisdom." Most of the rest of the book is a collection of individual proverbs—the short, memorable sayings that give the book its name. Not the work of one person, the pithy proverbs of the second part are the accumulated sayings of generations of wisdom teachers.

The Wisdom Poems in Proverbs 1–9

The poems in the first part of the book introduce us to the central metaphor of Israel's wisdom tradition: life as a "way" or "path." They abound in images related to moving along that path: walking, running, following, stumbling, falling. The poems develop the metaphor by contrasting two paths: the wise way and the foolish way, the path of wisdom and the path of folly. Other contrasting pairs are also used: the way of righteousness and the way of wickedness, the way of life and the way of death. The book as a whole develops the choice between the two ways.

The foundation and starting place of the wise way is announced in the first chapter: "The fear of the LORD is the beginning of knowledge; fools despise wisdom and instruction."[4] The phrase "fear of the LORD" does not mean "fright," as one might be frightened of a tyrannical ruler or parent. Rather, it refers to awe, wonder, and reverence in the presence of the One who is the maker of heaven and earth and the lord of life and death. The beginning of wisdom lies in taking seriously that we are dealing with a reality that transcends the world of the everyday, even as that reality is *known* in the world of the everyday.

These chapters also introduce us to the personification of "Wisdom" in female form, commonly called "the wisdom woman" or "Sophia." "Sophia" is not only the Greek word for *wisdom;* as a woman's name it better expresses the personification than the more abstract and neuter-sounding "Wisdom."

Wisdom/Sophia is of inestimable worth. Following her is the wise way, and that way leads to life, riches, honor, peace, and happiness:

Happy are those who find wisdom,
    and those who get understanding.

Her income is better than silver,
  and her revenue better than gold.
She is more precious than jewels,
  and nothing you desire can compare with her.
Long life is in her right hand;
  in her left hand are riches and honor.
Her ways are ways of pleasantness,
  and all her paths are peace.
She is a tree of life to those who lay hold of her;
  those who hold her fast are called happy.[5]

So important is Wisdom/Sophia that she is spoken of as having been with God at the creation of the world:

The LORD created me at the beginning of God's work,
  the first of God's acts of long ago.
Ages ago I was set up at the first,
  before the beginning of the earth.[6]

Wisdom/Sophia offers food and drink. She hosts a banquet of bread and wine to which she invites all who will come:

You who are simple, turn in here!
Come, eat of my bread,
  and drink of the wine I have mixed.
Lay aside immaturity, and live,
  and walk in the way of insight.[7]

This personification is the first stage of a process whereby Wisdom/Sophia becomes a female image for God in Jewish wisdom literature.[8] This development is the background for the New Testament's use of Sophia imagery to speak about Jesus as prophet of Sophia and as incarnation of Sophia. It is also the basis for the increasing attention paid to Sophia in recent Christian theology.[9]

There is a second personification in these poems. Namely, the way of folly is personified as "the strange woman" or "the alien woman." Often portrayed as an adulteress and seductress, she has an appeal that is described with remarkable literary elegance and psychological astuteness.[10] Not only does she invite people to follow a way, but she mimics Sophia. With the same words, she too calls people to her house and banquet: "You who are simple, turn in here!"[11] But her way leads to folly, wickedness, and death.

These two personifications symbolize the two ways of which the book of Proverbs as a whole speaks. Following Sophia and the way of wisdom leads to life:

> For whoever finds me finds life
>   and obtains favor from the LORD;
> But those who miss me injure themselves;
>   all who hate me love death.[12]

Following "the alien woman," on the other hand, leads to death:

> Do not let your hearts turn aside to her ways,
>   do not stray into her paths.
> For many are those she has laid low,
>   and numerous are her victims.
> Her house is the way to Sheol,
>   going down to the chambers of death.[13]

To avoid a possible misunderstanding, it is important to emphasize that the Jewish tradition did not yet affirm an afterlife. Belief in a heaven and hell beyond death was still two or three centuries in the future.[14] Thus the two ways—one leading to life, the other leading to death—are not about eternity (about heaven and hell), but about two different ways of living *this* side of physical death.

The Proverbs of Chapters 10–30
We turn now to the collection of individual proverbs that fill the rest of the book. Generally speaking, proverbs are short, wise

sayings designed to be memorable. To use a definition attributed to the Spanish author Cervantes, proverbs are short sentences founded upon long experience and containing a truth. As observations about life, proverbs are typically indicative rather than imperative statements, though an imperative is implied.

One of the best nonbiblical examples of a proverb is "A stitch in time saves nine." Short, rhythmical, and using repeating sounds, it is easy to remember.[15] Moreover, though it uses an image from sewing, it obviously refers to more than sewing. Finally, though the sentence is indicative, the imperative is clear: *make* the stitch in time.

We can only speculate about the origin of the proverbs collected together in the second part of the book of Proverbs. Some probably originated within family and village life, others may have been the product of sages (teachers of wisdom), and some were borrowed from other cultures.[16] As a completed collection in the postexilic period, they may have been taught in schools for young men of the upper classes. The method of instruction would have been oral, of course, and we might imagine the teacher saying the first line of a proverb and the students responding in unison with the second line.

These proverbs are like snapshots depicting the wise and foolish ways announced in the wisdom poems of the first nine chapters. The best way to understand what they are and how they work is to look at a number of them.

Proverbs Characterized by Elegance and Humor I have chosen some proverbs to illustrate central themes and others because of their linguistic elegance and occasional humor. In the latter category, on a miscellany of subjects:

> The words of a whisperer are like delicious morsels; they go
> down into the inner parts of the body. (18.8; repeated in
> 26.22)
> Like vinegar on a wound is one who sings to a heavy heart.
> (25.20)

The legs of a disabled person hang limp; so does a proverb in
the mouth of a fool. (26.7)
Like a dog that returns to its vomit is a fool who reverts to his
folly. (26.11)
As a door turns on its hinges, so does a lazy person in bed.
(26.14)
Whoever blesses a neighbor with a loud voice, rising early in
the morning, will be counted as cursing. (27.14)
Like somebody who takes a passing dog by the ears is one
who meddles in the quarrel of another. (26.17)

Proverbs Dealing with Children and Family A repeated message in these proverbs concerns the importance of training children in the paths of wisdom. For example:

Train children in the right way, and when old, they will not
stray. (22.6)

Physical discipline is part of this training. One of the best-known
proverbs is "Spare the rod, spoil the child." Its full form reads:

Those who spare the rod hate their children, but those who
love them are diligent to discipline them. (13.24)

The same theme is sounded in several more passages:

Do not withhold discipline from your children; if you beat
them with a rod, they will not die. (23.13)
Folly is bound up in the heart of a boy, but the rod of discipline drives it far away. (22.15)
Blows that wound cleanse away evil; beatings make clean the
innermost parts. (20.30)

The book of Proverbs also contains a number of sayings about
difficult wives and good wives. These sayings disclose the andro-
centric perspective of the book (and of the Bible as a whole, for

that matter): there are no sayings about good or difficult husbands.
Mentioned often is the contentious or quarrelsome wife:

> A wife's quarreling is a continual dripping of rain. (19.13)
> A continual dripping on a rainy day and a contentious wife are
>   alike. (27.15)
> It is better to live in a corner of the housetop than in a house
>   shared with a contentious wife. (21.9; repeated in 25.24)
> It is better to live in a desert land than with a contentious and
>   fretful wife. (21.19)

The sages also knew about *good* wives:

> A good wife is the crown of her husband. (12.4)
> He who finds a wife finds a good thing, and obtains favor
>   from the LORD. (18.22)
> House and wealth are inherited from parents, but a prudent
>   wife is from the Lord. (19.14)

The ideal wife is the topic of the acrostic poem that concludes
the book as a whole. She bears a remarkable resemblance to the
"wisdom woman" of chapters one through nine.[17]

Proverbs Dealing with Wealth and Poverty The book of Proverbs
has much to say about wealth and poverty. In general, prosperity is
seen as the result of following the wise way. The attitude toward
poverty is more complex. If possible, poverty is to be avoided, of
course. The wealthy are urged to be generous to the poor, but
sometimes the poor are virtually blamed for their poverty.

Some proverbs are simply observations about the way things
are for the poor, with no value judgment (other than sympathy)
implied:

> The poor are disliked even by their neighbors, but the rich
>   have many friends. (14.20)
> Wealth brings many friends, but the poor are left friendless.
>   (19.4)

If the poor are hated even by their kin, how much more are
   they shunned by their friends. (19.7)

Some proverbs recognize that wealth is not good in and of itself and that in some circumstances poverty is better:

Better is a dinner of vegetables where love is than a fatted ox
   and hatred with it. (15.17)
Better is a little with righteousness than large income with injustice. (16.8)
Better to be poor and walk in integrity than to be crooked in
   one's ways even though rich. (28.6)
Those who trust in their riches will wither, but the righteous
   will flourish like green leaves. (11.28)

One saying affirms that both wealth and poverty can be dan-
gerous snares:

Give me neither poverty nor riches; feed me with the food
   that I need, or I shall be full, and deny you, and say, "Who
   is the LORD?" or I shall be poor, and steal, and profane the
   name of my God. (30.8–9)

The poor are to be treated compassionately. In language that
anticipates Jesus' parable of the sheep and the goats, what one
does to or for the poor is done to God:[18]

Those who oppress the poor insult their Maker, but those who
   are kind to the needy honor God. (14.31)
Those who mock the poor insult their Maker. (17.5)
Whoever is kind to the poor lends to the LORD, and will be re-
   paid in full. (19.17)

Thus the wise will be generous to the poor:

Those who are generous are blessed, for they share their bread
   with the poor. (22.9)

Whoever gives to the poor will lack nothing, but one who
   turns a blind eye will get many a curse. (28.27)

Though none of the sayings directly blames the poor for their
poverty, the frequent association of prosperity with wisdom, diligence, industry, and prudence and of poverty with foolishness,
laziness, and drunkenness comes close. The lazy person (the
"sluggard," in older translations) is one of the villains of
Proverbs. In the first part of the book, the lazy person is told to
learn a lesson from the ant:

Go to the ant, you lazybones;
   consider its ways and be wise.
Without having any chief
   or officer or ruler,
it prepares its food in summer,
   and gathers its sustenance in harvest.
How long will you lie there, O lazybones?
When will you arise from your slumber?
A little sleep, a little slumber,
   a little folding of the hands to rest,
and poverty will come upon you like a robber,
   and want, like an armed robber. (6.6–11; last three lines
   also in 24.34)

Other sayings make the connection between laziness and
poverty:

A slack hand causes poverty, but the hand of the diligent
   makes rich. (10.4)
Do not love sleep, or else you will come to poverty;
   open your eyes and you will have plenty of bread.
   (20.13)
An idle person will suffer hunger. (19.15)

Drunkenness also leads to poverty:

The drunkard and the glutton will come to poverty, and
  drowsiness will clothe them with rags. (23.21)

More broadly, failure to follow the way of wisdom produces
poverty:

The LORD does not let the righteous go hungry. (10.3)
Anyone who tills the land will have plenty of bread, but one
  who follows worthless pursuits will have plenty of poverty.
  (28.19)
Misfortune pursues sinners, but prosperity rewards the righteous. (13.21)
The plans of the diligent lead surely to abundance, but everyone who is hasty comes only to want. (21.5)

There is some truth in these observations, of course. Laziness
and folly and drunkenness often do produce poverty and want.
But the corollary—that poverty is always the product of these—is
not true, though Proverbs comes close to drawing that inference.

Proverbs Dealing with the Rewards of Right Living The book
of Proverbs affirms with great frequency and confidence that following the way of wisdom will bring rewards. This is such a central theme of the book, and so important for understanding an
ongoing tension within Israel's wisdom tradition, that I report,
at the risk of tedious repetition, a selection of proverbs extolling
the rewards of virtue. A reminder: these sayings do not have an
afterlife in mind; they are speaking about *this* life.

The LORD's curse is on the house of the wicked, but God
  blesses the abode of the righteous. (3.33)
The blessing of the LORD makes rich. (10.22)
What the wicked dread will come upon them, but the desire of
  the righteous will be granted; when the tempest passes, the
  wicked are no more, but the righteous are established forever. (10.24–25)

The fear of the LORD prolongs life, but the years of the wicked will be short. (10.27)

The righteous will never be removed, but the wicked will not remain in the land. (10.30)

Righteousness delivers from death. (11.4)

The righteous are delivered from trouble, and the wicked get into it instead. (11.8)

Whoever is steadfast in righteousness will live, but whoever pursues evil will die. (11.19)

Be assured, the wicked will not go unpunished, but those who are righteous will escape. (11.21)

The good obtain favor from the LORD, but those who devise evil God condemns. (12.2)

The wicked are overthrown and are no more, but the house of the righteous will stand. (12.7)

No harm happens to the righteous, but the wicked are filled with trouble. (12.21)

Those who despise the word bring destruction on themselves, but those who respect the commandment will be rewarded. (13.13)

The house of the wicked is destroyed, but the tent of the upright flourishes. (14.11)

The perverse get what their ways deserve, and the good, what their deeds deserve. (14.14)

In the house of the righteous there is much treasure, but trouble befalls the income of the wicked. (15.6)

The LORD is far from the wicked, but he hears the prayer of the righteous. (15.29)

Commit your work to the LORD, and your plans will be established. (16.3)

Those who keep the commandment will live; those who are heedless of their way will die. (19.16)

The reward for humility and fear of the LORD is riches and honor and life. (22.4)

Do not envy the wicked, for the evil have no future; the lamp of the wicked will go out. (24.19–20)

One who walks in integrity will be safe, but whoever follows
crooked ways will fall into the Pit. (28.18)
The faithful will abound with blessings. (28.20)

Proverbs as Conventional Wisdom The repetition of this theme
has a rhetorical function, of course: the purpose of Proverbs is to
extol the importance of the path of wisdom, and it does this by
affirming again and again, "Follow this way, and your life will go
well." The cumulative effect of the repetition: Proverbs becomes
a book of conventional wisdom (or at least the most common
way of reading Proverbs turns it into conventional wisdom).

Conventional wisdom is the heart of every culture and of most
subcultures. As I use the term, it always has two defining meanings. On the one hand, conventional wisdom is "cultural wisdom" or "community wisdom" or "folk wisdom": it is "what
everybody knows" (or should know). It is collective wisdom, the
consensus of the culture or community about how life should be
lived. Its subject matter is vast, covering everything from etiquette to central values to images of the good life.

Included within "what everybody knows" is the second defining feature of conventional wisdom: the notion of rewards for
living life right. Not only is this claim that virtue will be rewarded central to Proverbs, but it is the core of all forms of conventional wisdom, religious and secular: follow this path, and life
will work out for you. Its variations are familiar, as this brief sam-
pling shows:

You reap what you sow.
Work hard and you'll succeed.
Do (or believe) X, Y, and Z and you'll go to heaven.
People get what they deserve.
What goes around comes around.
Follow the Lord and you'll be happy.
Follow the American way of life and you'll reap the fruits of
the American dream.
Lose fifty and pounds and you'll be happy.

Conventional wisdom thus leads to a performance-and-rewards view of life. The quality of our life depends upon our doing things right. By making this connection, conventional wisdom also images life as orderly and, to that extent, under our control: if we follow *this* path, we will not end up at a dead end.

There is, of course, truth in conventional wisdom. There *are* ways of living that do lead to dead ends. Pride often *does* go before a fall. Diligence, industry, honesty, humility, generosity, and integrity *are* virtues. Injustice, strife, deceit, and violence *should* be avoided. Etiquette *can* make dining more pleasant.

Not only does conventional wisdom often contain truth, but we could not live without it. We could not live together in groups without taken-for-granted expectations about human behavior, ranging from the taboo against cannibalism to confidence that people will stop at stop signs.

Moreover, some forms of conventional wisdom are better than others. One needs only to think of the conventional wisdom of the Third Reich versus the conventional wisdom of societies strong in human rights, or conventional wisdom about race in the United States now compared with that of fifty years ago. So conventional wisdom and its content *matter*.

But conventional wisdom has a cruel corollary. If your life fails to work out, it must be because you have done something wrong. Trouble is *your* fault. Just as conventional wisdom about the importance of disciplined work can often lead to the poor being blamed for their poverty, so those for whom life is hard are often seen (in their own mind or in the minds of others) as responsible for their hardship.

The problem posed by the corollary of conventional wisdom brings the central claims of Proverbs into question. *Do* things work out if you live right? (Always, or only sometimes?) *Are* the righteous rewarded and the wicked punished? (Always, or only sometimes?) *Is* life fair? (Always, mostly, sometimes, or seldom?)

As noted earlier in this chapter, the wisdom literature of the Hebrew Bible does not speak with one voice on these issues.

While Proverbs is fairly unambiguous, the other two wisdom books hint at randomness and chance. And if life is not so well ordered as Proverbs suggests, what does that say about how we should live? What does it say about the purpose of life? What does it say about the nature of God?

These are the questions with which the authors of Ecclesiastes and Job wrestle.

Ecclesiastes

For many modern people, Ecclesiastes is the most "user-friendly" book in the Hebrew Bible (and perhaps in the Bible as a whole). It requires of its readers no knowledge of Israel's history, its language strikes people as speaking immediately to life, and its melancholic tone seems to fit the modern spirit. Almost uniformly, my students report liking Ecclesiastes.

Its author is "Qoheleth," which is not a name in Hebrew but a title or office. Most likely, the word means "teacher"—more specifically, *"wisdom* teacher"—and in this case probably a teacher who lived in Jerusalem. The title of the book—Ecclesiastes—is the Greek word for Qoheleth. Though the words are thus interchangeable, I will follow the convention of referring to the author as Qoheleth and the book as Ecclesiastes.

Though Qoheleth writes as King Solomon in the first two chapters, this is clearly done for rhetorical effect rather than to reflect actual authorship by Solomon. The book is one of the latest in the Hebrew Bible, typically dated around 300 to 250 BCE.

Scholarly assessment of Ecclesiastes varies greatly. Some scholars find it so unrelievedly pessimistic that they wonder how it ever got into the Bible. They claim that the author's skepticism about generally accepted religious convictions is so thoroughgoing as to suggest that he might as well have been an atheist. Other scholars greatly admire Qoheleth, not just for his honesty but for his religious vision. Whether to think of him as a wisdom teacher gone bad (perhaps "burned out") or as among the wisest of the wise is the central issue in the interpretation of this book.

But before I turn to that, I will identify Qoheleth's two central metaphors and look at the themes raised in key passages of Ecclesiastes.

Central Metaphors

The first central metaphor is "Vanity of vanities: all is vanity." Not only does Qoheleth begin and end his book with this thematic metaphor, but it is a repeating refrain throughout.[19] The Hebrew word translated as "vanity" is *hebel*. Though sometimes translated with the quite abstract words "emptiness," "meaningless," or "absurdity," *hebel* has more concrete literal meanings that are the basis for its metaphorical meaning in Ecclesiastes: breath, vapor, mist, or fog. All is breath; all is vapor; all is mist; all is fog. The connotations are *insubstantiality* (one cannot get hold of breath, vapor, mist, or fog), *ephemerality* (insubstantial substances such as vapor come and go), and obscured vision (especially if mist or fog is emphasized).

A second metaphor—"chasing after wind"—also occurs frequently. That phrase is sometimes translated as "herding" or "shepherding" the wind. It is, of course, an image of futility.

The King's Speech

The two metaphors named above are central to the opening speech of the book. From the middle of the first chapter through the end of the second, Qoheleth speaks as King Solomon.[20] The strategy is brilliant.

As the traditional father of wisdom in Israel, Solomon had an unrivaled reputation for sagacity. Moreover, he was fabled for having everything a human being might desire: not only wisdom, but power, fame, wealth, reputation, security, possessions, sensual pleasure. Solomon had everything that the conventional wisdom of most cultures desires.

Qoheleth imagines Solomon turning to all of these in his search for a satisfying life. But they do not satisfy. About all that conventional wisdom prizes, the verdict is the same: they are "vanity" and "chasing after wind." Ten times in the speech, one or both of the metaphors occur. All that Solomon has is declared to be vapor or fog: insubstantial, ephemeral, unsatisfying. The final line of the speech brings the two metaphors together: "All is vanity and a chasing after wind."[21]

The Righteous Sometimes Do Not Prosper

Solomon's speech is the first stage in Qoheleth's indictment of conventional wisdom. The next step is the rejection of conventional wisdom's central claim: if you follow the path of righteousness—the wise way—you will do well and be rewarded.

> In my vain life I have seen everything: there are righteous
>   people who perish in their righteousness, and there are
>   wicked people who prolong their life in their evildoing.
> There is a vanity that takes place on earth, that there are righ-
>   teous people who are treated according to the conduct of
>   the wicked, and there are wicked people who are treated ac-
>   cording to the conduct of the righteous.
> Again I saw that under the sun the race is not to the swift, nor
>   the battle to the strong, nor bread to the wise, nor riches to
>   the intelligent, nor favor to the skillful; but time and chance
>   happen to them all.[22]

Qoheleth knows that people often suffer from oppression through no fault of their own; they are simply the victims of power:

> Again I saw all the oppressions that are practiced under the
>   sun. Look, the tears of the oppressed—with no one to com-
>   fort them! On the side of their oppressors there was
>   power.[23]

Qoheleth's perception of life's inequities leads to despairing statements about whether life is worthwhile at all:

> And I thought the dead, who have already died, more fortu-
>   nate than the living, who are still alive; but better than both

is the one who has not yet been, and has not seen the evil
deeds that are done under the sun.[24]

The Specter of Death

Ecclesiastes is haunted by death. The author returns to the subject again and again. He does not simply say that we are mortal;
he dwells on that fact, *emphasizes* it.

Qoheleth stresses the utter inevitability of death. We are no
different from the animals—one fate awaits us all:

> For the fate of humans and the fate of animals is the same; as
> one dies, so dies the other. They all have the same breath,
> and humans have no advantage over the animals; for all is
> vanity. All go to one place; all are from the dust and all turn
> to dust again.[25]

He also stresses the randomness of death. Not only are we
fated to die, but the timing of our death is as random as what
happens to fish and birds:

> For no one can anticipate the time of disaster. Like fish taken
> in a cruel net, and like birds caught in a snare, so mortals
> are snared at a time of calamity, when it suddenly falls upon
> them.[26]

The inevitability and randomness of death make our conventional pursuits meaningless. Death comes regardless:

> Yet I perceived that the same fate befalls all of us. Then I said to
> myself, "What happens to the fool will happen also to me.
> Why then have I been so very wise?" And I said to myself
> that this is also vanity. For there is no enduring remembrance
> of the wise or of fools, seeing that in the days to come all will
> have been long forgotten. How can the wise die just like
> fools? So I hated life, because what is done under the sun was
> grievous to me, for all is vanity and a chasing after wind.[27]

For Qoheleth, the certainty and randomness of death drive an arrow into the heart of conventional wisdom. Nothing that we do or have—none of what we spend our lives seeking to achieve, possess, and control—can forestall death, can alter its inevitability or timing. Moreover, when death comes, it takes away everything we have acquired: wisdom, wealth, honor, a good name, family, possessions.

Nothing can affect this, says Qoheleth. Neither wisdom nor righteousness nor goodness nor worship can change either the inevitability or the randomness of death:

> The righteous and the wise and their deeds are in the hand of God; whether it is love or hate, one does not know. Everything that confronts them is vanity, since the same fate comes to all, to the righteous and the wicked, to the good and the evil, to the clean and the unclean, to those who sacrifice and those who do not sacrifice. As are the good, so are the sinners; those who swear are like those who shun an oath. This is an evil in all that happens under the sun, that the same fate comes to everyone.[28]

Qoheleth's case against conventional wisdom is complete. The rewards of conventional wisdom do not satisfy; even Solomon, who had them all to a superlative degree, found them lacking. Reality is not organized in such a way that the righteous are rewarded and the wicked punished. Death comes to all, and comes randomly. Conventional wisdom, whether in Proverbs or elsewhere, affirms that reality is orderly. But in Qoheleth's view, God has made the world not orderly and straight, but crooked.[29]

Then How Live?

If this is the way things are, what then is life about? What should we concern ourselves with? Qoheleth's answer, surprisingly simple and brief, is repeated several times for emphasis. Here are its first two appearances:

There is nothing better for mortals than to eat and drink, and
find enjoyment in their toil. This also, I saw, is from the
hand of God. . . .
I know that there is nothing better for people then to be
happy and enjoy themselves as long as they live. Moreover,
it is God's gift that all should eat and drink and take pleasure in all their toil.

In its longest form:

Go, eat your bread with enjoyment, and drink your wine with
a merry heart; for God has long ago approved of what you
do. Let your garments always be white; do not let oil be
lacking on your head. Enjoy life with the wife whom you
love all the days of your vain life that are given you under
the sun, because that is your portion in life and your toil at
which you toil under the sun. Whatever your hand finds to
do, do with your might.[30]

But even this simple, world-affirming advice is followed immediately by the specter of death:

For there is no work or thought or knowledge or wisdom in
Sheol, to which you are going.[31]

Sheol does not mean "hell" as a place of punishment where
some go. Sheol is the land of the dead, where *all* go.

Reading Ecclesiastes and Hearing Qoheleth

What are we to make of this? As mentioned earlier, there is no
consensus among scholars regarding how to hear Qoheleth's
message. To some, his pessimism and gloom seem to speak of a
world from which God is absent. His disparagement of life's
common goals suggests aimlessness. His positive advice sounds
difficult to distinguish from the familiar "Eat, drink, and be
merry, for tomorrow we may die." Is this really wisdom, or is
this the way the world looks when someone has given up on life?

As we puzzle about how to hear Qoheleth, let me suggest that context and inflection make all the difference. I invite you to imagine three different ways of saying (and thus hearing) the best-known passage in Ecclesiastes. Because of its length, I will not quote it all:

> For everything there is a season, and a time for every matter
>   under heaven:
> a time to be born, and a time to die;
> a time to plant, and a time to pluck up what is planted;
> a time to kill, and a time to heal;
> a time to break down, and a time to build up;
> a time to weep, and a time to laugh;
> a time to mourn, and a time to dance . . .
> a time to embrace, and a time to refrain from embracing . . .
> a time to love, and a time to hate;
> a time for war, and a time for peace.[32]

1: *First scenario*. Because the words of this passage became the lyrics of a popular folksong, most of us have heard them sung. I can remember some performances that gave the text a moral meaning, expressing a preference for one half of each set of opposites: *this*, not *that*. The inflection made it clear that *this time* (our time) is a time for peace, *not* war; a time for love, *not* hate; a time to heal, *not* kill; a time to dance, *not* mourn. However, I do not imagine that Qoheleth meant this.

2: *Second scenario*. Imagine this passage as read by a depressed Swedish Lutheran pastor in an Ingmar Bergman movie. The church is almost empty, the cold light of a gray winter morning makes everything pale and colorless, the voice is flat with despair, and there is virtually no one to hear it. Life is bleak—unbearably so—an endless cycle of meaningless repetition. This is an exaggerated form of some scholarly ways of reading Ecclesiastes.

3: *Third scenario*. Imagine these same words as read by the Dalai Lama. The meaning would be very different. Not *"this* versus *that,*" and not "everything is meaningless." Rather: live fully, whatever time it is. Be present to what is.

This third scenario is how I hear Qoheleth. His critique of conventional wisdom is similar to what we hear in the writings of Lao-tzu, a sixth-century BCE Chinese wisdom teacher whose teaching is preserved in the *Tao-te-ching.* Lao-tzu's thought is similar to that of Buddhism, especially Zen Buddhism. Like Qoheleth, Lao-tzu offers a radical critique of conventional wisdom.

The Tao (pronounced "dow") is Lao-tzu's word for both ultimate reality and "the way" of living in accord with it. Language cannot capture or domesticate the Tao as ultimate reality, as the opening line of the *Tao-te-ching* makes clear: "The Tao that can be named is not the eternal Tao." The Tao is thus intrinsically ineffable, "Mystery" with a capital *M.* The way of living in accord with the Tao is "not grasping." The way most of us live most of the time—the way of conventional wisdom—is the way of grasping. We grasp not only by seeking to domesticate reality, but also by seeking those satisfactions that convention urges us to seek. But grasping is futile. Indeed, in Buddhism, it is the primary source of suffering.

The similarities to Qoheleth are striking. Qoheleth's claim that we cannot make straight what God has made crooked points to the Mystery of the sacred. For Qoheleth, God is not absent; God is simply beyond all of our attempts to domesticate the divine.

His central metaphors of "all is vanity" (vapor, mist, fog) and "chasing the wind" point to the futility of grasping: we cannot lay hold of that which is insubstantial and ephemeral. Moreover, that which we can *momentarily* possess is ultimately unsatisfying.

His emphasis on death also fits this way of reading Ecclesiastes. For Qoheleth, death is not only the specter that haunts conventional wisdom, pointing to the futility of grasping. Death is also the master teacher who teaches us how to live:

> It is better to go to the house of mourning
>   than to go to the house of feasting;

> for this is the end of everyone,
>> and the living will lay it to heart.
> The heart of the wise is in the house of mourning;
>> but the heart of fools is in the house of mirth.[33]

The striking poem with which Qoheleth ends the book makes the same point. Filled with images of aging and decline, it includes the line, "Remember your grave in the days of your youth."[34] This injunction reflects not a melancholic, pessimistic attitude that robs even youth of its joy, but the belief that the awareness of death teaches us about what is important in life. Death is the teacher of true wisdom.

In this context, Qoheleth's admonition to live the life of simplicity does not sound like a cynical or burned-out "Eat, drink, and be merry, for tomorrow we may die"; rather, it comes across as genuine wisdom:

> Go, eat your bread with enjoyment, and drink your wine
>> with a merry heart. . . . Enjoy life with the wife whom you
>> love. . . . Whatever your hand finds to do, do with your
>> might.[35]

To do whatever you do "with your might" suggests living strongly, not tentatively; living fully, not holding back. Thus, in Ecclesiastes, life is not about pursuing the rewards promised by the path of conventional wisdom (religious or secular), but about living in the present. Seeing the futility of grasping and the inevitability and yet unpredictability of death drives us into the present.[36] True wisdom means *carpe diem:* "seize the day." Don't miss it; don't let it slip by unnoticed; don't live it in the fog; don't waste it chasing the wind.

And so I see Qoheleth as among the great wisdom teachers of the world. If it is not too bold a claim, I see him as a Jewish Lao-tzu. I do not think the similarities between Qoheleth's thought and Eastern thought are due to cultural contact with Eastern religions. I doubt that he had any awareness of the *Tao-te-ching* or

Buddhist teachings. Rather, I think the similarities flow out of similar reflections on human experience, perhaps even out of similar experiences of the sacred.

The wisdom of Qoheleth is thus a subversive wisdom. His teaching undermines and subverts "the way" taught by conventional wisdom. It is also an alternative wisdom, for it points to another way, one that leads beyond convention. To use a familiar phrase from Robert Frost, the subversive and alternative wisdom of Qoheleth is "the road less traveled."

Job

The dialogue and conflict within Israel's wisdom tradition continue in the book of Job. Radical questioning of conventional wisdom is this document's central feature—a document whose magnificent language, provocative content, and stunning climax make it one of the most remarkable books in the Bible.

Job has received extraordinary accolades. Martin Luther spoke of it as magnificent and sublime as no other work of Scripture. Alfred Lord Tennyson, a famous poet of the nineteenth century, called it the greatest poem of ancient and modern times. Another nineteenth-century Englishman, the historian Thomas Carlyle, said that nothing that has ever been written, in the Bible or out of it, is of equal merit.[37]

As mentioned earlier, the book of Job was probably written during the Babylonian exile in the sixth century BCE or shortly thereafter. It begins with a brief prose prologue (the first two chapters) and concludes with an even briefer prose epilogue (42.7–17). In between is the main body of the book, cast in the form of poetry and running almost forty chapters long (3.1–42.6). The prose prologue may be an old folktale adapted by the author of the poetic body as the framework for his work.

There is no scholarly consensus about either the relationship of the prose prologue to the poetic body or the literary unity of the book as a whole. Some scholars see considerable tension between the prologue and the poetic body, and some see the poetic body itself as containing the work of more than one author.

Without trying to resolve any of these questions, I will treat the book as a whole in its present form.

It is common to see the book of Job as wrestling with the problem of innocent suffering. This common view is only partly correct. On the one hand, it is true that the main character, Job, suffers intensely and does not know why; he cannot see that he has done anything to deserve the intensity of his pain and loss. On the other hand, I do not see that the author provides any answer to that question—nor, I am convinced, does he intend to do so. His purpose, I will suggest, is quite different.

The Prose Prologue: Chapters 1–2

The prologue introduces the character Job and the situation that led to his predicament. The first verse reminds us of the "once upon a time" of folktales about long ago and far away: "There was once a man in the land of Uz whose name was Job." The next two verses tell us that he was a very good and prosperous man—one who lived the life of wisdom: he was "blameless and upright, feared God and turned away from evil." Life was going well for him. Not only a paragon of wisdom and virtue, he was blessed with ten children and great prosperity: "seven thousand sheep, three thousand camels, five hundred yoke of oxen, five hundred donkeys, and very many servants." Indeed, he "was the greatest of all the people of the east."

With that groundwork laid, the prologue then turns from earth to heaven, where the dramatic action of the book is set in motion. There, we are told, a meeting is held between the heavenly beings and God. Among them is a figure called "Satan"—not yet the evil power opposed to God of later Jewish and Christian tradition, but a servant of God whose task is patrolling the earth as a kind of espionage agent. God brags to Satan about his righteous servant Job:

> There is no one like him on the earth, a blameless and upright
> man who fears God and turns away from evil.[38]

Satan is unimpressed. After all, why shouldn't Job be faithful—God has given him everything. So Satan says to God:

Does Job fear God for nothing? Have you not put a fence [a
positive image of protection] around him and his house
and all that he has, on every side? You have blessed the
work of his hands, and his possessions have increased in the
land.[39]

Satan then challenges God to a wager. Take away everything
Job has, he says, and see how faithful Job is then. God agrees,
and the wager is on.[40]

Job's life of blessedness then ends. In two stages, Satan takes it
away. In stage one, Job's flocks are all stolen or destroyed, most
of his servants are killed, and his children all die as a house col-
lapses on them. But Job's response is impeccable:

Naked I came from my mother's womb, and naked shall I return there; the LORD gave, and the LORD has taken away;
blessed be the name of the LORD.[41]

In stage two, Satan (with God's permission) goes after Job's
own body, inflicting him with "loathsome sores from the sole of
his foot to the crown of his head." His possessions gone, his children dead, he is reduced to sitting among the ashes, scraping his
sores with a broken piece of pottery. But he remains faithful to
God: "Shall we receive the good at the hand of God and not receive the bad?" The narrator hardly needs to add, "In all of this,
Job did not sin with his lips."[42] God has won the wager.

If we interpret the book of Job within the framework of the
question, "Why do the righteous suffer?" the answer provided
by the prologue is very strange. Job's suffering was caused by
something that happened completely "over his head": a wager in
the heavenly council between God and one of God's servants. I
doubt that Job would have been impressed with this explanation. Neither should we be.

Rather, the prologue and the book have another purpose.
That purpose is expressed in the question Satan asks God: "Does
Job fear God for nothing?" The question is both provocative and
profound, and it signals the author's probing of conventional

wisdom. Why be religious? Why take God seriously? Is it because "there's something in it for me"?

That is the answer of conventional religious wisdom, ancient and modern, Jewish and Christian, and as found in other religions. Follow *this* way—it will take you to a good place, whether internally or externally, whether in this life or the next. Its Christian forms are many: believe in God and Jesus and you'll go to heaven, or you'll prosper, or you'll have peace of mind, or you'll be fulfilled. All of these turn taking God seriously into a means to some other end. But Satan's question leads us to reflect on the central issue raised by the prologue: Is there such a thing as religion unmotivated by self-interest? What would it mean to take God seriously not as a *means,* but as the ultimate *end?*

The prologue has another purpose as well. It sets up the dialogue between Job and his friends that fills most of the poetic main body.

Eliphaz, Bildad, and Zophar arrive at the end of the second chapter; their purpose is to comfort Job. So shocked are they at his miserable appearance that they sit on the ground with him in silence for seven days.

The Poetic Dialogue between Job and His Comforters

The author has structured the poetic body of the book as a series of interchanges between Job and his friends. Job speaks, then Eliphaz; Job speaks, then Bildad; Job speaks, then Zophar; and the cycle repeats itself three times. Though the language is often magnificent, the content is quite repetitious. Rather than expositing all three cycles, then, I will provide passages that illustrate the depths of Job's suffering and questioning and the core of his friends' responses.

Job's Torment The portrait of Job in the prologue is responsible for the proverbial "patience of Job," a phrase first used in the letter of James in the New Testament.[43] As we turn now to the Job of the poetic main body, we will see that he is anything but patient.

Job speaks first. His suffering is so great that he curses the day he was born:

Let the day perish in which I was born,
    and the night that said, "A man-child is conceived."
Let that day be darkness! . . .
That night—let thick darkness seize it!
Let it not rejoice among the days of the year. . . .
Yes, let that night be barren:
    let no joyful cry be heard in it. . . .
Why did I not die at birth,
    come forth from the womb and expire? . . .
Why was I not buried like a stillborn child? . . .
For my sighing comes like my bread,
    and my groanings are poured out like water.[44]

Job's suffering is relentless. Even sleep gives him no relief: "When I lie down, I say, 'When shall I arise?' But the night is long, and I am full of tossing until dawn". He accuses God of giving him no rest:

When I say, "My bed will comfort me, my couch will ease my
    complaint,"
    then you terrify me with dreams and terrify me with visions,
    so that I would choose strangling and death rather than
    this body.
I loathe my life. . . .
Will you not look away from me for a while,
    let me alone until I swallow my spittle?
Why have you made me your target?[45]

Job cannot understand why he is suffering. He knows that he has done nothing to deserve this degree of torment and accuses God of destroying the righteous as well as the wicked:

I am blameless; I do not know myself.
I loathe my life.
It is all the same. Therefore I say,
    God destroys both the blameless and the wicked.

When disaster brings sudden death,
 God mocks at the calamity of the innocent.

Then Job addresses God directly:

You know that I am not guilty,
 and there is no one to deliver out of your hand.
Your hands fashioned and made me,
 and now you turn and destroy me.[46]

Job's Friends' Responses Eliphaz, Bildad, and Zophar consistently respond with the same refrain: you must have done something wrong. They defend the honor of God by reaffirming the claim that God rewards the righteous and punishes the wicked. Eliphaz says to Job:

Think now, who that was innocent has ever perished?
Or where were the upright cut off?
As I have seen, those who plow iniquity
 and sow trouble reap the same.

Eliphaz, who sees what is happening to Job as divine discipline, offers his advice. If I were you, he says:

I would seek God, and to God I would commit my cause. . . .
God sets on high those who are lowly,
 and those who mourn are lifted to safety. . . .
How happy is the one whom God reproves;
 therefore do not despise the discipline of the Almighty. . . .
We have searched this out; it is true.
Hear, and know it for yourself.[47]

Bildad makes the same point:

If you will seek God and make supplication to the Almighty, if
 you are pure and upright, surely then God will rouse up for

you and restore to you your rightful place. . . . God will not reject a blameless person.[48]

Zophar, the third friend to speak, is beginning to lose his patience. Accusing Job of being "full of talk" and "babble," he mocks Job and says that Job should suffer more than he already is:

You say, "My conduct is pure, and I am clean in God's sight."
But oh, that God would speak and open his lips to you,
    and tell you the secrets of wisdom!
Know then that God exacts of you less than your guilt deserves.[49]

Like Eliphaz and Bildad, he also suggests that repentance is the way to get back on God's good side and bring about a reversal of Job's misfortune.

Not surprisingly, Job does not find much comfort in all of this. He calls his friends "worthless physicians" and "miserable comforters." About their wisdom and counsel, he says, "Your maxims are proverbs of ashes."[50]

The central issue in the long section of the book reporting the exchanges between Job and his friends is the inadequacy of conventional wisdom. The friends are, of course, the voice of Israel's conventional wisdom. Their point of view, perhaps in hardened form, is the conventional wisdom of the book of Proverbs: the righteous will flourish; the wicked will wither. The friends draw the obvious corollary: if you are not flourishing but withering, you must be doing something wrong. Indeed, the friends are the voices of conventional wisdom in other times and places as well: if your life's not going right, it's your fault; if your life's not going right, fix it.

They also demonstrate the peril of quoting all parts of the Bible as if they reflect God's point of view. According to the book of Job, what Job's friends say at considerable length reflects a point of view that not only the character of Job and the author reject, but that God also rejects.[51] Conventional wisdom, whether biblical or secular, offers an inadequate explanation of suffering; it fails to account for the way the world is ordered.

Job's Dialogue and Encounter with God Throughout the long central section, Job not only rejects the wisdom of his friends, but expresses a strong desire to meet God face-to-face that he might confront God with the unfairness of his suffering.

Job's desire is granted, but the meeting turns out different than he had imagined it. The last five chapters contain God's answer to Job, expressed in the most remarkable nature poetry in the Hebrew Bible. God answers Job "out of the whirlwind." In a series of rhetorical questions, God displays the wonders of creation to Job: the foundations of the earth, the sea, the dwelling place of light, the storehouses of snow and hail, the constellations, clouds and rain and lightning, lions, mountain goats, deer, the wild ass and wild ox, the ostrich, the war horse, the hawk and the eagle, and ultimately the mythological sea monsters of Behemoth and Leviathan.[52]

The language is marvelous, the display magnificent. The effect of the latter is twofold. On the one hand, the display speaks of the absolute difference (though not distance) between the creator and the created. On the other hand, it speaks of the world of undomesticated nature—the nonhuman world of creation beyond culture—as an epiphany or disclosure of God.

The display stuns Job into smallness and silence:

> I am of small account; what shall I answer you?
> I lay my hand on my mouth; I have spoken once,
>> and I will not answer;
>> twice, but will proceed no further.[53]

Then Job does speak to God one more time. His words are the climax of the book:

> I had heard of you by the hearing of the ear,
>> but now my eye sees you.[54]

Seeing God is classical language for a mystical experience: an intense, immediate experience of the sacred. In many traditions, the "vision of God" is the peak experience of the religious quest. Here, in the climax of the book, the author of Job presents the character of Job as having a firsthand experience of the sacred. I am persuaded that the author knew this kind of experience in his own life. I have difficulty imagining how he could have written the climax as he does if he had not.

The contrast between *hearing* and *seeing* is the key to the book's climax. What Job had *heard* was the conventional understanding of God as conveyed by tradition. No doubt he had accepted it until his time of calamity began.[55] Then it no longer made sense to him, despite the fervent repetition of it by his well-intentioned friends. It did not fit his experience, and he was resolute enough not to agree with those who put it forward. But his rejection of conventional wisdom called everything he had once believed into question. Now, at the end of the book, he *sees* God—he experiences the sacred. In the words of an older translation, "But now *my eye beholds you.*"

Job's experience of God gave him no new answers or explanations for the problem of suffering. But his experience convinced him that God was real in spite of the human inability to see fairness in the world.

His experience of God changed him: "Therefore I melt into nothingness, and repent in dust and ashes," he said. As his old construction of the world (and himself) melted away, he "repented"—that is, he changed.[56]

A century ago, William James made a distinction that perfectly illuminates the climax of the book of Job. The most brilliant and influential American psychologist and philosopher of his day (and brother of the novelist Henry James), James distinguished between secondhand and firsthand religion. Secondhand religion is religion as learned from others. It is religion as a set of teachings and practices to be believed and followed—in other words, religious conventional wisdom. Firsthand religion is the religion that flows from the firsthand experience of God. At the end of the book of Job, the main character moves from second-hand religion—from what he had learned—to firsthand religion: "I had heard of you with the hearing of the ear, but now my eye beholds you."

Secondhand religion as religious conventional wisdom is not bad. It can and does produce good. The Spirit of God can and does work through it. Indeed, secondhand religion can be a sacrament of the sacred. But it is not the same as firsthand religion. The *experience* of the sacred shatters and transforms secondhand religion.

This distinction also helps us to understand the dialogue and conflict within ancient Israel's wisdom tradition. Israel's conventional wisdom, as seen in the cumulative effect of the book of Proverbs, is secondhand religion: religion as an orderly set of teachings about how things are and how things go. The alternative voice of Israel's wisdom—the wisdom of Job and Ecclesiastes—is grounded in the experience of God.

The conflict within Israel's wisdom tradition is one of two major conflicts within the Hebrew Bible. The other we have already seen: the conflict between the imperial theology of Egypt and exodus theology, between the royal theology of Israel's monarchy and the message of Israel's prophets. The New Testament, to which we now turn, continues the story of these conflicts. It does not resolve them, however; if anything, it intensifies them. It also names the central tensions and conflicts that run through subsequent Christian history.

NOTES

1. The most accessible introduction to Israel's wisdom literature is Kathleen M. O'Connor, *The Wisdom Literature* (Wilmington: Michael Glazier, 1988). Other books I have found especially helpful are James Crenshaw, *Old Testament Wisdom: An Introduction*, rev. ed. (Louisville: Westminster John Knox, 1998); Roland Murphy, *The Tree of Life: An Exploration of Biblical Wisdom Literature*, 2nd ed. (Grand Rapids: Eerdmans, 1996); Roland Murphy and Elizabeth Huwiler, *New International Biblical Commentary: Proverbs, Ecclesiastes, Song of Songs* (Peabody, MA: Hendrickson, 1999); Leo Perdue, *Wisdom and Creation: The Theology of Wisdom Literature* (Nashville: Abingdon, 1994).

2. For a persuasive argument that Israel's wisdom tradition is centered in God as creator, see Leo Perdue, *Wisdom and Creation* (Nashville: Abingdon, 1994).

3. Usually abbreviated as either "Sir." or "Ecclus." Note how close the latter is to the common abbreviation of Ecclesiastes: "Eccles."

4. Prov. 1.7.

5. Prov. 3.13–18. She is first introduced in 1.20–33, where she speaks like a prophet.

6. Prov. 8.22–23. The poem, which continues through v. 31, stresses Wisdom/Sophia's presence with God at the creation: "When there were no depths, I was brought forth. . . . Before the mountains had been shaped . . . when God established the heavens, I was there," and so forth.

7. Prov. 9.4–6; the banquet passage begins in 9.1.

8. Other primary texts in the Jewish wisdom tradition: Sir. 24; Wisd. of Sol. 7.7–8.16, esp. 7.22–8.1, and chap. 10.

9. For my chapter-length treatment of Sophia imagery and its application to Jesus, see *Meeting Jesus Again for the First Time* (San Francisco: HarperSanFrancisco, 1994), chap. 5.

10. See the seduction scenario in Prov. 7.6–23. Other relevant texts: 2.16–19, 5.3–14.

11. For her banquet, see Prov. 9.13–18; the invitation is in 9.16.

12. Prov. 8.35–36.

13. Prov. 7.25–27. See also 2.16–19, 5.3–14, 9.18.

14. The first unambiguously clear affirmation of an afterlife is in Daniel (see chap. 12), a book commonly dated around 165 BCE.

15. For a masterful exposition of how this proverb works, see John Dominic Crossan, *In Fragments: The Aphorisms of Jesus* (San Francisco: Harper and Row, 1983), pp. 12–13.

16. Notably Prov. 22.17–24.22, a collection that borrows freely from an Egyptian wisdom text known as the Instruction of Amenemope.

17. Prov. 31.10–31. An acrostic poem is one in which each line begins with a successive letter of the alphabet (in this case, of course, the Hebrew alphabet).

18. Matt. 25.31–46. The major point of the parable: whatever is done "for the least of these" (the hungry, thirsty, strangers, naked, sick, imprisoned) is done to Jesus.

19. Eccles. 1.2, immediately following the superscription of the book; 12.8, ending Qoheleth's words and preceding the brief epilogue probably added by an editor.

20. Eccles. 1.12–2.26.

21. Eccles. 1.14, 17; 2.1, 11, 15, 17, 19, 21, 23, 26.

22. Eccles. 7.15, 8.14, 9.11.

23. Eccles. 4.1.

24. Eccles. 4.2–3.

25. Eccles. 3.19–20.

26. Eccles. 9.12. See also 8.8: "No one has power over the day of death."

27. Eccles. 2.14–17.

28. Eccles. 9.1–3.
29. Echoing Eccles. 1.15. Elizabeth Huwiler, *New International Biblical Commentary: Proverbs, Ecclesiastes, Song of Songs* (Peabody, MA: Hendrickson, 1999), p. 159, comments that for Qoheleth, human experience is not "meaningful, controllable or predictable." She adds, as I also will, that for Qoheleth human well-being and enjoyment are nevertheless possible.
30. Eccles. 2.24, 3.12–13, 9.7–10. White garments and the act of anointing one's head with oil are associated with festive meals. See also 3.22, 5.18–20, and 8.15.
31. Eccles. 9.10.
32. Eccles. 3.1–8.
33. Eccles. 7.2, 4.
34. Eccles. 12.1–8. Though the first verse is commonly translated "Remember your *Creator* in the days of your youth," several commentators note that the Hebrew word translated as "creator" more likely means "grave" or "cistern" (as a metaphor for "grave").
35. Eccles. 9.7–10.
36. Thus I hear Qoheleth's wisdom as positive and not as unrelieved pessimism. For an equally positive reading, see Kathleen O'Connor, *The Wisdom Literature* (Wilmington: Micahel Glazier, 1988), pp. 114–33; see her note 6 on p. 123 for a citation of negative readings.
37. Cited by Samuel Terrien in *The Interpreter's Bible* (New York: Abingdon, 1954), vol. 3, p. 877.
38. Job 1.6–12. Quoted passage is v8.
39. Job 1.9–10.
40. Job 1.11.
41. The first calamities are narrated in Job 1.13–22. Quoted words are from 1.21.
42. The second stage is described in 2.1–10. Quoted words are from vv. 7, 10.
43. James 5.11.
44. His first speech is in chap. 3. Quoted passages are from vv. 3–4, 6–7, 11, 16, 24.
45. From Job's second speech, chaps. 6–7. Quoted passages are from 7.4, 13–16, 19–20.
46. From Job's third speech, chaps. 9–10. Quoted passages are from 9.21–23, 10.7–8.
47. From Eliphaz's first speech, chaps. 4–5. Quoted passages are from 4.7–8; 5.8, 11, 17, 27.
48. From Bildad's first speech, chap. 8. Quoted passages are from vv. 5–6, 20.
49. From Zophar's first speech, chap. 11. Quoted words are from 11.2–6; subsequent section on repentance and the reversal of fortune it will bring is from vv. 13–21.
50. Job 13.4, 16.2, 13.12.
51. Explicitly in Job 42.7.
52. Job 38.1–41.34. The display is interrupted by a brief dialogue between God and Job in 40.1–5; then it resumes.
53. Job 40.4–5.

54. Job 42.5.
55. Explicitly affirmed in chap. 29, esp. vv. 18–20.
56. Job 42.6. English translations commonly read "I despise myself" instead of "I melt into nothingness." But the latter phrase better expresses the meaning. The meaning of the final line, "I repent in dust and ashes," is difficult to express. It does not mean that Job finally realized he was guilty of great sins after all; minimally, it means that the experience changed Job.

Part Three

THE NEW TESTAMENT

8

Reading the
Gospels Again

We now move from the Hebrew Bible to the New Testament. There is far more continuity between the two than the later division between Judaism and Christianity suggests. Not only is the Hebrew Bible part of the Christian Bible, but it was *the* sacred scripture for Jesus, his followers, the early Christian movement, and the authors of the New Testament.

For all of them—Jesus and those who followed and wrote about him—the Hebrew Bible provided the language of the sacred imagination, that place within the psyche in which images of God, the God-world relationship, and the God-human relationship reside. They referred to the Hebrew Bible frequently, sometimes by quoting it but more often by alluding to its stories and texts dealing with Israel's past. They grew up with the Hebrew Bible and throughout their lives lived within the symbolic universe constituted by its words, images, and stories. It shaped their identity and their vision, their sense of who they were and their way of seeing, as individuals and as a community.

Though I will follow common practice and use the phrases "early Christianity" and "the early Christian movement," it is not clear historically when we should begin using the words "Christian" and "Christianity," if we mean by that a religion distinct from Judaism. Jesus and his early followers were all Jewish and saw themselves as doing something within Judaism, not as founding a religion separate from Judaism. Paul did not regard himself as converting to a new religion, but saw himself as a Jew all of his life. Most (and perhaps all) of the authors of the New Testament were Jewish. The word "Christianity" does not occur in the New Testament.[1]

Yet a "parting of the ways" began to become visible near the end of the first century.[2] Several factors accounted for the division: Gentile converts who did not become Jewish, a growing concern within Judaism to exclude Jews who saw Jesus as the messiah, and Roman perceptions of the Christian movement as a new religion separate from Judaism. But we should not see the emerging division as a complete divorce or imagine that Gentiles soon dominated the movement. A recent study suggests that the majority of Christians were still Jewish in origin as late as the middle of the third century.[3]

Judaism and early Christianity were "Rebecca's children," twin offspring of Israel's ancestors Rebecca and Isaac, to use the Jewish scholar Alan Segal's apt phrase.[4] Though Rebecca's twins were fraternal and not identical, they did have the same mother. Thus we understand the New Testament best when we see it within the world of first-century Judaism, including the way that world was shaped by the Hebrew Bible. And we understand early Christianity best when we see it as a way of being Jewish.

The Historical Transition

From Ecclesiastes, the latest of the wisdom books in the Hebrew Bible, we move forward in time about three centuries. The Jewish people regained their national independence in 164 BCE after a heroic war of revolt against the Hellenistic Empire of Antiochus

Epiphanes. The book of Daniel, the latest book in the Hebrew Bible, was written shortly before the revolt. The books of the Maccabees, Jewish documents in the Christian Apocrypha but not in the Hebrew Bible, tell the story of the revolt and its aftermath.

Independence lasted only a century, however. In 63 BCE, the Jewish homeland was incorporated into the Roman Empire. Roman imperial control was administered for a while by "client kings" appointed by Rome. The most famous of these was Herod the Great, who became king in 37 BCE. At his death in 4 BCE, his kingdom was divided into three parts ruled by his sons. In 6 CE, one part—Judea—came under direct Roman rule through prefects, or governors, sent from Rome. The most famous of these was Pontius Pilate, prefect from 26 to 36 CE.

During these centuries, the great majority of Jews did not live in the Jewish homeland itself, but in the "Diaspora," a term referring to Jewish communities outside of Palestine. Estimates vary, but perhaps as many as eighty percent or more lived in the Diaspora. The number of Jews living in the homeland at that time is commonly estimated at about one million, whereas four to six million lived in the Diaspora.[5] Some were descendants of Jews who had not returned from exile; others had emigrated more recently. Most Jews living in the Diaspora were urban, and they and their synagogues provided the primary network for Christian growth well into the third century.

In the Jewish homeland itself, the first century was a restive and violent time. The violence took several forms. There was the institutional and structural violence of Herodian and Roman rule, including economic and taxation policies that deprived more and more Jewish peasants of their ancestral landholdings and drove them into severe poverty, turning many into landless artisans, tenant farmers, or day-laborers and some into beggars. There was the violence of social bandits, groups of Jews who attacked and robbed Romans and the wealthy of their own people. (These social bandits were more than just *gangs* of bandits; the latter would have been simply outlaws, whereas the former were more like Robin Hood many centuries later.)

There was also the violence of armed revolutionary movements. In 4 BCE, when Herod the Great died, armed revolts
broke out in most parts of his kingdom, including Galilee.
Roman reprisal was quick and brutal. Sepphoris, the capital of
Galilee (and only four miles from Nazareth), was burned to the
ground, and many of the survivors were sold into slavery. Revolutionary violence simmered throughout much of the first century CE, culminating in the catastrophic war of revolt against
Rome in 66. The Romans brutally reconquered the Jewish
homeland and destroyed Jerusalem and the temple in 70. With
the destruction of the temple, Jewish sacrificial worship ceased.
The temple was never rebuilt, and Judaism changed forever.

An Introduction to the New Testament

Most of the twenty-seven documents that eventually became the
New Testament were written between 50 CE and the end of
the first century, although a few were written from the early to
middle second century.[6] Whereas the Hebrew Bible was written
over a period of around eight hundred years and is the literature
of a nation, the New Testament was written in one hundred
years or less and is the literature of a sectarian movement num-
bering only a few thousand people. A recent estimate suggests
that there were only about two thousand Christians in the year
60, by which time Paul's genuine letters had been written. By
the year 100, when most of the New Testament had been written, there were only 7,500 Christians.[7] It is an impressive literary
production from such a small group.

It is common to refer to these documents as the twenty-seven
"books" of the New Testament, and I will sometimes follow
this convention. But to call them "books" is somewhat misleading. Many of them are very short. (Two are only a page long,
for example, and the longest are only about forty pages in most
English translations.)[8] Moreover, a "book" in the modern sense
of the term is written for a general public not known personally
to the author.[9] But all of the New Testament documents were

written to persons or communities personally known to the authors.

These documents fall into four categories. The largest category is letters or epistles (twenty-one, thirteen of them attributed to Paul). The next largest category is gospels (four). The last two categories are represented by one book each: an apocalypse (the Revelation or Apocalypse of John), and a history of the movement (the Acts of the Apostles, or simply Acts).

An Introduction to the Gospels[10]

Among these documents, the four gospels are foundational, even though they are not the earliest writings in the New Testament. All of the genuine letters of Paul were written earlier, and much of the rest of the New Testament was written about the same time as the gospels.

They are foundational because they tell the story of Jesus. Just as the story of the exodus is ancient Israel's primal narrative, so the gospels are the early Christian movement's primal narratives in both senses of the word: "foundational" and "of first importance."

Jesus lived in the first third of the first century. Born around 4 BCE, he was executed by the Romans around the year 30 CE. The gospels were written in the last third of the first century, between approximately 65 and 100 CE. The earliest is almost certainly Mark, and the latest is probably John. Though we call the gospels Matthew, Mark, Luke, and John, we are not sure who wrote any of them. The author of Mark did not begin his gospel by writing "The Gospel according to Mark" at the top. Names were not assigned to these writings until sometime in the second century. For us they are anonymous documents, but presumably their authors were known in the communities for which they wrote.[11]

Although scholarly debate about their more particular literary form continues, the gospels are at a very general level "public biographies": accounts of the public life—the message and activity—of Jesus. They show little interest in his personal life before his public activity began. Two (Mark and John) do not even mention Jesus' early years. The other two (Matthew and Luke) have birth stories, and Luke has a story about Jesus at age twelve, but that's all.[12]

Like the historical narratives of the Bible generally, the gospels are the product of a developing tradition, containing earlier and later layers of material and combining history remembered and history metaphorized. They preserve the Jesus movement's memory of Jesus and use the language of metaphor and metaphorical narrative to speak about what Jesus had become in their experience, thought, and devotion in the decades after his death.

As developing traditions combining historical memory and metaphorical narrative, they can be read in two different ways. On the one hand, as virtually our only source of information about the historical Jesus, they can be read for the sake of reconstructing a sketch of what Jesus of Nazareth was like as a figure of history. On the other hand, they can be read as late-first-century documents that tell us about Christian perceptions and convictions about Jesus some forty to seventy years after his death.

The first way of reading focuses on "the historical Jesus": the Jesus of the early layers of the developing tradition behind or beneath the surface level of the gospels. The second way focuses on "the canonical Jesus": the Jesus we encounter on the surface level of the gospels in their present form. We do not need to choose between these two ways of reading the gospels. Both are legitimate and useful.[13]

But we do need to be clear about when we are doing one and when we are doing the other. When we do not distinguish between the historical Jesus and the canonical Jesus, confusion results, and we risk losing both. When what the gospels say about the canonical Jesus is taken as historical reporting about Jesus of Nazareth, as both natural literalism and conscious literalism do, Jesus becomes an unreal human being, and we lose track of the utterly remarkable person he was. Anybody who can multiply loaves, walk on water, still storms, change water into wine, raise the dead (including someone who has been dead four days), and call down twelve legions of angels from heaven is not a credible human being. He is not one of us.

Moreover, when what is said about the canonical Jesus is taken literally and historically, we lose track of the rich metaphorical meanings of the gospel texts. The gospels become factual reports about past happenings rather than metaphorical narratives of present significance. But when we are clear about the distinction between the historical Jesus and the canonical Jesus, we get both. And both matter.

Most of my previous books on Jesus have focused on the historical Jesus.[14] In radical shorthand, I see the pre-Easter Jesus as a Jewish mystic, healer, teacher of unconventional wisdom, social prophet, and renewal-movement initiator. Thus I see him as standing in continuity with the following strands of the Hebrew Bible:

- The experiential stream of the tradition that emphasizes the firsthand experience of the sacred
- The exodus and prophetic strands of the tradition, with their emphasis upon social justice and critique of and liberation from domination systems
- The critique of conventional wisdom in the subversive wisdom of Israel as represented by Ecclesiastes and Job
- The affirmation of an alternative social vision and vision of community that flows out of the above

I also see Jesus, in radical shorthand, as the Christian messiah. I think it most likely that the perception of him as messiah (and Son of God, and so forth) emerged among his followers after and because of Easter. By "Easter," I mean the experience among his followers of Jesus as a living reality after his death, and the conviction that God had exalted him to be both messiah and Lord. This Jesus—the canonical Jesus—is the Jesus we meet on the pages of the New Testament.

In this chapter I focus on the canonical Jesus. My purpose is to illustrate how to read the gospels in their present form as the primal narratives of the early Christian movement. I will introduce each gospel and then comment more extensively on selected texts. I will emphasize reading the gospels as metaphorical narratives, incorporating a historical approach that adds to the metaphorical meanings of gospel texts in their late-first-century settings.

The Gospels as Thematic Constructions

As documents written in the last third of the first century in different Christian communities, the gospels are thematic constructions, each with its own distinctive themes, purpose, and emphasis. As I introduce each, I will not seek to be comprehensive; rather, I will simply highlight its thematic construction.

As I do so, I will integrate the inaugural scene of Jesus' public activity in each, to show how the author has constructed it to crystallize his vision of what Jesus was most centrally about. By "inaugural scene" I mean the first public words or public deed attributed to Jesus. In each case, the inaugural address or inaugural deed functions as a thematic introduction. Thus it is an aperture through which we are given an advance glimpse of the evangelist's perception of Jesus and his significance.

I begin with the synoptic gospels of Matthew, Mark, and Luke. They are known as "the synoptics" because they are similar enough to be seen together (as the root of the word "synoptic" suggests). The reason for their similarity: they have written sources in common. Matthew and Luke both used the gospel of Mark, incorporating most of Mark's material as well as his narrative structure of the public activity of Jesus: a period of teaching and healing in Galilee in the north of the country followed by a journey south to Jerusalem and death, all occurring within one year. Matthew and Luke also used an early collection of Jesus' teachings known as "Q." Their use of Mark and Q accounts for the family similarity of the synoptic gospels. The gospel of John, as we will see, is very different.

Mark

The gospel of Mark was written around 70 CE, the year that Jerusalem and the temple were reconquered and destroyed by the Roman Empire as the Jewish war of revolt led to its virtually inevitable climax. That event casts its shadow on the gospel, either because it had recently happened or because it was soon to happen; in fact, Mark has aptly been referred to as "a wartime gospel."[15]

Apocalyptic Eschatology We see the impact of the war and its climax especially in the thirteenth chapter of Mark, called "the little apocalypse." (An apocalypse commonly deals with "the end," and the "big apocalypse" is, of course, the book of Revelation.) The chapter begins with a warning of the temple's destruction. As the disciples look at the temple, one exclaims, "Look, teacher, what large stones and what large buildings!" The Jesus of Mark then says to him, "Do you see these great buildings? Not one stone will be left here upon another; all will be thrown down."[16]

The disciples ask when this will happen and what the sign will be that the time is near. As the little apocalypse continues, the Jesus of Mark speaks of false messiahs, wars and rumors of war, nation rising against nation, persecution and betrayal, and finally says, "When you see the desolating sacrilege set up where it ought not to be—let the reader understand—then those in Judea must flee to the mountains." The phrase "desolating sacrilege" echoes the book of Daniel, where that wording refers to a previous foreign empire taking over the temple and there offering sacrifice to a foreign god.[17] In Mark, the phrase refers to what has just happened (or is soon to happen) to the temple, an event that Mark says will be followed by suffering "such as has not been from the beginning of creation."

Then, in language that Mark almost certainly understood to refer to the second coming of Jesus, the Jesus of Mark speaks of "the Son of Man coming in clouds with great power and glory":

> But in those days, after that suffering,
>   the sun will be darkened,
>   and the moon will not give its light,
>   and the stars will be falling from heaven,
>   and the powers in the heavens will be shaken.

Then they will see "the Son of Man coming in clouds" with great power and glory. Then he will send out his angels to gather his elect from the four winds, from the ends of the earth to the ends of heaven.

When will all of this happen? Soon. A few verses later, the Jesus of Mark says, "Truly I tell you, this generation will not pass away until all these things have taken place."[18] Thus Mark viewed the events of 70—the suffering of the final stages of the war, the destruction of Jerusalem and the temple—as signs that "the end" was at hand.

In short, Mark's gospel has an apocalyptic eschatology.[19] Apocalyptic eschatology appears earlier in his gospel as well, in a "kingdom of God" saying. In the middle of Mark, immediately after a passage about the Son of Man coming in glory with his angels, the Jesus of Mark speaks of the imminence of the kingdom: "Truly I tell you, there are some standing here who will not taste death until they see the kingdom of God coming with power."[20] In other words, some of those still alive will see this.

Jesus' Inaugural Scene   The imminence of the kingdom of God is the theme of Jesus' brief inaugural address in Mark:

The time is fulfilled,
   and the kingdom of God is at hand.
Repent and believe in the good news.

Though Jesus often spoke about the kingdom of God, this passage is Mark's thematic construction, announcing a major emphasis of his gospel. "The time is fulfilled"; the kingdom of which Jesus spoke is now "at hand."

Yet though the events of 70 account for Mark's emphasis on the imminence of the kingdom, they account for surprisingly little of his gospel's contents. The rest of Mark does not often use the phrase "the kingdom of God."[21] Instead, much of his gospel is about another major theme: the way—that is, the "way" or "path" or "road" of following Jesus.[22]

In what is virtually the title of the gospel, Mark opens with a citation from Isaiah 40: "In the wilderness, prepare *the way* of the Lord."[23] The language takes us back to the exile: the gospel of Mark is about a way of return from exile. The way of return is the way of Jesus, as the pivotal central section of the gospel emphasizes. The story of Jesus' journey from Galilee to Jerusalem is filled with teaching about the "way" of discipleship, which means "following" Jesus on his "way." That way leads to Jerusalem, the place of confrontation with the domination system, death, and resurrection. As Jesus journeys on his way, he solemnly speaks three times of his own impending death and resurrection and after each invites his disciples to follow him.[24] For Mark, the "way" of Jesus is the path of death and resurrection.

The emphasis on a way of return connects to the final element in Jesus' inaugural address in Mark: "Repent." Repentance here does not mean contrition for sin, as it often has in later Christian theology. Rather, its meaning is rooted in the exile story: to repent is to return from exile. To connect that concept back to kingdom of God language: to repent—to embark on the journey of return—is to enter the kingdom of God.[25]

Thus, for Mark, the canonical Jesus calls his followers to the way of the cross, the path of death and resurrection. The way of Jesus—the way of repentance and return from exile—involves dying to an old way of being and being born into a new way of being. Taken literally, it is the path of martyrdom, which may have been an issue when Mark was written.[26] Taken metaphorically, it refers to the internal process at the center of the way of Jesus and the life of discipleship.

Matthew

Matthew's gospel is written about ten to twenty years later than Mark's. Its content points to a late-first-century community of Christian Jews in conflict with other Jews. Of the synoptic gospels, Matthew is both the most Jewish and the most hostile to Judaism.

Hostility to Judaism Jews are referred to as if separate from Matthew's community. Synagogues are "their" synagogues, for example.[27] Matthew intensifies Jesus' criticism of scribes and Pharisees by turning it into invective. In a lengthy chapter of condemnation, the formula "Woe to you, scribes and Pharisees, hypocrites!" is used six times, and scribes and Pharisees are called "blind guides, "blind fools," "serpents," and "brood of vipers."[28]

To Mark's version of the parable of the wicked tenants, Matthew adds a verse addressed to the leaders of the Jewish people: "The kingdom of God will be taken away from you and given to a nation [or people] producing the fruits of it."[29] He adds to Mark's account of the trial of Jesus the scene of Pilate washing his hands of the blood of Jesus and thus declares Pilate to be innocent of Jesus' death. Instead, he assigns responsibility for Jesus' condemnation to the Jewish crowd and their descendants: "All the people answered, 'His blood be on us and our children.'"[30] Ever since Christianity became the dominant religion of Western culture, the words have been a text of terror for Jewish people.

The intensity of the conflict with Judaism in Matthew reflects the situation of his community. After the Roman reconquest of the Jewish homeland, the survivors sought to consolidate and preserve Jewish identity in spite of the loss of the temple. Along with the Torah, the temple had been one of the two centers of Jewish practice and identity. Soon after the temple's destruction, the Jewish community began to ostracize Jews who followed Jesus as the messiah, claiming that they were no longer true Jews. One of Matthew's central concerns is to claim the opposite: that his community of Christian Jews is faithful to the traditions of Israel.

Continuity with Judaism Matthew does this by emphasizing continuity with Jewish tradition. He quotes the Hebrew Bible more than any other gospel-writer. Not counting allusions or echoes, he quotes forty times with an explicit phrase such as "It is written" and another twenty-one times without such a phrase.[31]

He traces Jesus' genealogy back to Abraham, the father of the Jewish people. He reports that Jesus during his lifetime restricted his mission to Jews and ordered his disciples to do the same: "Go nowhere among the Gentiles, and enter no town of the Samaritans, but go rather to the lost sheep of the house of Israel."[32]

In a saying found in Matthew alone, Jesus is said to affirm the enduring validity of the Law and the Prophets, the two divisions of the Hebrew Bible regarded as sacred by Jews by the first century:

> Do not think that I have come to abolish the law or the
> prophets; I have not come to abolish but to fulfill. For truly
> I tell you, until heaven and earth pass away, not one letter,
> not one stroke of a letter, will pass from the law until all is
> accomplished.[33]

In addition, Matthew uses a Moses typology to construct his gospel. Matthew uses ninety percent of Mark as he writes, and to Mark's narrative he adds the teachings of Jesus as collected in Q, as well as some material not found in either Mark or Q. But he does so in a distinctive way. Namely, he gathers the teaching of Jesus into five major blocks of material and concludes each with a similar formula: "When Jesus had finished saying these things. . . ."[34] The arrangement of Jesus' teaching into five blocks calls to mind the five books of the Pentateuch.

In presenting the story of Jesus' birth, Matthew echoes the story of Moses' birth. Just as the life of Moses was threatened by Pharaoh's command that all male Hebrew babies be killed, so Jesus' life as an infant is threatened by King Herod's command that all male infants in the area of Bethlehem are to be killed. Matthew's meaning is clear. Jesus is like Moses, Herod is like Pharaoh, and what is happening in and through Jesus is like a new exodus.

Jesus' Inaugural Scene   The Moses typology is also reflected in Jesus' inaugural address. On a superficial level, Jesus' first public words in Matthew are virtually the same as those in Mark. Matthew condenses and slightly changes Mark's advance summary of Jesus' message to "Repent, for the kingdom of heaven is at hand."[35]

But we encounter what is distinctive about Jesus' inaugural address in Matthew in the next scene: the famous "Sermon on the Mount." Three chapters long, it is the first of the five blocks of Jesus' teachings in Matthew. It begins with the beatitudes ("Blessed are the . . .") and concludes with a parable contrasting two ways: one way is the wisdom of building your house on rock; the other way is the folly of building your house on sand.[36] In between, the sermon describes the "way" of Matthew's community, sometimes contrasting it with "what was said to those of ancient times."[37] These three chapters contain some of the most striking and radical teachings of Jesus.

They are called "the Sermon on the Mount" because of Matthew's narrative introduction: "Seeing the crowds, Jesus went up *on the mountain* and taught them."[38] Matthew is responsible for locating this teaching on a mountain; some of it is also found in Luke, where it is spoken "on a level place" and commonly called "the Sermon on the Plain."[39] Why does Matthew set this teaching on a mountain? Doing so fits his Moses typology: just as Moses ascended Mt. Sinai to receive the Torah, so Jesus now goes up on a mountain to deliver his teaching.

Thus Matthew constructs the inaugural scene of Jesus' public activity to disclose one of the central themes in his portrait of Jesus: Jesus is one like Moses.[40] Together with Matthew's frequent quotation of the Hebrew Bible and his structuring of Jesus' teaching into five blocks like the five books of Moses, the inaugural scene suggests that his gospel functioned like the Pentateuch for his community. It was their foundational document, combining their primal narrative (the story of Jesus) with teachings about the way of life that flowed out of taking Jesus seriously. This is the way Matthew and his community told and understood the story of Jesus.

Yet though the gospel of Matthew functioned for that community like the Pentateuch, it did not replace the Pentateuch. As mentioned earlier, according to Matthew 5.17–20, every letter and stroke of the Law and the Prophets remained valid. Matthew was not a supercessionist.[41] Rather, by presenting Jesus as the fulfillment of prophecy and as one like Moses, Matthew claimed the traditions of Israel for his community. He did not set out to prove that Jesus was the messiah; he and his community already believed that. Instead, in a late-first-century setting of conflict with other Jews, he claimed that the traditions of Israel belonged to his Christian Jewish community, not to "the scribes and Pharisees." In Matthew, we see an early stage of "the parting of the ways" that ultimately led to Judaism and Christianity as separate religions. But for Matthew and his community, it was still an intra-Jewish struggle.

Luke-Acts

Like Matthew, Luke was most likely written a decade or two after Mark and includes material from both Mark and Q. Unlike Matthew (and unlike any other gospel), the gospel of Luke is the first volume of a two-volume work, the second of which is the book of Acts. The two volumes together are an intricately integrated thematic construction.

Luke's gospel narrates Jesus' mission to the Jewish people in the Jewish homeland; Acts describes the spread of early Christianity into the Roman Empire beyond the Jewish homeland, beginning with Jews of the Diaspora and soon including a mission to Gentiles as well. The gospel begins and ends in Jerusalem; Acts begins in Jerusalem and ends in Rome.[42] The movement of Luke's two volumes is thus from Jerusalem to Rome.

The Spirit: Promise and Fulfillment   Central to Luke's thematic construction is repeated emphasis on the Spirit of God. Though Matthew and Mark also frequently speak of the Spirit, Luke does so even more often. The first two chapters of Luke not only narrate Jesus' conception by the Spirit, but also report that Elizabeth and Zechariah (the parents of John the Baptizer) are filled with the Holy Spirit, as is the aged Simeon, who praises God after he sees the infant Jesus in the temple.[43]

Like Matthew and Mark, Luke reports that the Spirit descended upon Jesus at his baptism and led him into the wilderness. Then Luke adds another reference to the Spirit as Jesus begins his public activity: "Then Jesus, filled with the power of the Spirit, returned to Galilee."[44] Near the end of the gospel, the final words of the dying Jesus are, "Father, into your hands I commend my spirit."[45] The gospel ends with the risen Jesus promising to send the Spirit upon his followers: "I am sending upon you what my Father promised; so stay here in the city [Jerusalem] until you have been clothed with power from on high."[46]

Acts opens with a twofold repetition of Jesus' promise of the Spirit.[47] And that promise is soon fulfilled. In Jerusalem on the day of Pentecost (the Jewish "Festival of Weeks," held fifty days after Passover), the Spirit descends on the community:

> They were all together in one place. And suddenly from
>   heaven there came a sound like the rush of a violent wind,
>   and it filled the entire house where they were sitting. Di-
>   vided tongues, as of fire, appeared among them, and a
>   tongue rested on each of them. All of them were filled with
>   the Holy Spirit and began to speak in other languages, as
>   the Spirit gave them ability.[48]

The gift of "other languages" enabled Jews from many nations and languages who were living in Jerusalem to understand the speakers.[49]

This text is full of rich symbolism. "Wind" and "fire" are classic images for the Spirit in the Hebrew Bible. The gift of universally intelligible language deliberately echoes the story of the Tower of Babel in Genesis, in which humanity was fragmented into language groups. The coming of the Spirit is the reversal of Babel, the beginning of the reunion of the human community. Then Peter speaks and interprets the descent of the Spirit as the fulfillment of God's promise for "the last days": "In the last days it will be, God declares, that I will pour out my Spirit upon all flesh."[50]

In the rest of Acts, the Spirit is so central that it is virtually the book's main character. Not only does the Spirit give birth to the community at Pentecost, but the Spirit directs significant advances in the community's mission: Philip's conversion of an Ethiopian eunuch, Paul's conversion, Peter's conversion of a Roman centurion named Cornelius, Paul and Barnabas's commissioning for their first missionary journey, the directive to Paul to take the gospel to Europe, and more.[51]

The Spirit also guides the decision of the Jerusalem council about whether to impose conditions on Gentiles who are joining the movement. In words that have been the envy of church committees ever since, the council concludes, "It has seemed good to the Holy Spirit and to us. . . ."[52] In addition, Luke frequently writes about the community and individuals as filled with the Spirit.[53] Thus in Acts, the same Spirit that conceived, empowered, and guided Jesus now does the same within the Christian community as it spreads from Jerusalem (the center of the Jewish world) to Rome (the center of the Gentile world).

Jesus' Inaugural Scene The centrality of the Spirit and a foreshadowing of the Gentile mission are crystallized in the inaugural scene of Jesus' public activity in Luke. Luke replaces Mark's inaugural text ("The time is fulfilled, and the kingdom of God is at hand. Repent . . .") with the story of Jesus in the synagogue in Nazareth, his hometown.[54] The scene begins with Jesus reading a passage from the book of Isaiah, the first words of Jesus' public activity in Luke:

> The Spirit of the Lord is upon me,
>> because God has anointed me to bring good news to the
> poor,
>> and has sent me to proclaim release to the captives
>> and recovery of sight to the blind,

          to let the oppressed go free,
to proclaim the year of the Lord's favor.[55]

This is a remarkably apt summary portrait of Luke's Jesus: in the rest of the gospel, he is a Spirit-anointed social prophet whose activity is directed especially to the poor and oppressed.

As the inaugural scene continues, Jesus speaks about two prophets from the Hebrew Bible who were sent to Gentiles: Elijah to a widow at Zarepath in Sidon, and Elisha to a Syrian leper named Naaman. The crowd in the synagogue who a few verses earlier had heard him gladly now turns on him and the people seek to kill him by hurling him off a cliff. But Jesus "passed through their midst and went on his way."

This is not history, of course. We are not to think that Jesus' mission began with his neighbors in Nazareth trying to kill him—an attempt that anticipates his eventual execution. Rather, like the inaugural addresses in Matthew and Mark, the whole scene is a thematic construction created by Luke.[56] It announces in advance the theme of Luke-Acts as a whole: the mission of Jesus to Israel in the gospel and the extension of that mission to Gentiles by the early Christian movement in Acts. All of this is the work of the Spirit: the same Spirit that anoints Jesus at the beginning of his mission goes on to anoint the Christian community at Pentecost at the beginning of its mission. For Luke, the Spirit active in Jesus continues in the mission of the community. By implication, then, the community is to continue Jesus' activity in the world.

John

The awareness that John (also called "the Fourth Gospel") is very different from the synoptic gospels is a foundation of modern study of the gospels. But the awareness itself is not modern. Clement of Alexandria, an early Christian theologian writing around the year 200, distinguished John from the other gospels and called it "the spiritual gospel."

John as Distinct from the Synoptics   The differences between John and the other gospels include the following:

- *Chronology.* In the synoptics, Jesus' public activity fits into a year; in John, three to four years. In the synoptics, overturning the tables of the moneychangers in the temple occurs in the last week of Jesus' life and is the cause of his arrest; in John, the event occurs at the beginning of Jesus' public activity.[57]
- *Geography.* In the synoptics, most of Jesus' public activity occurs in Galilee; in John, Jesus is more often in Judea and Jerusalem.
- *Jesus' message.* In the synoptics, Jesus' message is about the kingdom of God, not about himself; in John, much of it is about himself. Declarations such as "I and the Father are one" and "Whoever has seen me has seen the Father" are found in John, as are the familiar "I am" sayings: I am the light of the world, the bread of life, the resurrection and the life, the way and the truth and life, and so forth.
- *Style of Jesus' teaching.* In the synoptics, Jesus teaches in parables and short memorable sayings; in John, long and remarkably dense theological discourses. John is very "wordy," as my students say.

Yet alongside the dense wordiness of the discourses is the richest symbolic language about Jesus in the New Testament: Jesus as the Word made flesh, as the light of the world, as the Lamb of God, as the bread of life, as the true vine, as the door, as the good shepherd. John also uses a set of dualistic symbols to present the significance of Jesus and his work: darkness/light, below/above, flesh/spirit, death/life, falsehood/truth, earth/heaven. He also sometimes uses the term "the world" to refer not simply to the created order, but to a negative way of being, just as he often uses the phrase "the Jews" as a negative symbol (about which I will say more later in this chapter).[58]

Though both the synoptics and John are a mixture of history and symbol, in John metaphorical narrative dominates history remembered and historical memory. Of course Jesus of Nazareth as a historical figure lies behind John, but he is further removed than in the synoptics. Put positively, John is the most symbolic of the gospels.

Jesus' Inaugural Scene Thus it is not surprising that the inaugural scene of Jesus' public activity in John is a richly symbolic narrative. Rather than an inaugural address as in the synoptics, it is an inaugural deed: Jesus changes water into wine at a wedding banquet.[59] The story is well known: Jesus, his mother, and his disciples are at a wedding in Cana, a village in Galilee; the wine runs out; Jesus changes a large amount of water into very good wine. Indeed, the steward, thinking that the groom has provided the wine, says to him, "Everyone serves the good wine first. . . . But you have kept the best wine until now." This, John says, was "the first of Jesus' signs" and "revealed his glory, and his disciples believed in him."

The text reports a miracle, of course: the transformation of a large quantity of water (120 to 180 gallons) into wine. But if we focus on the event's "happenedness," we easily become distracted and miss the point. We then wonder if such a thing could really happen; and if we think it could and did, we then marvel about what Jesus did on a particular day in the past. But the meaning of this story does not depend upon its "happenedness." Instead, it is a "sign," as John puts it. Signs point beyond themselves; to use a play on words, they *sign*-ify something, and what they signify is their significance.

So what is the meaning of this story as a "sign"? What is its significance? A number of its details have caught the attention of scholars: the odd exchange between Jesus and his mother; the detail that the water was "for the Jewish rites of purification"; the anticipation of Jesus' death.[60] Though these details matter, they should not divert attention from the primary symbolic feature of the text: a wedding banquet.

Wedding banquets were the most festive occasions in the

world of first-century Palestine, especially in the peasant class (and Cana was a peasant village). Wedding banquets commonly lasted seven days. They featured dancing, wine, and vast quantities of food. The normal peasant diet was meager: grains, vegetables, fruit, olives, eggs, and an occasional fish. Meat and poultry were infrequently eaten, since people were reluctant to kill the few animals they had. But at a wedding banquet, there were copious amounts of food of all kinds.

Given the above, what is this text—which John places as the inaugural scene of Jesus' public activity—saying? What is Jesus about? What is the gospel—the good news—of Jesus about? John's answer: it is about a wedding banquet at which the wine never runs out and the best is saved for last.

To this metaphorical meaning of a wedding banquet can be added historical associations of banquet and wedding imagery in Jewish and early Christian traditions. In Judaism, a banquet was a frequent symbol for the messianic age. Marriage was also used as a metaphor for the relationship between God and Israel.[61] In the New Testament, Jesus is sometimes spoken of as the bridegroom and the community of his followers as the bride.[62] The book of Revelation refers to "the marriage supper of the Lamb" (Jesus) and ends with a vision of the New Jerusalem descending from the sky "prepared as a bride adorned for her husband."[63] A wedding could thus symbolize the intimacy of the divine-human relationship and the marriage between heaven and earth. It is a common mystical symbol, and John is the most mystical gospel.[64]

Did John intend to build all of these meanings into his inaugural scene? There is no way of knowing. But it is the nature of metaphorical language to convey more meanings than the author intended. In any case, it is clear what John is *saying:* the story of Jesus is about a wedding banquet at which the wine never runs out.

Selected Texts: Metaphorical Narratives

We move now from seeing the gospels as thematic constructions to reading individual texts as metaphorical narratives. As we do so, we will attend to two levels or kinds of metaphor: *intrinsic metaphor* and *historical metaphor*.[65]

Intrinsic metaphor is shorthand for the metaphorical meanings intrinsic to the story itself—the meanings that occur to a reader sensitive to the language of metaphor prior to taking into account (or even knowing) the specific historical associations of the language. *Historical metaphor* is shorthand for the additional metaphorical meanings that flow out of the specific historical associations of the language.

I illustrate the distinction by returning briefly to the story of the wedding at Cana. The intrinsic metaphorical meaning of that story is that Jesus is about a wedding banquet at which the wine never runs out. The historical metaphorical meanings are those additional meanings that flow out of knowing about the specific associations of banquet and marriage/wedding imagery in Judaism and early Christianity.

The texts I have selected for this section of the chapter are all, in my judgment, purely metaphorical narratives. I do not think a particular historical event in the life of Jesus lies behind any of them, even though I think all of them speak powerfully and truthfully about the significance of Jesus and his vision.

Using different language to make the same point, John Dominic Crossan calls stories like these "parables." Jesus, he says, told parables about God. The early Christian movement likewise told parables about Jesus.[66] He suggests that we ask the following question about the stories in the gospels: "Whether you read the story as history or parable, what is its meaning—for then, for now, for always?"[67]

Walking on Water

The story of Jesus walking on the water is one of only two miracle stories found in both John and the synoptics.[68] With small variations, the details are remarkably similar in Mark and John. It is night, and the disciples are rowing across the Sea of Galilee in a small boat by themselves. There is a strong wind, the sea is rough, and they make little headway. Then they see Jesus walking on the sea. Initially, they are terrified. But he says to them, "It is I—do not be afraid." Then they are safe.

Intrinsic Metaphorical Meanings What metaphorical meanings are intrinsic to the story and not dependent on either the "happenedness" of the story or the specific historical associations of the imagery? As with any good metaphorical story, the meanings of this one cannot be reduced to a single understanding. I provide a short list of possible meanings —a list whose purpose is not to be comprehensive but to illustrate metaphorical thinking. There is nothing special about my list; generating it required no scholarly expertise. You are invited to reflect on the story to see what other intrinsic meanings occur to you.

- Without Jesus, you don't get anywhere.
- Without Jesus, you're at sea and in the dark.
- Following Jesus may put you in difficult situations.
- Jesus takes away fear.
- Jesus comes to you in distress.
- Jesus stills storms.

I think I see some sermon possibilities here.

As Matthew narrates this story, he adds an episode: Peter walks on the water as well. After Jesus says, "It is I, have no fear," Matthew tells us:

> Peter answered him, "Lord, if it is you, bid me come to you on the water." Jesus said, "Come." So Peter got out of the boat and walked on the water and came to Jesus; but when he saw the wind, he was afraid, and beginning to sink he cried out, "Lord, save me!" Jesus immediately reached out his hand and caught him, saying to him, "O man of little faith, why did you doubt?"[69]

I strongly doubt that Matthew's point is literal: if you have enough faith in Jesus, you can literally walk on water. Rather, his

point is metaphorical, and the intrinsic metaphorical meanings
might include the following:

- Without faith in Jesus, fear takes over.
- Without faith in Jesus, you sink.
- With faith in Jesus, you can walk on water (metaphorically).
- When you're sinking, call out, "Lord, save me!"—and he
  will.

Historical Metaphorical Meanings Additional meanings can be
added to the above if we factor in the specific historical associations of sea imagery in the Hebrew Bible. Those associations
were ominous. The sea was a mysterious and threatening force
opposed to God. Thus, when the ancient Hebrews wanted to
stress God's power and authority, they spoke of God's mastery
over the sea. The authors of the book of Psalms exclaimed, "You
rule the raging of the sea; when its waves rise, you still them,"
and "The sea is God's, for God made it."[70] In the book of Job,
the voice from the whirlwind declares that it was God who "shut
in the sea with doors" and said to it, "Thus far you shall come,
and no farther, and here shall your proud waves be stopped."[71]
Indeed, the plight of the disciples echoes a psalm that may
have been the model for the gospel story:

The stormy wind lifted up the waves of the sea.
They mounted up to heaven, they went down to the depths.
The courage of those in the boat melted away in their
     calamity;
          they reeled and staggered like drunkards,
          and were at their wits' end.
Then they cried to the LORD in their trouble,
          and God brought them out of their distress;
God made the storm be still,
          and the waves of the sea were hushed.
Then they were glad because they had quiet,
          And God brought them to their desired haven.[72]

So what more do we see and hear in the gospel story by being aware of the historical associations of the imagery? The primary additional meaning is christological. The story's portrait of Jesus walking on the water and calming the waves makes the claim that Jesus participates in the power and authority of God: that which was said about God in the Hebrew Bible is now said about Jesus.

Finally, the disciples of Jesus were sometimes a symbol for the Christian community, and a boat was an early Christian symbol for the church. This suggests that the story is also about the relationship between Jesus and the church.

The story thus witnesses to what the post-Easter Jesus had become in the life of early Christian communities: one with God. The canonical Jesus is one who stills storms, takes away our fear, rescues us—and does so because he participates in the power of God.

Feeding the Multitude

The second miracle story found in both the synoptics and John is the feeding of five thousand people with five loaves and two fish.[73] In both, the story is remarkably similar, and its basic outline is familiar. Jesus, the disciples, and a crowd are in the countryside (the synoptics call it "a lonely place"), and the crowd has nothing to eat. The disciples cannot imagine that feeding them—as Jesus wants to do—is possible and ask, "Shall we go and buy 200 denarii worth of bread?"[74] Instead, five loaves and two fish are found. According to Mark, Jesus then took the food, "looked up to heaven, and blessed, and broke the loaves and gave them to the disciples to set before the people." According to John, "Jesus took the loaves, and when he had given thanks," he distributed them to the crowd himself. All ate and were satisfied. Afterward, twelve baskets of food were left over.[75]

Here the similarities between John and the synoptics end. Unlike the synoptics, John uses the story as a springboard for a long discourse by Jesus.[76] Its subject matter is one of the "I am" statements attributed by John to Jesus: "I am the bread of life." Because John's interpretation of the feeding story is significantly different from that of the synoptics, I will treat the two interpretations separately.

The Synoptic Story: Intrinsic Metaphorical Meanings Again I invite you to reflect on the metaphorical meanings intrinsic to the story. As I did so myself, the following occurred to me:

- Without Jesus, you go hungry.
- With Jesus, there is more than enough.
- Feeding the multitude matters to Jesus.
- Jesus commands his followers to feed the multitude.
- Jesus' followers resist feeding the multitude: How is it possible, they ask?[77]

Though the narrative is metaphorical, real food for real people mattered to Jesus.

The Synoptic Story: Historical Metaphorical Meanings The historical metaphorical associations with the Hebrew Bible are especially rich in this story. The principal association is with Israel's primal narrative, the exodus story. Just as God fed the Israelites with manna from heaven as they journeyed through the wilderness, so now Jesus provides bread in the wilderness. The exodus story is happening again. Just as Second Isaiah viewed what was happening in his time as a new exodus, so now the gospels view what is happening in Jesus as a new exodus.[78] And though the feeding part of the exodus story is emphasized, the fuller story is also called to mind: Jesus is like Moses, the leader of Israel who liberated his people from bondage and deprivation in imperial Egypt and brought them to the promised land.

John's Story: Intrinsic Metaphorical Meanings In the long discourse and dialogue following the story of the feeding, the Jesus of John says, "I am the bread of life" and "the bread of God" that "comes down from heaven and gives life to the world."[79] Jesus himself is that bread; people are to eat him. The language in John becomes even more graphic:

> Unless you eat the flesh of the Son of Man and drink his
> blood, you have no life in you. Those who eat my flesh and
> drink my blood have eternal life. . . . For my flesh is true
> food and my blood is true drink.[80]

Obviously, John's story uses the language of metaphor. If taken literally, this passage would smack of cannibalism. So what are the intrinsic metaphorical meanings of eating Jesus' flesh and drinking his blood?

The imagery of eating and drinking connects to a central religious metaphor for our deepest human yearning: hunger, and the closely related metaphor thirst. There are those who hunger and thirst for God, for justice, for meaning, for life. For John, Jesus is the answer to that hunger: Jesus himself is the bread of life who satisfies our hunger. Eat this bread and you will never be hungry: "I am the bread of life; whoever comes to me will never be hungry." The next line of the verse invokes the thirst metaphor: "And whoever believes in me will never thirst."[81]

The metaphors remind us of the Christian eucharist, of course. But one should not reduce their meaning to the bread and wine of the central Christian sacrament. Although John's language adds resonances of meaning to the eucharist, to see this language as conveying simply "Eat the bread and drink the wine of the eucharist" flattens the varied metaphors into a single prosaic meaning.

The metaphors also connect to the wisdom literature of Israel, especially to the banquet of Wisdom/Sophia in Proverbs: "Come, eat of the bread and drink of the wine I have mixed!"[82] For John, Jesus is the incarnation not only of the Word of God but also of the Wisdom of God. To take Jesus in, to digest Jesus, is to partake in Jesus as the Wisdom of God.

John's Story: Historical Metaphorical Meanings The metaphors also connect to the mysticism of John's gospel. Eating and drinking Jesus is the way of becoming one with Jesus: "Those who eat my flesh and drink my blood abide in me, and I in them."[83] By taking in and digesting the flesh and blood of Jesus, we live in Jesus and Jesus lives in us: we become one with Jesus.

Abiding or dwelling in Jesus is also the theme of another mystical metaphor in John: Jesus as the true vine and his followers as branches. The branches are joined to the vine and depend on the vine for their life. They are to bear fruit; and the fruit, John tells us, is love: just as Jesus abides in God's love, so Jesus' followers are to abide in his love. Thus the consequence of having Jesus within and being in Jesus is to "Love one another as I have loved you."[84] And part of loving one another is feeding the multitude.

The implicit connection between the feeding of the five thousand and the exodus story is made explicit in John. In his discourse, John explicitly refers to Israel's ancestors being fed with manna in the wilderness. But John's point is not simply *similarity* to the exodus; he also emphasizes contrast. While Jesus "gives life to the world" as "the bread of life," the manna of the exodus did not give life: "Your ancestors ate the manna in the wilderness, and they died." What Moses gave them was not the true bread from heaven.[85] But Jesus is "the true bread" and "the living bread," and "whoever eats of this bread will live forever."[86]

Thus in John the point is not really that Jesus now feeds people in the wilderness as God did in the exodus story. The point, rather, is that Jesus provides that which was not provided in the time of the exodus: living bread.

Sight to the Blind

I have already commented briefly about two synoptic "sight to the blind" stories as metaphorical narratives that also reflect history remembered.[87] Here I will focus on a story in John's gospel that deals with Jesus giving sight to a man blind from birth. I leave unaddressed the question of whether this particular healing happened. For a metaphorical reading, the question does not matter.

John devotes the whole of his ninth chapter to the story and its aftermath. The first part of the chapter narrates the healing itself. Jesus gives sight to the man "born blind" by making a paste of clay and spittle and spreading it on his eyes. The second part concerns the interrogation of the once-blind man and his parents by "the Pharisees" and "the Jews." The response of the man's parents to the interrogation is cautious and careful, because, we are told, "they were afraid of the Jews; for the Jews had already agreed that anyone who confessed Jesus to be the Messiah would be put out of the synagogue." Then the formerly blind man is interrogated again, and when he unambiguously affirms that Jesus is from God, he is driven out of the synagogue.[88]

Intrinsic Metaphorical Meanings The intrinsic metaphors in this story are "light" and "seeing." As John often does, he makes the intrinsic metaphors explicit. He does so in words attributed to Jesus and the blind man:

> *Jesus:* "I am the light of the world."
> *The blind man:* "Once I was blind, but now I see. . . . Jesus opened my eyes."[89]

The metaphors connect to a major theme of John's story of Jesus: Jesus is the light who brings enlightenment. One chapter before this blind-man-healed story, some of the same language is used: "I am the light of the world. Whoever follows me will never walk in darkness but will have the light of life."[90]

This theme is prominently announced in the elegant prologue to John's gospel. The Word (and Wisdom) of God that became incarnate in Jesus is the life and light of all people:[91]

> The light shines in the darkness,
>   and the darkness did not overcome it. . . .
> The true light which enlightens everyone
>   was coming into the world.[92]

Darkness and light, blindness and seeing, light and enlightenment—these are archetypal religious metaphors common to many traditions. Though the imagery is used in the Hebrew Bible, the archetypal associations are more important for our

purposes than the specifically historical associations.[93] "Being in
the dark" and "blindness" are frequent cross-cultural images for
the human condition, just as "light," "seeing," and "enlightenment" are images for the deliverance from that state of affairs.

Enlightenment as an archetypal religious metaphor belongs to
a mystical way of being religious. Outside of the Jewish and
Christian traditions, the best-known enlightenment experience is
the Buddha's mystical experience. Such an experience leads to
seeing everything differently. It is not simply an intellectual or
mental "seeing," as when we say, "Oh, I see what you mean."
Rather, enlightenment as a religious experience involves communion or union with what is, an immediate "knowing" of the sacred that transforms one's way of seeing.

So it is in John: enlightenment is a central metaphor for salvation. To have one's eyes opened, to be enlightened, is to move
from the negative pole of John's contrasting symbols to the positive pole. To move from darkness to light is also to move from
death to life, from falsehood to truth, from life in the flesh to life
in the Spirit, from life "below" to life "from above."[94]

To be enlightened is to be born "from above" and "of the
Spirit"—in other words, to be "born again." Thus the "born
again" experience in John is an enlightenment experience.[95]

The language of enlightenment connects to John's emphasis
upon knowing God. For John, such knowing is the primary
meaning of "eternal life"—not a future state beyond death but
an experience in the present. To know God is eternal life: "This
is eternal life, that they may know you, the only true God." Of
course, for John, the true God is known in Jesus, and so the second half of the verse continues with "and Jesus Christ, whom
you have sent."[96] For John, the Christian enlightenment experience is knowing God in Jesus.

Historical Metaphorical Meanings   In the judgment of most
scholars, the interrogation in the second part of John 9, with its
language of being "put out of the synagogue," points to the historical context in which the gospel was written: late in the first

century.[97] A synagogue, of course, was a local Jewish assembly of teaching and worship. In that world, being "put out" (expelled) from the synagogue was far more serious than being expelled from a Christian congregation or denomination is in our world. Whereas we can simply find and join another church, those who were expelled from the synagogue were no longer considered Jews (or at least not *acceptable* Jews). In a traditional society where most people lived their entire life in the same village or town, this was a powerful social sanction. Those who were expelled faced social ostracism: among other things, expulsion disrupted relationships within families and with neighbors and made marriage to "proper" Jews difficult or impossible.

Followers of Jesus were not threatened with expulsion from the synagogue during his lifetime. At the earliest, this happened a decade or two after the destruction of the temple in 70. John 9 thus not only suggests an approximate date for the gospel but also points to the historical situation with which John and his community were dealing: bitter conflict between Jews and Christian Jews. As it did in the gospel of Matthew, this conflict shapes John's story of Jesus. In particular, it accounts for John's use of "the Jews" as a negative symbol of disbelief. And worse: though "the Jews" claim to have Abraham and God for their father, they are neither Abraham's children nor God's children. Rather—and somewhat shockingly—the Jesus of John says, "You are from your father the devil."[98] The conflict situation helps us to understand this language, even as we must also regret and reject it.

Jesus as "the Way"

Jesus said, "I am the way, and the truth, and the life; no one comes to the Father except through me."[99]

The last text we shall explore is also from John. It is troubling to many mainline Christians in our time because of how it has commonly been heard and read through the Christian centuries: it has been the classic "proof text" for Christian exclusivism—the notion that salvation is possible only through Jesus, and thus only through Christianity.

Intrinsic Metaphorical Meanings   Although this text, like the
others we have looked at, has specific historical relevance, it also
has universal meanings. We gain access to those meanings by
paying attention to the metaphor at the heart of the text: Jesus is
"the way." A way is a path or a road or a journey, not a set of beliefs.[100]

So Jesus is "the way." But what does this metaphor, applied to
a person, mean? More specifically, what is Jesus' "way" in John's
gospel (or what is "the way" which Jesus is)? The answer is
found in the movement or dynamic of the gospel as a whole as
well as in a single verse:

• *In the gospel as a whole:* From the inaugural scene onward,
  Jesus' way leads to his death—which is also, for John, his
  glorification.[101] The way to life in the presence of God is
  through death.
• *In a single verse:* The Jesus of John says, "Very truly I tell
  you, unless a grain of wheat falls into the earth and dies, it
  remains just a single grain; but if it dies, it bears much
  fruit."[102]

In short, for John the way or path of Jesus is the path of death
and resurrection understood as a metaphor for the religious life.
That way—the path of dying to an old way of being and being
born into a new way of being—is the only way to God.

The same point is made in a story I once heard about a sermon preached by a Hindu professor in a Christian seminary several decades ago. The text for the day included the "one way"
passage, and about it he said, "This verse is absolutely true—
Jesus is the only way." But he went on to say, "And that way—of
dying to an old way of being and being born into a new way of
being—is known in all of the religions of the world." The way of
Jesus is a universal way, known to millions who have never heard
of Jesus.

The way of Jesus is thus not a set of beliefs about Jesus. That
we ever thought it was is strange, when one thinks about it—as if

one entered new life by believing certain things to be true, or as if the only people who can be saved are those who know the word "Jesus." Thinking that way virtually amounts to salvation by syllables. Rather, the way of Jesus is the way of death and resurrection—the path of transition and transformation from an old way of being to a new way of being.

Finally, the language of incarnation, so central to John, is crucial for understanding the threefold affirmation of this verse: Jesus is not only "the way," but also "the truth, and the life." Incarnation means embodiment. Jesus is the way—Jesus is what the way embodied in a person looks like. Jesus is the truth—Jesus is what the truth embodied in a person looks like. Jesus is the life— Jesus is what life (*real* life) embodied in a person looks like. Taking Jesus seriously is not about a set of beliefs but about a person in whom we see embodied the way, the truth, and the life.

Historical Metaphorical Meanings   As in John's gospel generally, though "I am the way, and the truth, and the life" is attributed to Jesus, it does not go back to Jesus himself. Rather, it is the product of a later stage in the developing tradition and was perhaps created by the author of John himself.

One key to reading this text is to set it in the historical context of John's gospel: a situation of bitter conflict in which John's community of Christian Jews was experiencing sharp social ostracism from non-Christian Jews. As a result, some of John's community may have been tempted to return to their community of origin.

In that setting, John wrote these words. He was thinking not of all the religions of the world, but of the synagogue across the street. He was saying, in effect, Stay within the community of Jesus. Don't go back to the way you left behind. Jesus is the way; that way isn't.

Even as we understand the text this way, it is important not to turn it into a rejection of Judaism, as if other religions might be all right, but not Judaism. In short, reading the verse in historical context relativizes it. It is not an absolute pronouncement about all other religions or about all other forms of Judaism for all time; rather, it is a pastoral exhortation in a particular historical setting.

Conclusion

The gospel portraits of the canonical Jesus make extraordinary claims about him. He is one with God and shares in the power and authority of God. He is the revelation of God. He is also the revelation of "the way," not only in John but also in the synoptics. He is the bread of life who satisfies the deepest hunger of human beings and the light shining in the darkness who brings enlightenment. He lifts us out of death into life. He is the Word and Wisdom of God embodied in a human life. He is the disclosure of what a life full of God—a life filled with the Spirit—looks like.

This is who Jesus is for us as Christians. Some modern Christians have been uncomfortable with these claims because they seem to partake of Christian triumphalism. But for Christians, these claims should not be watered down. For us as Christians, Jesus is not less than this—he is *all* of this. And we can say "This is who Jesus is for us" without also saying "And God is known only in Jesus."

The gospels—as particular documents, as a collection of documents, and as individual stories within them—are Christianity's primal narratives. To say this means that these are the most important stories we know, and we know them to be decisively true.

NOTES

1. The word "Christian" does occur, but only three times: I Pet. 4.16 and Acts 11.26 and 26.28. Formed from the Greek or Latin word for "messiah," in this early usage it meant a follower of Jesus as the Jewish messiah. Thus it did not yet mean a member of a new religion. See Michael J. Wilkins, "Christian," *The Anchor Bible Dictionary,* ed. David Noel Freedman (New York: Doubleday, 1992), vol. 1, pp. 925–26.
2. The phrase "the parting of the ways" echoes the title of a fine book by James D. G. Dunn, *The Partings of the Ways. Between Christianity and Ju-*

daism and Their Significance for the Character of Christianity (Philadelphia: Trinity Press International, 1991).

3. Rodney Stark, *The Rise of Christianity* (San Francisco: HarperSanFrancisco, 1997), chap. 3.

4. Alan Segal, *Rebecca's Children: Judaism and Christianity in the Roman World* (Cambridge: Harvard University Press, 1986).

5. Stark, *The Rise of Christianity*, p. 57.

6. Typically dated to the early second century are I and II Timothy, Titus, and II Peter, with the last commonly seen as the latest book of the New Testament.

7. Stark, *The Rise of Christianity*, chap. 1.

8. The two shortest documents are Philemon and Jude.

9. See the illuminating comments of Eugene Boring, *Revelation* (Louisville: Knox, 1989), p. 6.

10. Excellent accessible introductions to the gospels include Mark Allan Powell, *Introduction to the Gospels* (Minneapolis: Fortress, 1998), and W. Barnes Tatum, *In Search of Jesus*, rev. ed. (Nashville: Abingdon, 1999).

11. We are virtually certain that none was written by any of the twelve disciples or other eyewitnesses. There is a strong scholarly consensus that Matthew and John were not written by disciples named Matthew and John. With Mark and Luke, a reasonable (though not decisive) case can be made that they were written by people named Mark and Luke, in part because there was no particularly good reason for second-century Christians to name the gospels after these men if they were not the authors. Neither Mark nor Luke was among the twelve disciples, nor was either an eyewitness to the public activity of Jesus.

12. Moreover, most mainline scholars see the birth stories and the story of Jesus at age twelve as metaphorical narratives. Historically speaking, they are thus legendary, even though as metaphorical narratives they make significant affirmations about Jesus.

13. Thus I reject the either-or choice that has marked a fair amount of Jesus and gospel scholarship: that only the historical Jesus matters or only the canonical Jesus matters. *Both* matter. For a vigorous presentation of the case for the primacy of the canonical Jesus, see Luke Timothy Johnson, *The Real Jesus* (San Francisco: HarperSanFrancisco, 1995). For my summary of the two positions in the history of scholarship, see *Jesus in Contemporary Scholarship* (Valley Forge, PA: Trinity Press International, 1994), chap. 9.

14. My understanding of the historical Jesus is described most fully in the following books: *Conflict, Holiness, and Politics in the Teaching of Jesus* (Harrisburg, PA: Trinity Press International, 1998; first published in 1984); and, all published by HarperSanFrancisco: *Jesus: A New Vision* (1987), *Meeting Jesus Again for the First Time* (1994), and, with N. T. Wright, *The Meaning of Jesus: Two Visions* (1998). The last one in particular also treats post-Easter perceptions of Jesus within the early Christian movement.

15. Dating Mark to the late 60s or early 70s is widely accepted. I owe the phrase "wartime gospel" to Daryl Schmidt, *The Gospel of Mark* (Sonoma, CA: Polebridge, 1990).

16. Mark 13.1–2. A historical comment: I think it is likely that the historical Jesus did address threats to Jerusalem and the temple as the center of the native domination system, just as many of the classical prophets of the Hebrew Bible warned of the destruction of the kingdoms that they addressed. Thus my position is not that Mark has created these warnings but that Mark has composed his thirteenth chapter with the events of the Jewish war in mind. In short, Mark may be using historical material here, even as he applies it to his own time.

17. Mark 13.4 and following. Quoted passage is 13.14, echoing Dan. 9.27, 11.31, and 12.11. In Daniel, the foreign empire is the Hellenistic Empire of Antiochus Epiphanes IV; his desecration of the temple around 165 BCE sparked the Maccabean revolt. Some scholars, including the well-known German scholar Gerd Theissen, have argued that elements of Mark 13 may have originated in connection with the crisis of 40 CE, when the Roman emperor Caligula planned to have a statue of himself erected in the temple in Jerusalem. See Theissen, *The Gospels in Context*, trans. Linda Maloney (Minneapolis: Fortress, 1991), pp. 125–65. I regard this as possible (maybe even plausible), even as I also think it is clear that Mark is applying this language to the events of 70.

18. The first and longer quoted passage is Mark 13.24–27; the quoted phrase within it is taken from Dan. 7.13–14. The second quoted passage is Mark 13.30.

19. When speaking about "apocalyptic" and "eschatology," terminological problems abound. Here I use "eschatology" as a fairly broad umbrella term to refer to "the end of things"; adding the adjective "apocalyptic" refers to an eschatology that sees "the end" as imminent, dramatic, and brought about by divine intervention.

20. Mark 9.1, immediately following the Son of Man saying in 8.38. Mark 9.1 occupies a strategic place in the gospel, either as the end of the first half or as the beginning of the second half. Note that it is followed immediately by the story of Jesus' transfiguration, in which the same voice that declared Jesus to be God's beloved Son at the beginning of the gospel in the story of Jesus' baptism (Mark 1.11) is heard again: "This is my Son, the Beloved" (Mark 9.7, in the context of 9.2–8). Just as the first half of Mark begins with a declaration of Jesus' identity at his baptism, so the second half begins with a declaration of his identity at his transfiguration.

21. In addition to Mark 1.15 and 9.1, only eleven more times in words attributed to Jesus in Mark: 4.10–12 (the "mystery" of the kingdom); 4.26–29, 30–32 (two brief parables of the Kingdom); six sayings in Mark 9 and 10 (9.47; 10.14, 15, 23, 24, 25); 12.34; and 14.25. Comparisons: Matthew has thirty-six "kingdom of God" sayings attributed to Jesus, and Luke has thirty-two.

22. Behind all three English words is the Greek word *hodos,* used frequently by Mark.

23. Mark 1.3.

24. The central section of Mark is 8.27–10.45 (or 8.22–10.52, if the two stories of blind men regaining their sight—stories that frame the section—are included). John Donahue, in *Harper's Bible Commentary* (San Francisco:

Harper & Row, 1988), p. 984, highlights the section's centrality by comparing the construction of Mark's gospel to the design of a Roman triumphal arch: the side panels point to what is most central, the panel in the middle of the arch. Mark's central section is the middle panel. The three predictions of Jesus' death and resurrection are Mark 8.31, 9.31, and 10.33–34.

25. All of Mark's sayings about entering or being in the kingdom of God are found in his central section: 9.47; 10.14, 15, 23, 24, 25.

26. Shortly before Mark was written, the first persecution of Christians by the Roman Empire occurred. Instigated by the emperor Nero in 64, it happened in Rome itself, and apparently not elsewhere. Though we do not have any specific evidence of persecution and martyrdom of Christians in connection with the Jewish war of revolt against Rome, it is plausible to think that it happened.

27. Matt. 4.23, 9.35. In 7.29, Matthew refers to "their" scribes. See also Matt. 6.2 and 6.5, where those in synagogues are called "hypocrites."

28. Matt. 23. The formula occurs in vv. 13, 15, 23, 25, 27, 29. "Blind guides," "blind fools," "blind men," and "blind Pharisee": vv. 16, 17, 19, 24, 26. "Serpents" and "brood of vipers": v. 33. "Child of hell": v. 15. Luke 11.37–52 contains some of the same material, and thus Matt. 23 is based on Q; but in Luke (and Q), the criticisms are specific indictments and not broadside invective.

29. Matt. 21.43.

30. Matt. 27.24–25. These verses are a Matthean editorial addition to Mark's account of the trial. So also is Pilate's wife's dream in 27.19, which declares Jesus to be a righteous man.

31. See the excellent excursus on Matthew as interpreter of scripture in Eugene Boring's commentary on Matthew in *The New Interpreter's Bible* (Nashville: Abingdon, 1995), vol. 8, pp. 151–54.

32. Matt. 10.5; see also 15.24. Matthew is not against a mission to the Gentiles, but he attributes the command for such a mission to a post-Easter setting: Matt. 28.18–20.

33. Matt. 5.17–18.

34. The five blocks of teaching material are Matt. 5.1–7.27, 10.5–42, 13.1–52, 18.1–35, and 24.3–25.46. The formula is found in 7.28, 11.1, 13.53, 19.1, and 26.1.

35. Matt. 4.17. Matthew's use of "kingdom of *heaven*" instead of "kingdom of *God*" here and elsewhere in his gospel requires a brief comment. Whereas Mark and Luke consistently use the phrase "kingdom of God," Matthew substitutes "heaven" for "God." But Matthew does not mean a kingdom in another world after death, or heaven as afterlife. Rather, the substitution is another reflection of his continuity with Jewish tradition: out of reverence for God, he seeks to avoid using the name "God" and so substitutes "heaven" as an alternative (incidentally, he uses the plural: kingdom *of the heavens*). Matthew's piety has unfortunately led centuries of Christians to think that the center of Jesus' message was the kingdom of heaven understood as afterlife. But Jesus' focus was on the kingdom of God, which is not at all the same as heaven.

36. Matthew's nine beatitudes are in 5.3–12; Luke has four in Luke 6.20–23. The parable of the wise and foolish builders at the end of the Sermon on the Mount is in Matt. 7.24–27.

37. The contrasts are called "the antitheses" of the Sermon on the Mount, and are in 5.21–48.

38. Matt. 5.1–2. The Sermon on the Mount as a whole is in Matt. 5–7.

39. Luke 6.17. The Sermon on the Plain is in Luke 6.20–47.

40. For Matthew, Jesus is more than this. He is also, for example, the messiah and Son of God. My concern here is not to present Matthew's christology as a whole, but simply to illustrate how Matthew's Moses typology is reflected in Jesus' inaugural address.

41. A *supercessionist* is one who thinks that Israel and the Jewish people *were* the people of God until the time of Jesus but no longer are, and that Christians are now the people of God (in other words, that Christians have superseded Jews as God's "chosen"). Much of conventional Christian belief throughout the centuries has been supercessionist, consciously or unconsciously, though most often without using that label. In our time, supercessionism has been explicitly rejected by the Catholic Church and by many mainline Christians, including most mainline Christian theologians.

42. A "roadmap" of the spread of early Christianity in Acts is programmatically stated in Acts 1.8: the risen Christ just before his ascension says to his followers, "You will be my witnesses in Jerusalem, in all Judea and Samaria, and to the ends of the earth."

43. Luke 1.35, 41, 67; 2.25–27.

44. Luke 4.14. References to the Spirit descending at Jesus' baptism and leading him into the wilderness (both paralleled in Mark and Matthew) are found in 3.22 and 4.1.

45. Luke 23.46. It is unclear whether we should understand the words to mean that the Spirit that had guided and empowered Jesus during his life now returns to God, or whether the statement is simply a confession of trust in God as Jesus dies. Both meanings are possible.

46. Luke 24.49. Luke goes on to end his gospel with the story of Jesus' ascension, which he speaks of as having occurred the night after Easter. Then Luke begins Acts with another story of Jesus' ascension—this one some forty days later. The two ascension stories are a bit of a puzzle, especially since they are set forty days apart. Perhaps the contradiction suggests that Luke does not see the ascension story as reporting a literally factual event.

47. Acts 1.5, 8. The Spirit is also mentioned in v. 3.

48. Acts 2.1–4.

49. Thus this is quite different from "speaking in tongues" (*glossolalia*) as reported in the churches of Paul, where what is heard is unintelligible language. In Acts, the gift is universally intelligible language.

50. The story of the first Christian Pentecost continues through Acts 2.41. Quoted words are from 2.17, an approximate citation of Joel 2.28.

51. Acts 8.29, 9.17, 10.19, 13.2, 16.6–7.

52. Acts 15.28.

53. Examples in addition to those already cited: Acts 2.38, 4.8, 4.31, 6.3, 7.55, 8.15–17, 9.31, 10.44, 11.15, 11.24, 13.9, 19.2–6, 19.21, 20.22–23, 21.11.

54. Luke 4.16–30.
55. Luke 4.18–19, quoting Isa. 61.1–2 and 58.6.
56. To avoid a possible misunderstanding, let me add that to say that the inau-
    gural addresses were constructed by the evangelists does not mean that the
    evangelists made them up out of nothing. Jesus really did proclaim the king-
    dom of God, and Jesus did say much of what is included in the Sermon on
    the Mount. But portraying "the kingdom of God is at hand" and the Ser-
    mon on the Mount as the inaugural addresses of Jesus is the product of
    Mark and Matthew. So also here in Luke: historically speaking, Jesus was a
    Spirit-anointed prophet who proclaimed good news to the poor, and so
    forth. But Luke 4.16–30 is a Lucan product.
57. John 2.13–22; Mark 11.1–10, with parallels in Matt 21.1–9 and Luke
    19.28–38.
58. For an accessible and illuminating treatment of John's contrasting symbols, see
    Robert Kysar, *John: The Maverick Gospel*, rev. ed. (Louisville: Westminster/
    Knox, 1993), pp. 58–77. For comments about John's treatment of "the
    Jews," see my section later in this chapter on John 9.
59. John 2.1–11. Immediately preceding it is the preparation for Jesus' public
    activity in the first chapter: the witness of John the Baptizer and Jesus' call
    of his first disciples.
60. John 2.3–4, 6. The "hour" in the phrase "My hour has not yet come" (v. 3)
    refers in John to the hour of Jesus' death.
61. In the Hebrew Bible, see Hos. 2.14–20, Isa. 54.5, Jer. 2.2. See also Song of
    Songs; its erotic love poetry has been understood from ancient times as a
    metaphor for the God-Israel and divine-human relationship.
62. See, for example, Mark 2.19–20, John 3.29, II Cor. 11.2, Eph. 5.21–32.
63. Rev. 19.7–9, 21.2.
64. The story of the wedding at Cana may also have metaphorical associations
    with the wine of the Christian eucharist. Just as later in the gospel Jesus pro-
    vides bread when there is no bread, here he provides wine.
65. Because I am not aware of standard terminology for these two kinds of
    metaphorical meaning, these are my own terms.
66. John Dominic Crossan, *A Long Way from Tipperary* (San Francisco:
    HarperSanFrancisco, 2000), pp. 136, 168. Crossan is thus using the word
    "parable" with a broader (but defensible) meaning than its normal mean-
    ing. Normally in gospel and Jesus scholarship, the word "parable" refers to
    an oral form of speech used by Jesus: a memorable short story that is not
    factually true whose purpose is to invite the hearer into the world of the
    story and then to see something in light of that story. In an important sense,
    parables are "fictions"; they do not report something that happened. But
    they are nonetheless "true" fictions. Crossan's point is that the more spec-
    tacular "miracle stories" might be thought of the same way.
67. From the published description of a lecture he gave on the feeding of the
    multitude at Trinity Cathedral in Portland, Oregon, in September of 2000.
68. Mark 6.45–52, Matt. 14.22–33, John 6.15–21. The synoptics (but not
    John) also have a second "sea" story: the stilling of the storm in Mark
    4.35–41 = Matt. 8.23–27 = Luke 8.22–25. In this story, Jesus is with the
    disciples in the boat, but asleep. When a storm comes up and the boat is in

danger of sinking, they call out to him, "Do you not care if we are perishing?" He then stills the storm.
69. Matt. 14.28–31; the full story in Matthew is found in 14.22–33.
70. Ps. 89.9, 95.5.
71. Job. 38.8, 11.
72. Ps. 107.25–29.
73. John 6.1–14; Mark 6.30–44 = Matt. 14.13–21 = Luke 9.10–17. Mark and Matthew also narrate a second bread miracle, though Luke and John do not: feeding four thousand people in Mark 8.1–10 and Matt. 15.32–39.
74. A denarius was a unit of money (a coin) commonly understood to be a day's wages. Hence the NRSV translates the phrase "six months' wages."
75. Among the few variations: only John mentions that the five loaves and two fish are supplied by a boy. In John, Jesus himself distributes the food; in the synoptics, the disciples do. The striking similarities include the same numbers throughout: five loaves, two fish; five thousand people; two hundred denarii worth of bread; twelve baskets of food left over. Moreover, in both John and the synoptics, this story is followed immediately by the story of Jesus walking on water. These similarities have led some scholars to think that the author of John knew one of the synoptic gospels or, alternatively, that both John and the synoptics knew a common "signs source." It is also possible that a common oral tradition used by both John and Mark may account for the similar details.
76. John 6.22–59.
77. For Crossan's powerful exposition of this point, see *A Long Way from Tipperary*, pp. 167–68. I condense it to its essentials. Jesus tells the disciples, "You give them something to eat." But "they almost jeer at him." They virtually have to be forced "kicking and screaming, as it were," into the process. "It is the duty of the disciples, the Twelve, the Church to make sure that food is distributed fairly and equitably to all. And, the Church is very reluctant to accept that responsibility.... Reluctant then, reluctant now. This [the story of the feeding of the five thousand] is a parable not about charity, but about justice, about the just distribution of the material bases of life, about the sharing of that which is available equitably among all."
78. See chap. 6 above, p. 136.
79. John 6.35, 48, 33.
80. John 6.53, 55.
81. John 6.35. The thirst metaphor is also found in the story of Jesus and the Samaritan woman at the well in John 4.1–42. There Jesus speaks of "living water" (vv. 10–11) in contrast to the water from Jacob's well and says, "Everyone who drinks of this water [from Jacob's well] will be thirsty again, but those who drink of the water that I will give them will never be thirsty" (vv. 13–14).
82. Prov. 9.5. See chap. 7 above, p. 150.
83. John 6.56.
84. John 15.1–12.
85. John 6.49, 32; see also 6.58.

86. John 6.32, 51.
87. See chap. 3 above, p. 45–46.
88. John 9.22, 34–35.
89. John 9.5, 25, 30.
90. John 8.12.
91. Though John's prologue refers explicitly only to "the Word of God" and not to "the Wisdom of God," I use both here because, as many scholars have pointed out, the two phrases are close equivalents in John: what John says about the former is also said about the latter in the Jewish wisdom tradition.
92. John 1.5, 9.
93. Imagery of darkness and light is used in passages such as "The people who walked in darkness have seen a great light; those who lived in a land of deep darkness—on them has light shined" (Isa. 9.2); "Arise, shine for your light has come" (Isa. 60.1); "Your word is a lamp to my feet and a light to my path" (Ps. 119.105). Imagery of blindness and sight is used, for example, in these passages: "The eyes of the blind shall see" (Isa. 29.18); "Then the eyes of the blind shall be opened" (Isa. 35.5); "You that are blind, look up and see" (Isa. 42.18); "Bring forth the people who are blind, yet have eyes" (Isa. 43.8). In all of these cases, blindness and seeing are used metaphorically, not literally.
94. See earlier in this chapter.
95. The "born again" or "born from above" text is the story of Jesus and Nicodemus in John 3.1–10. It is interesting to note that the story begins with Nicodemus coming to Jesus "by night"—that is, he is in the dark.
96. John 17.3.
97. Persuasively argued about thirty years ago by J. Louis Martyn in *History and Theology in the Fourth Gospel* (Nashville: Abingdon, 1968), it is now widely accepted by Johannine scholars.
98. See John 8.31–59, esp. 39–44.
99. John 14.6.
100. "Way" or "path," as noted in the previous chapter, is a central image in the Jewish wisdom tradition. It is also a central image in Mark (as well as the other synoptics), as argued in this chapter: to follow Jesus is to follow him *on his way*.
101. The death of Jesus is anticipated already in John's inaugural scene, the wedding at Cana; "my hour" in v. 4 refers to Jesus' death.
102. John 12.24.

9

Reading Paul Again

As I begin this chapter, I sit at a sidewalk café on a busy street in the city of Thessaloniki in northern Greece.

Around the year 50, Paul wrote a letter to a small community of Christians in this city. Now called I Thessalonians, that letter is the earliest document of what eventually became the New Testament. Nothing remains of the city that Paul knew; the centuries have covered it over. And as I sit here, I wonder again: What was he like?

Next to Jesus, Paul is the most important individual in the birth of what became Christianity. More of the New Testament documents were written by him than by any other person. And, more than anybody else, he was responsible for the spread of the Jesus movement into the Gentile world.

But despite his importance, Paul has a very mixed press today, even among Christians. Some love and admire him, others keep their distance, and still others despise him. Though all Christians have heard of him, many do not know much about him.

I encountered this mixture of attitudes while teaching a seminary course on the New Testament. During the first part of the course on Jesus and the gospels, the students were attentive, engaged and excited. Then we got to Paul, and the mood of the class changed. Whereas everybody had felt positive about Jesus, most were wary of Paul. Though some had a definite (and sometimes favorable) interest, the majority were indifferent or grumpy or even hostile.

A number of factors feed the negativity regarding Paul. Some people (including some historians) see Paul as the perverter of the gospel of Jesus, someone who turned Jesus of Nazareth into a divine being and distorted Jesus' message into a complex and convoluted abstract mythological-theological belief system. In the view of these particular critics, Jesus is good, Paul is bad. Certain other critics see Paul as a puritanical moralist preoccupied with sin and guilt, sacrifice and atonement. Still others are put off particularly by passages about gender and sex. The most negative statement about women in the New Testament is found in a letter attributed to Paul, and other passages commonly attributed to Paul speak about the duty of wives to submit themselves to their husbands.[1] Paul is frequently quoted negatively about homosexuality and even about sexuality in general.[2] Moreover, Paul's letters are often difficult and obscure, opaque rather than luminous.

I grant that Paul is flawed (though no more so than the rest of us) and often difficult to understand. He has often been used in ways that are injurious. Yet I acknowledge that I am an admirer of Paul. My appreciation flows in part out of my Protestant and Lutheran heritage, though I hope that more than my early conditioning is involved. When we separate the genuine letters of Paul from those attributed to him, some of the more disturbing passages disappear. Moreover, when we take seriously Paul's own religious experience, the historical context of his letters, and the central metaphors that shaped his message, we find an apostle whose teaching and passion stand in considerable continuity with Jesus.

Our primary sources for glimpsing Paul are seven of the thirteen letters attributed to him. About these seven there is a strong consensus that he was the author. They are, in approximate chronological order, I Thessalonians, Galatians, I and II Corinthians, Philemon, Philippians, and Romans. Most likely all of these were written in the decade of the 50s. The authorship of another three letters is disputed, though a majority of scholars maintain that they were written not by Paul but in his name after his death: Colossians, Ephesians, and II Thessalonians. Finally, there is a near-consensus that the remaining three are definitely not by Paul. Called the "Pastoral Epistles," they are I and II Timothy and Titus.

The book of Acts serves as a secondary source. More than half of that document is about Paul, though there is a wide range of scholarly opinion about the historical accuracy of its account. Acts reports much that Paul's letters do not, for example. This is not surprising or particularly significant, given the different literary genres. However, when there is overlap between Acts and the letters, Acts is sometimes consistent with the letters and sometimes not, making it difficult to assess the historical accuracy of Acts when there is *no* overlap. Some scholars think that the author of Acts was a companion of Paul and therefore an eyewitness to some of what he reports, whereas other scholars think that the story of Paul in Acts is dominated by literary and not historical concerns. Thus, for Paul's teaching, I will use only his genuine letters, though I will occasionally use Acts for other matters.

On the Damascus Road

The decisive event in Paul's life was his experience of the risen Christ on the road to Damascus. That experience transformed Paul. Before Damascus, he was a zealous persecutor of the Jesus movement; afterward, he became its foremost apostle.

This life-changing experience happened around the year 35, about five years after Jesus' execution. The author of Acts tells the story three times with minor differences of detail—once as part of his narration and twice in speeches attributed to Paul.[3]

According to the first and fullest account in Acts 9, Paul was on his way to Damascus in Syria, authorized by Jewish authorities to seek out followers of Jesus (those who belonged to a fledgling movement called "the Way") and bring them bound to Jerusalem. Then he experienced a brilliant light and heard a voice:

> Now as Paul was approaching Damascus, suddenly a light
> from heaven flashed around him. He fell to the ground and
> heard a voice saying to him, "Saul, Saul, why do you perse-
> cute me?" He asked, "Who are you, Lord?" The reply
> came, "I am Jesus, whom you are persecuting."[4]

Paul had a vision—a vivid subjective sense of momentarily seeing and hearing another reality. The men traveling with Paul did not experience exactly what he did. In Acts 9, we are told that they heard the voice but saw no one; in Acts 22, we are told that they saw the light but heard nothing.[5]

The vision blinded Paul. The voice commanded him to go into Damascus, where he would be told what to do. In that city, Jesus appeared in another vision to a disciple named Ananias, directed him to find Paul, and disclosed to him that Paul had been chosen as an instrument to bring Jesus' name "before Gentiles and kings and the people of Israel."

Ananias did as he was told and found Paul, who had now been blind for three days. Laying his hands on Paul, he said, "The Lord Jesus has sent me so that you may regain your sight and be filled with the Holy Spirit." The result: "Something like scales fell from Paul's eyes, and his sight was restored."[6] Whether Ananias's restoration of sight to Paul is history remembered or metaphorical narrative, its metaphorical meaning is provocatively appropriate: filled with the Spirit, Paul saw anew as the scales fell from his eyes. Then he was baptized, and his life as an apostle of Jesus began.

Paul's experience on the Damascus Road is one of the most famous in religious history. Even in the secular culture, people speak of dramatic, life-changing experiences as "Damascus Road experiences." It included features reported in other visions in the history of religions: a "photism" and an "audition," technical terms for an experience of brilliant light and a voice.

Commonly called Paul's conversion experience, it is and is not, depending upon what we mean by "conversion." In a religious context, the word has three meanings. The first is conversion from being nonreligious to being religious, the second is conversion from one religion to another, and the third is conversion within a religious tradition. Paul's experience is neither of the first two. Clearly, he was deeply religious before Damascus. Moreover, he did not convert from one religion to another. Not only was Christianity not yet seen as a separate religion, but Paul continued to regard himself as a Jew after his conversion and for the rest of his life. But it was a conversion within a tradition: from one way of being Jewish to another way of being Jewish.

In an important sense, his conversion was his "call story" to the rest of his life-work. All three accounts in Acts report Paul's commissioning to his vocation as an apostle to the Gentiles. In his own words from Galatians:

> God, who had set me apart before I was born and called me
> through divine grace, was pleased to reveal God's Son to
> me so that I might proclaim him among the Gentiles.[7]

This dramatic experience changed not only Paul, but eventually the world.

I have begun with the story of Paul on the Damascus Road in part because that experience was the turning point in his life, but also because I am convinced that we best understand Paul when we take his religious experience seriously as our starting point for understanding his message. Moreover, because he also refers to dramatic religious experiences in his own letters, he is one of only two first-century followers of Jesus (and perhaps the only one) from whom we have firsthand reports of such experiences.[8] Unless we ground Paul's theology in his conversion experience, it easily becomes an abstract and unpersuasive intellectual construction.

Before we turn to Paul's message, let us take a closer look at his life. Because of the importance of the Damascus Road experience—its life-changing impact—I will speak of the pre-Damascus Paul and the post-Damascus Paul as we review his life.

The Pre-Damascus Paul: His Life

Paul's life before Damascus equipped him exceptionally well for his vocation as a Jewish apostle to the Gentile world.[9] Born to Jewish parents, he grew up in a Hellenistic city in the Diaspora. Well-educated in both the Jewish tradition and Hellenistic rhetoric, he was fluent in Greek and at least bilingual (and probably more). Urban and cosmopolitan, he was also a Roman citizen by birth, a relatively uncommon status.

Though we do not know when Paul was born, it was probably in the first decade of the first century.[10] He was born and grew up in Tarsus, a city on the south coast of Asia Minor (present-day Turkey). Tarsus, the capital of Cilicia, was located on the major north-south trade route leading from the Middle East to Asia Minor and the Aegean Sea.[11] Paul refers to it as "no mean city," and writers from the time support his judgment. Tarsus flourished in the age of Augustus (emperor of Rome from 31 BCE to 14 CE) and was well known as a center of Hellenistic culture. One ancient author referred to its reputation for philosophy and learning, claiming that it surpassed both Athens and Alexandria, though another criticized its frivolous and luxury-loving atmosphere.[12]

Paul received his early education in Tarsus, and he seems to have been well taught. As his letters written many decades later attest, he was brilliant. According to a well-known twentieth-century scholar:

> The intellectual range of his gospel . . . soared to incomparable heights, today still unconquered. Small wonder that many readers are left gasping at his letters, loaded to the line with a

heavy cargo of thought; and that not a few who yield themselves to his gospel are left feeling like a traveler overcome by vertigo in an Alpine region surrounded by steep cloud-covered peaks, who often does not know how to follow on and how he is going to last the journey.[13]

A scholar of ancient Greek refers to his "writing as a classic of Hellenism."[14] Though both are referring to the post-Damascus Paul, the pre-Damascus Paul must also have been intellectually gifted. Conversion changes the way one *sees*, but it does not make one brighter.

According to Acts, as a young man Paul went to Jerusalem to study and spent a significant amount of time there. Acts reports that he studied under the famous Jewish teacher Gamaliel, that he was present at the martyrdom of Stephen before his Damascus experience, and that he had a sister living in Jerusalem. But Paul's letters say nothing about any of this, so some uncertainty must remain.[15]

But his letters do make it clear that he was thoroughly educated in the Jewish tradition. He quotes and alludes to the Hebrew Bible (in Greek translation) over and over again, and his use of that text indicates that he was familiar with Jewish methods of interpretation. He was also passionately committed to Judaism. In his own words:

> You have heard no doubt of my earlier life. . . . I was violently
> persecuting the church of God and was trying to destroy it.
> I advanced in Judaism beyond many among my people of
> the same age, for I was far more zealous for the traditions of
> my ancestors.[16]

In another passage about his life before Damascus, he describes himself with obvious pride as "circumcised on the eighth day, a member of the people of Israel, of the tribe of Benjamin, a Hebrew born of Hebrews." He then refers to himself as a Pharisee: "as to the law a Pharisee." The Pharisees were a Jewish sectarian movement committed to an intensified form of Torah observance, especially the extension of priestly standards of purity to everyday life. We do not know when Paul became a Pharisee, but if he did spend time in Jerusalem, it probably happened there. The fact that he chose Pharisaism points to the earnestness of his religious quest and the depth of his conviction. After once again mentioning the zeal with which he persecuted the church, he concludes the passage with the words, "as to righteousness under the law, blameless."[17] Though Paul's claim to be "blameless" under the law sounds strange to many Protestant Christians, there is no reason to doubt it, just as there is no reason to think that Paul found his pre-Damascus life as a Pharisee either oppressive or unsatisfying.

At some time in his life, Paul learned a trade. He became a tentmaker, which involved making tents and awnings out of leather and cloth. The trade gave him great mobility, requiring only a few lightweight tools (a knife, an awl, and curved needles) that could be carried anywhere. He was thus able to support himself everywhere, as he did in his life as a missionary.

The Post-Damascus Paul: His Life

Now we turn to Paul's life and activity as a follower of Jesus and apostle to the Gentiles.

A Jewish Christ-Mystic

A mystic is a particular type of religious personality. Mystics do not simply *believe* in God; they *know* God. The defining core of mysticism is thus experiential: mystics have direct, vivid, and typically frequent experiences of the sacred. Sometimes the sacred is experienced in another level of reality beyond the visible world; other times it is experienced as a luminous reality shining through the visible world. Mysticism intrinsically involves a nonordinary state of consciousness—nonordinary in the sense that such experience is radically different from ordinary everyday consciousness. Mystical consciousness is *ecstatic* in the root sense of the word: in Greek, *ek* means "out of" and *stasis* means "state of being." To be ecstatic in this sense does not mean to be thrilled or happy or jubilant (as in the term's common usage today), but to be out of one's ordinary state of being. Thus, to use an approximate synonym, a mystic is a religious ecstatic.

Paul was clearly a mystic—a Jewish mystic. His experience on the Damascus Road (as well as subsequent experiences) put him in this category. Mystical experience in the Jewish tradition is ancient, going back well beyond the first century. Reflected in several books in the Hebrew Bible, it continued into the post-biblical period and has endured through the centuries ever since. But in the history of Jewish mysticism, Paul occupies a special place: he is the first Jewish mystic from whom we have a first-hand account, and the only one prior to about 1000 CE.[18]

We do not know how frequently Paul had such experiences. The Damascus Road experience was certainly one. Another one is reported in Second Corinthians. Defending his credentials as an apostle, he says, "I will go on to visions and revelations of the Lord," and then uses third-person language to refer to himself:

> I know a person in Christ who fourteen years ago was caught
> up to the third heaven—whether in the body or out of the
> body I do not know, God knows. And I know that such a
> person—whether in the body or out of the body I do not
> know; God knows—was caught up into Paradise and heard
> things that are not to be told, that no mortal is permitted to
> repeat.[19]

It is a classic description of a particular kind of mystical experience: a journey into another level of reality ("the third heaven") named as Paradise (the place of God's presence), a sense of being out of one's body, and an inability (or prohibition?) to disclose what was experienced there.[20]

Does this passage suggest that Paul had many such experiences? As he introduces it, he uses the plural *visions* and *revelations* and concludes by using the plural again as he refers to "the exceptional character of the *revelations.*" [21] Perhaps not much weight should be given to this, but the language suggests that the experience was one of several.

Strikingly, Paul regarded his mystical experience of Jesus as a resurrection experience—an appearance of the risen Christ similar to those experienced by the original followers of Jesus. In I Corinthians 15, in the earliest passage in the New Testament referring to those to whom the risen Christ appeared, Paul includes himself. Similarity is also suggested by the use of the same verb throughout:

> Jesus *appeared* to Cephas [Peter], then to the twelve. Then he
> *appeared* to more than five hundred brothers and sisters at
> one time, most of whom are still alive, though some have
> died. Then he *appeared* to James, then to all the apostles.
> Last of all, as to one untimely born, he *appeared* also
> to me.[22]

When and how did the risen Christ first appear to Paul? The answer, of course, is in his mystical vision on the Damascus Road.

In addition to these reports of mystical experience, there are passages in Paul that reflect the consciousness of a mystic. In Galatians, he uses classical mystical language that points to a mystical identity—the death of an old self and the birth of a new self spoken of as Christ living in him: "I have been crucified with Christ; it is no longer I who live, but Christ who lives in me."[23] Of the many passages in Paul whose language makes best sense within a mystical framework, I cite one more. In a dense but luminous passage, Paul uses phrases characteristic of one who has had mystical experiences: "unveiled faces" and "beholding the glory of the Lord" ("glory" means "radiant presence"). He also speaks of the transforming effect of such experience:

> And we all, with unveiled faces, beholding the glory of the
> Lord, are being changed into his likeness from one degree

of glory to another; for this comes from the Lord who is
the Spirit.[24]

Thus Paul was not just a Jewish mystic, but a Jewish *Christ*-
mystic. In my judgment, his mystical experience was the source
of everything he became as a follower of Jesus. It was the ground
of his conviction that Jesus was not a dangerously misleading
and cursed figure of the past but a living reality of the present
who had been raised by God; it was the basis of his identity and
of his call to be an apostle; and, as we will see, it was the foundation of his message.

An Apostle and Missionary of Jesus

Paul's life as a missionary of Jesus lasted about twenty-five years.
Most of it was spent in Asia Minor and Greece. On the road
much of the time, he established Christ communities in urban
areas and then stayed in touch with them by writing letters.

Paul's Travels   Paul's travels as an apostle may have totaled
about ten thousand miles—miles that he covered mostly by foot
and occasionally by boat.[25] As an itinerant, he supported himself
as a tentmaker, though he occasionally received some additional
support from the communities he founded.

After his experience on the Damascus Road, he spent three
years in "Arabia," which in those days meant Nabatea (in present-
day Jordan; its ancient capital was Petra). He spent the 40s of the
first century as a missionary in Asia Minor, including the area of
Galatia. Around the year 50, he left Asia Minor for Europe. In
Greece, beginning in the north, he established Christ communities in Philippi, Thessaloniki, and Beroea. In the south, he apparently had no success in Athens, though he did in the cosmopolitan
city of Corinth, where he spent a couple of years and to whose
Christians much of his correspondence was directed.[26] During the
50s, he crossed back and forth between Greece and Asia Minor,
where he spent considerable time in the important city of Ephesus. During this decade, he wrote most or all of his letters.

Paul's life as an apostle was often arduous, filled with controversy, and marked by suffering. He describes it in a well-known
passage in which he defends himself against Christian opponents:

> Are they ministers of Christ? I am talking like a madman—I
> am a better one: with far greater labors, far more imprison-
> ments, with countless floggings, and often near death. Five
> times I have received the forty lashes minus one. Three
> times I was beaten with rods. Once I received a stoning.
> Three times I was shipwrecked; for a night and day I was
> adrift at sea; on frequent journeys, in danger from rivers,
> danger from bandits, danger from my own people, danger
> from Gentiles, danger in the city, danger in the wilderness,
> danger at sea, danger from false brothers and sisters; in toil
> and hardship, through many a sleepless night, hungry and
> thirsty, often without food, cold, and naked. And besides
> other things, I am under daily pressure because of my anxi-
> ety for all the churches.[27]

Paul wrote the above before his final imprisonment, which was
to last at least four years. Near the end of the 50s, he returned to
Jerusalem with a collection of money for "the poor," gathered
from his largely Gentile communities. There, according to Acts,
he was arrested on the charge of bringing a Gentile into the part
of the temple forbidden to Gentiles. Imprisoned in Caesarea on
the coast for about two years, he was then transported as a pris-
oner to Rome around the year 60 (and shipwrecked again). In
Rome he was under house arrest for another two years, though
people were able to come to him to hear the gospel. There the
book of Acts ends, and we learn nothing more about what happened to Paul next.[28]

The Christ Communities of Paul The common image of Paul as
a street-corner preacher proclaiming the gospel to all and sundry
is probably not an accurate reflection of the way he did things.
According to Acts, Paul followed a consistent missionary strat-

egy. When he arrived in a new city, he began by going to the Jewish synagogue. There he would address Jews, of course, but also Gentiles who were loosely associated with the synagogue. Commonly called "God-fearers," these were Gentiles who were attracted to Judaism and worshiped in the synagogue but did not fully convert to Judaism.[29] (We might call them "seekers.") Paul sought them out, most likely engaging them in one-on-one or small-group conversation. Most of Paul's Gentile converts seem to have come from this category.

Paul's converts would begin a community life of their own, gathering regularly for worship and instruction and life together. Later in this chapter I will say more about the life of these communities. For now, I note that they were small, for two reasons. The first was the relatively small number of Christians. According to a recent estimate of early Christian growth, there were only about two thousand Christians in the whole of the Roman Empire by the year 60, by which time Paul's missionary activity was basically over.[30] Assuming that half of these were in the Jewish homeland, about a thousand were spread out over the rest of the empire. Thus in any given locality, with perhaps an exception or two, the number of Christians would have been well under a hundred (and perhaps more like ten to thirty).

The second reason for the small size of Paul's communities was space limitation. These communities were "house churches" whose members met in private dwellings of two kinds: tenements (often with shops on the ground floor) or villas. A tenement or shop house church might meet in a space as small as ten-by-ten feet or as large as ten-by-twenty feet and thus could accommodate only a small group of people. A villa house church (possible only if one of the converts was wealthy enough to own a villa) would meet in the courtyard of a villa, which might accommodate as many as a hundred people.[31]

Paul's strategy also included moving on. Though he remained in Corinth and Ephesus for a couple years each, he generally moved on to a new city soon after a local community had been established. He also used a teamwork approach, not only traveling with other missionaries but also incorporating any Christians who already lived in a city into his efforts.

Paul's Letters Paul's letters were an integral part of his life as an apostle and community-founder. Through them he kept in touch with his communities after he had moved on.[32] They represented him in his absence, and they were read aloud in the gathering of the community. They were not intended for the silent reading of individuals but were addressed to the community, which heard them together.

Paul's letters are "conversations in context"—conversations with communities he founded in the context of his life as an apostle of Jesus.[33] Indeed, they are only one-half of a conversation, for in them Paul is most often responding to a letter he has received from a community or to news of that community he has heard by other means.

This recognition is essential to reading the letters, and it has more than one implication. It means that we should not see Paul's letters as a summary of his message. With one exception (Romans), Paul does not use his letters for that purpose, since he is writing to people who have already heard his message in person. Thus the content of his letters has little to do with what he thinks most important and more to do with specific issues arising within his communities. The agenda for Paul's letters is set not by him but by them. This helps us to understand why his letters often treat issues that seem obscure or relatively unimportant to us—why, for example, he spends more time writing about whether women should be veiled in Christian gatherings, or whether one may eat food that has been sacrificed to idols, than he does writing about the teaching of Jesus.[34]

Moreover, as Paul responds to a letter he has received, he sometimes quotes or echoes words from it. When we do not realize this, serious misunderstanding can result. A classic example occurs in I Corinthians:

> Now concerning the matters about which you wrote. It is
>   well for a man not to touch a woman. But because of

temptation to immorality, each man should have his own
wife and each woman her own husband. The husband
should give to his wife her conjugal rights, and likewise the
wife to her husband.[35]

How much of this is Paul's point of view? In particular, does
the second sentence—"It is well for a man not to touch a
woman"—express Paul's position, or is it a point of view expressed in the letter to which he is responding? Ancient Greek
does not use quotation marks, so the text does not tell us.

If we see it as Paul's point of view, then it follows that Paul
sees sexuality as less desirable than abstinence and his acceptance
of sexual behavior as a concession to human weakness. Through
most of the Christian centuries, the passage has been read this
way (no wonder, then, that Paul has been thought of as anti-sex
and that Christians have often struggled with sexuality). But if
Paul is quoting from a letter sent to him, then he is countering
the statement rather than affirming it. (Try it; note the difference it makes to put quotation marks around the second sen
tence.) Modern scholars are virtually unanimous that this is the
correct way to read it.[36]

The Post-Damascus Paul: His Message

Now I am sitting beside a small stream just outside the city wall
of ancient Philippi in northern Greece. It is very quiet here.
Though Philippi was an important city in antiquity, it is now a
magnificent ruin, and few people are here on this day in May.
The meadows around the ruins are full of red-orange poppies.
According to the book of Acts, it was next to this stream that
Paul made his first convert in Europe. Her name was Lydia, and
she was a businesswoman and a dealer in purple cloth, much
prized in the ancient world. She was, Acts tells us, a "worshiper
of God," a God-fearer, one of those Gentiles attracted to Judaism and the God of Israel.

And as I sit here, I wonder, What did Paul say to Lydia? Acts
does not tell us. It compresses the story into a few verses:

> On the sabbath day we [referring to Paul and his missionary
> companions Silas and Timothy, and possibly the narrator as a
> fourth] went outside the gate [of Philippi] by the river, where
> we supposed there was a place of prayer; and we sat down and
> spoke to the women who had gathered there. A certain
> woman named Lydia, a worshiper of God, was listening to us;
> she was from the city of Thyatira and a dealer in purple cloth.
> The Lord opened her heart to listen eagerly to what was said
> by Paul. Then she and her household were baptized.[37]

So what *did* Paul say to her? My question may seem fruitless to
some, because we do not know the answer and have no way of
learning it. But to me the question seems useful, for it raises the
more general question of what Paul's message was. What was it
that appealed to a Gentile God-fearer like Lydia to such an extent that she became part of a new form of Judaism?

I assume that Paul talked to her more than once. It is hard to
believe that Lydia made such a momentous decision after one
conversation. As a God-fearer, Lydia would have known something about the practices, beliefs, and hopes of Judaism, including the notion of a messiah. Her familiarity with Judaism would
have been the framework for their conversations.

As I try to imagine what Paul most likely said, three things
occur to me. First, Paul would have told her that Jesus was the
messiah. But for this to mean anything to her, he would also
have had to tell her about the kind of person Jesus was. Otherwise, the claim that Jesus was the messiah would have been a ci-
pher, a claim without content. Thus I assume that what Jesus
was like—his subversive wisdom, his healings, his passion for social justice for the poor and marginalized, his indictment of the
domination system, his goodness—mattered to Paul and would
have been central to his message.[38]

Second, after telling her about Jesus, Paul would have said,
"And then the rulers crucified him." As Paul emphasized in his
writings, and I will emphasize later, "Christ crucified" was utterly central to Paul. And third, I imagine Paul would have told

her his own conversion story: that he had been hostile to Jesus and the Jesus movement; that Jesus had then appeared to him in a vision, just as he had appeared to others; and that this meant that God had vindicated Jesus as messiah and Lord.

There would be more, of course, especially that the community of Jesus was open to both Jew and Gentile: that one could become part of this Jewish community without observing the sharp boundaries that separated Jews from Gentiles. This was certainly part of the appeal of Paul's message.

Paul may also have told her that the end of the age was at hand. He believed that Jesus would return soon, though the heart of his message does not seem to have been, "Repent, for the last judgment is coming soon."[39] He does not sound like an "end of the world" evangelist as we think of such people today. His emphasis seems to have been that God through Jesus had inaugurated a new age and that the rule of "the powers" (including the reign of the Roman empire) would soon be over.

I have begun by trying to imagine Paul's conversation with Lydia because, as already mentioned, I do not think that Paul's letters contain the whole of his message. Nor do I think that he replaced the message of Jesus with his own. Rather, I think that he added to the message of Jesus his own post-Easter and post-Damascus convictions and conclusions. Like other major figures in the biblical tradition, he conveys a message that has both religious and political meanings, both spiritual and social dimensions. To some of the central themes of Paul's post-Easter understanding and message I now turn.

"Jesus is Lord"

For Paul, the central meaning of his experience of the risen Christ was "Jesus is Lord." Both affirmations—Jesus lives, and Jesus is Lord—were immediate inferences from his Damascus Road experience; indeed, perhaps one should say that they were *given* with the experience. Thus for Paul the resurrection of Jesus was not primarily about an afterlife through the defeat of death. Nor was its central meaning that we also will be raised someday; as a Pharisee, the *pre*-Damascus Paul had already believed that. Rather, Easter meant, in an affirmation that Paul shared with the Jesus movement as a whole, "Jesus is Lord."

Paul refers to Jesus as "Lord" (Greek: *kyrios,* pronounced "kurios") with great frequency. He uses that designation more often than "Son" or "Son of God," for example; indeed, he uses it more often than any other affirmation about Jesus other than "Christ" (meaning "messiah"), which for Paul is virtually Jesus' second name. For Paul, "Jesus is Lord" is the primary confession of Jesus' significance and status.[40]

The connection between Jesus' resurrection, his status as Lord, and the cosmic extent of his lordship is magnificently made in a passage from Paul's letter to the Philippians that is probably based on a pre-Pauline hymn of praise. Immediately after it speaks of the death of Jesus, it affirms that God "exalted" Jesus, which means "raised up"; and it then speaks of Jesus' dominion as Lord as extending through all three levels of the three-story universe of the ancient worldview:

> Therefore God also highly exalted him
> > and gave him the name that is above every name,
> so that at the name of Jesus every knee should bend,
> > in heaven and on earth and under the earth,
> and every tongue should confess
> > that Jesus Christ is Lord,
> > to the glory of God the Father.[41]

In the first century, "Lord"/*kyrios* had a range of meanings along a "spectrum of dignity."[42] Four of these meanings are the most relevant:

- It was a term of respect—one that could, for example, be used to address a teacher. This use is reflected in the synoptic gospels when Jesus is occasionally addressed as Lord.
- It was a term used by slaves to address their master.
- It was used as a term for gods, including the God of Israel.

In particular, in the Greek translation of the Hebrew Bible, *kyrios* was used as the name of God.

• It was also one of the titles of the Roman emperor: Caesar is Lord.

Thus, in Paul's world, calling Jesus "Lord" had both religious and sociopolitical meanings (and the two were connected in ways that we often separate in the modern world).

Though I think Paul would agree that Jesus as teacher may properly be addressed as "Lord," as the first meaning suggests, this use does not play much (if any) role in Paul's message. But the rest of the meanings are present.

If Jesus is Lord, masters of slaves are not. In a passage to which I will return, Paul affirmed the second meaning of "Lord"/*kyrios*, saying that in Christ Jesus "there is no longer Jew or Gentile, there is no longer *slave or free*, there is no longer male and female."[43] In calling Jesus "Lord," Paul also affirmed that the risen Christ participated in the power and authority of God and that the other gods were not lords—the third meaning of "Lord"/*kyrios*.[44]

This affirmation and negation also countered the imperial ideology in which "Lord"/*kyrios* (in its fourth meaning) referred to the Roman emperor. When applied to the emperor, the term not only highlighted his political role but also suggested divine status. Thus to say "Jesus is Lord" meant "Caesar is *not* Lord"; the statement affirmed the status of Jesus even as it challenged the imperial domination system. There is, as recent scholarship shows, an anti-imperial theology at the center of Paul's understanding of the lordship of Christ.[45] Religion and politics are combined for Paul, as for Moses, the prophets, and Jesus: the domination system is not lord. Rather, Jesus, whom God has vindicated and exalted as the disclosure of God, is Lord. Thus the affirmation claims both our religious and our political loyalties.

"In Christ"

The short phrase "in Christ" is one of the two most important metaphors Paul uses for his vision of the Christian life. (The other is "justification by grace," which we will consider next.) In his letters, Paul uses "in Christ" (including the phrase "in the Lord") 165 times and the roughly synonymous phrase "in the Spirit" about twenty times. As a metaphor for the Christian life, "in Christ" has several dimensions of meaning. I begin with its opposite.

Life "in Adam" Paul is a dialectical thinker; he often thinks in contrasts or oppositions. The opposite of life "in Christ" is life "in Adam." The two metaphors refer to different and sharply contrasting ways of life: humanity "in Adam" is nothing like humanity "in Christ."

Life "in Adam" is one of Paul's primary metaphors for the human condition. Within the sacred imagination of the Hebrew Bible, Adam is the first human, the being whose primal act in the Garden of Eden began the human story of grasping, exile, sin, and death. Adam sought to seize or grasp equality with God.[46] The result was exile from paradise and lost intimacy with God. Life "in Adam" is thus the life of separation or estrangement from God.

It is also the life of sin and death, which Paul says came into the world through Adam. What does he mean by this? Does he mean simply that, beginning with Adam, people started sinning and dying, and they have been sinning and dying ever since? No, his language is too strong for that: he calls sin and death "powers" that have "dominion" over us. What does he have in mind? Is sin a "power"? Do we experience it as a "power"?

I do not know if everybody does, but I strongly suspect that Paul did—and that's why he uses this language.[47] To explain by contrast, there is a "free will" understanding of sin: we are free in each situation to choose right or wrong. When we choose the wrong, we have sinned. But this is not how Paul understood matters. Rather, life "in Adam" is life under the *dominion* of sin. Sin controls us; we are not free.

Paul describes the lordship of sin over life "in Adam" in an extended and powerful passage. Though sometimes interpreted autobiographically, the "I" of the passage is best understood as referring to what life "in Adam" is like for anybody. It is a life of bondage and internal conflict.[48]

> I do not understand my own actions. For I do not do what I
> want, but I do the very thing I hate. . . . I can will what is
> right, but I cannot do it. The good that I would do, I do
> not do; but the evil that I would not do, that I do. Now if I
> do what I do not want, it is no longer I that do it, but sin
> that dwells within me.

Life "in Adam" is "captive to the law of sin"; it is not free. For Paul, we are not sinners because we do wrong things; rather, we do wrong things because sin rules over life "in Adam."[49] Paul concludes this impassioned passage with the words, "Wretched man that I am! Who will rescue me from this body of death?"[50] Paul's metaphor of life "in Adam" thus combines central images for the human condition in the Hebrew Bible: sin, death, exile, and bondage.

Life "in Christ"   Life "in Christ" is the opposite of the above. It is the new way of being that Paul knew in his own experience and that he sought to incarnate in the life of his communities. To be "in Christ" is to be free, no longer enslaved to the dominion of sin and death.[51] Strikingly, "freedom" is for Paul one of the most central characteristics of the Christian life. It means being reconciled with God and thus brings the end of exile.[52] To be "in Christ" is to live in the presence of God as Christ lives in the presence of God. In language that continues to echo the theme of creation and Adam, to be "in Christ" is to be a new creation:

> Whoever is in Christ is a new creation. Everything old has
> passed away; see, everything has become new! All this is
> from God, who reconciled us to God through Christ.[53]

The contrast between life "in Adam" and life "in Christ" is the same as Paul's contrast between "life according to the flesh" and "life according to the Spirit."⁵⁴ The contrast is not between physical life and spiritual life, as if the former were bad and the latter good. "Flesh" here does not mean our physical bodies, as if there were something wrong with physical existence or enjoying our bodies. Rather, "life according to the flesh" and "life according to the Spirit" refer to "life in Adam" and "life in Christ" as two ways of living our embodied existence. Paul's list describing the former does include what are often thought of as bodily sins: "fornication, impurity, licentiousness, drunkenness, and carousing." But it also includes traits that cannot be reduced to indulging our bodies: "idolatry, sorcery, enmities, strife, jealousy, anger, quarrels, dissensions, factions, and envy."⁵⁵

On the other hand, the characteristics of life according to the Spirit—life "in Christ"—are "freedom" and "love, joy, peace, patience, kindness, generosity, faithfulness, gentleness and self-control." They are not achievements of the will but "the fruit of the Spirit."⁵⁶ Even more compactly, in the familiar language of Paul's great love poem in I Corinthians 13 set in the context of spiritual gifts, life in the Spirit is marked by "faith, hope and love, and the greatest of these is love."⁵⁷

The Way from Life "in Adam" to Life "in Christ" Paul's description of life "in Adam" strikes me as disturbingly (but accurately) dark, while his description of life "in Christ" is enormously attractive. Who would not want a life marked by freedom, love, joy, and peace? And thus the question becomes imperative: How does one move from life "in Adam" to life "in Christ"? For Paul, the new way of life is created by God through Christ. And the way one participates in that new way of life is by dying with Christ and being raised with Christ.

In Galatians, Paul writes about his own internal death and the birth of a new self within him: "I died to the law, so that I might live to God." He then makes the connection to the language of crucifixion: "I have been crucified with Christ." Thus the old Paul has died, and a new reality lives within Paul: "It is no longer I who live, but Christ who lives in me."⁵⁸

In Romans, Paul develops Jesus' death and resurrection as a metaphor for the way of transition from Adamic existence to life in Christ at greater length and connects death and resurrection to the ritual of baptism. To be baptized symbolizes and ritually embodies dying to an old way of life and being resurrected into a new way of life:

> Do you not know that all of us who have been baptized into Christ Jesus were baptized into his death? Therefore, we have been buried with him by baptism into death, so that, just as Christ was raised from the dead by the glory of the Father, so we too might walk in newness of life.[59]

The metaphor of dying to an old way of being is also central to Paul's ethic of transformation. We are to become "sacrifices," an obvious image for death. The result is to be no longer conformed to this age, but to be transformed:

> I appeal to you, therefore, brothers and sisters, by the mercies of God, to present your selves as a living sacrifice, holy and acceptable to God, which is your spiritual worship. Do not be conformed to this age, but be transformed by the renewing of your minds, so that you may discern what is the will of God—what is good and acceptable and perfect.[60]

In Philippians, Paul writes, "Let the same mind be in you that was in Christ Jesus." He then speaks of Jesus' death on the cross as involving self-emptying, humbling (roughly synonymous with self-emptying), and obedience unto death, followed by Jesus' exaltation. This is the pattern Paul commends to his community *for their own lives*.[61] This kind of self-emptying and humbling should not be confused with the kind that goes with an Adamic way of being, where it can mean simply giving in to the will of others. Paul is advocating neither autonomy (centering in one's self) nor heteronomy (centering in others), but theonomy (centering in God as known in Christ)

In short, the way we become "in Christ" is by dying and rising with Christ, by participating in the path of death and resurrection—the same path that we saw in the synoptic gospels and John, and in the Hebrew Bible (with different metaphors), especially in the subversive wisdom of Ecclesiastes and Job. Becoming "in Christ" involves a new identity, a new way of seeing, and a new way of living.

How did this transformation happen in practice in Paul's communities? A variety of instrumental means were involved, including Paul's teaching and the radical perceptual shift it sought to bring about. The transformation was also embodied and enacted in baptism. Finally, it was mediated through life together in community: not only were the communities of Paul Spirit-filled, but they also functioned as communities of resocialization in which the new identity and way of seeing and living were internalized.

The Social Vision of Life "in Christ" Life "in Christ" also has concrete social implications. The new humanity in Christ subverts and negates the social boundaries that mark conventional human existence. Those who are "in Christ" are all "one body."[62] The solidarity in Christ overcomes the primary divisions that Paul knew in his world, including especially (but not only) the sharp social boundary between Jew and Gentile:

> In Christ Jesus you are all children of God through faith. As many of you as were baptized into Christ have clothed yourselves with Christ. There is no longer Jew or Gentile, there is no longer slave or free, there is no longer male and female; for all of you are one in Christ Jesus.[63]

Of course, people continued to be Jew or Gentile by birth, and slave or free, and male or female, but within the community these distinctions were not to matter.[64] Life "in Christ" involved an egalitarian social vision. In the context of Paul's world, it was a new social reality.

In I Corinthians, the challenge to social distinctions extended to rich and poor. The context is the celebration of "the Lord's supper," which involved a real meal within which the ritual remembrance of the final meal of Jesus occurred. The Christ community in Corinth, which included some wealthy people, was a villa house church that met in the home of a wealthy patron. Paul learned that the rich had been eating their own meal separate from the poor (or before the poor could arrive from work). His indictment in I Corinthians is harsh:

> When you come together it is not for the better but for the
> worse. . . . When you come together, it is not really to eat
> the Lord's supper. For when the time comes to eat, each of
> you goes ahead with your own supper, and one goes hungry
> and another becomes drunk. What! Do you not have homes
> to eat and drink in? Or do you show contempt for the
> church of God and humiliate those who have nothing?

Then he warns them of eating the Lord's supper in an unworthy manner—that is, "without discerning the body" (meaning the community).[65] The issue is not the centuries' later Christian concern with discerning the "real presence" of Jesus in the elements of the eucharist, but the betrayal of "the body"—namely, the egalitarian social reality of life "in Christ."

Thus life "in Christ" is a remarkably comprehensive metaphor in Paul. It speaks of the new way of life in both its personal and social dimensions, as well as the path to the new life. It is also the subject of one of Paul's most eloquently lyrical passages. In Christ, we are indissolubly united with the love of God:

> Who will separate us from the love of Christ? Will hardship, or
> distress, or persecution, or famine, or nakedness, or peril or
> sword?
> . . . I am convinced that neither death, nor life, nor angels, nor
> things present, nor things to come, nor powers, nor height,
> nor depth, nor anything else in all creation, will be able to
> separate us from the love of God in Christ Jesus our Lord.[66]

"Justification by Grace"

Paul's other central metaphor for speaking of the Christian life is drawn from the legal world. The literal meaning of "justification" is found in a court of law: to be "justified" is a legal verdict that means "to be found in the right" or "to be acquitted." It is the verdict one would want to hear if one were on trial.

Paul uses justification as a metaphor to speak about the divine-human relationship. His most important expositions of it are in Galatians and Romans (especially the first four chapters). The dialectical character of his thought is again apparent. Just as life "in Adam" and life "in Christ" and life according to the flesh and life according to the Spirit are sharply contrasted, here "justification by works of the law" and "justification by grace through faith" are placed in sharp opposition to each other. What is the basis for being found in the right by God? Paul's answer: grace, not law; faith, not works. Justification is a free gift, not a reward for achievement.

In Galatians, the issue is particular. Paul had founded a Christ community in Galatia. After his departure, Christian Jewish opponents of Paul insisted that Gentiles who wished to be part of the Christ community had to be circumcised. The issue was therefore this: On what basis could Gentiles become part of this new Jewish movement? Paul's opponents had a reasonable case. After all, this was a Jewish movement, and God's law as disclosed in the Torah clearly required circumcision.

Paul stridently opposed his Christian Jewish opponents. Insisting that Gentiles were justified by their faith in Christ, he saw the issue as one of grace versus law, faith versus works:

> A person is justified not by the works of the law but through faith in Christ Jesus. . . . No one will be justified by the works of the law. . . . All who rely on the works of the law are under a curse. . . . Now it is evident that no one is justified before God by the law; for "The one who is righteous will live by faith." . . . I do not nullify the grace of God; for if justification comes through the law, then Christ died for nothing.[67]

As his letter nears its close, Paul cuttingly contrasts the demand for circumcision with grace: "You who want to be justified by the law have cut yourselves off from Christ; you have fallen away from grace." A few verses later, he goes further: "I wish those who unsettle you [by demanding circumcision] would castrate themselves."[68] In Galatians, justification by grace through faith is the basis for Gentiles becoming part of the community without becoming Jewish through circumcision.

In Romans, the issue is more general. Much of the first three chapters is an indictment of all humanity—Jews and Gentiles alike—as sinners:

> All, both Jews and Gentiles, are under the power of sin. . . .
> So that every mouth may be silenced and the whole world
>   may be held accountable to God. For "no human being will
>   be justified in God's sight" by works of the law . . . since all
>   have sinned and fall short of the glory of God.[69]

Instead, all "are now justified by God's grace as a gift through the redemption that is in Christ Jesus," made "effective through faith."[70]

Then Paul invokes Abraham, the father of the Jewish people, as a paradigm of faith, not works: "Abraham believed God, and it was reckoned to him as righteousness." And, Paul emphasizes, "Faith was reckoned to Abraham as righteousness" before he was circumcised and apart from works of the law.[71]

Justification by grace is radical. Though the language has been domesticated by familiarity, it is extraordinary: "God justifies the ungodly," Paul says. A few verses later: "Christ died for the ungodly." Then: "While we were yet sinners" and "enemies" of God, "Christ died for us."[72] God's love for us is prior to our worthiness. It need not be earned—indeed, cannot be earned.

Justification by grace has been more important in some periods of Christian history (and among some Christian groups) than others. It became particularly important in the Protestant Reformation. Though the understanding of it by Luther and Calvin has been criticized by many modern scholars as a misunderstanding of Paul and a projection upon Paul of the introspective conscience of early modern Western culture, it seems to me that there is insight in the radical Protestant understanding of grace.

Though I am not at all sure that I have understood Paul's message of justification adequately, and am quite sure that there is *more* to understand, I want to clarify it here by identifying some important misunderstandings.

First, justification by grace in opposition to justification by works of the law is not about the inadequacy of the Jewish law or Judaism. When Paul indicts life under the law, he is not attacking the Torah in particular. On the contrary, he saw the Torah as "holy, just and good."[73] The failure to recognize this has erroneously led Christians to think of Judaism as a religion of law, works, and judgment and Christianity as a religion of grace, faith, and love. But the way of being that Paul indicts—life under the law—is as present in Christianity as it is in Judaism. So also, grace is as present within the Jewish tradition as it is within the Christian tradition.

Rather, Paul's attack on "the law" subverts a more universal way of being, found not only within Christianity and Judaism but also within secular culture. Life under the law is the life of "measuring up" in which our well-being depends upon how well we do. If we are religious, we see our standing before God as dependent upon the earnestness of our religious life. Do we have enough faith? Are we good enough? If we are not religious, life under the law means seeing our identity and self-esteem (whether in positive or negative terms) as dependent upon our measuring up to cultural standards of achievement or appearance or worth. Life under the law is, as one contemporary scholar puts it, living according to the "performance principle."[74]

Second, justification by grace is not about forgiveness; it is not simply an affirmation that God will forgive those who repent. Forgiveness was a given for Paul even *before* his Damascus Road experience. The Judaism he knew did not teach that one had to observe the law perfectly; rather, it taught that God forgives repentant sinners, and it provided means for mediating forgiveness.

Third, justification by grace is not about who goes to heaven, or how. The notion that it *is* flows out of conventional Christianity's preoccupation with the afterlife throughout the centuries, as if that were most central to the message of Jesus and Paul and the New Testament. When justification by grace is thought about in this context, it leads to questions such as: Does this mean that everybody goes to heaven, regardless of what they believe or how they have lived (which strikes most people as unfair)? And if it *doesn't* mean that, what distinguishes those who do go to heaven from those who don't? If it's something we do, then we are back to works. But if going to heaven *doesn't* depend on something we do, then God must *arbitrarily* decide who goes to heaven—and then notions of predestination emerge. Here, as in much else, preoccupation with the afterlife has profoundly distorted Christianity.

Fourth, Paul's understanding of justification is not about the replacement of one requirement with another. This frequently happens in Christianity when "faith" replaces "good works" as what God requires of us. The system of requirements remains; only the content has changed. Of course, faith in God and Jesus was central for Paul. But it was not a new requirement; rather, faith in God's grace—in the God who justifies the ungodly—is the abolition of the whole system of requirements. It is thus a radically new way of seeing.

So what, then, is justification by grace about? Very simply, it is about the basis of our relationship to God in the present. Is it constituted by something we do or believe? Or is it a gift, a given? For Paul, of course, the answer is by now obvious. Justification is a gift of God, not a human accomplishment. Within the framework of justification by grace, the Christian life is about becoming conscious of and entering more deeply into an already existing relationship with God as known in Jesus. It is not about meeting requirements for salvation later but about newness of life in the present. And living by grace produces the same qualities as life "in Christ": freedom, joy, peace, and love.

Thus far I have spoken primarily about the personal meaning of justification by grace, perhaps because of my Protestant conditioning. But it also has a radically egalitarian social meaning. It did for Paul, for whom it was the basis for including Jews and Gentiles as equals within his communities. Along with his metaphor of "in Christ," it was the theological foundation of a new social reality. The logic is impeccable: within the framework of grace, there are no privileged few, no elites, no favored ones. Grace means that we are all equal before God. Indeed, even Paul's emphasis in Romans that "all have sinned and fall short of the glory of God" is a radically egalitarian notion.

"Christ Crucified"

For Paul, the death of Jesus was utterly central. When he wrote to the community in Corinth and reminded its members of what he had preached to them, he said, "I decided to know nothing among you except Jesus Christ and him crucified," and, even more compactly, "We proclaim Christ crucified."[75]

Paul's crystallization of his message as "Christ crucified" illustrates the combination of history and metaphor that characterizes so much of the Hebrew Bible and the New Testament. On the one hand, "Christ crucified" is a straightforward historical fact: Jesus, whom we as Christians confess to be the messiah, was crucified. On the other hand, Paul invests this historical fact with a wide range of symbolic meanings that go far beyond a historical assertion. As a symbol or metaphor, "Christ crucified" has multiple resonances of meaning. They are political as well as theological, and they sum up much of Paul's message.

For Paul, "Christ crucified" is an indictment of the imperial system of domination that executed Jesus. "The rulers of this age . . . crucified the Lord of glory." And for Paul, the resurrection was God's yes to Jesus and God's no to the domination system. The consequence: the rulers of this world are "doomed to perish." It is not simply that emperors and kings will die. Rather, the domination system itself must end.[76]

"Christ crucified" also discloses the wisdom of God and counters the wisdom of this world. How does the cross expose the wisdom of this world? Through paradox: the notion of a crucified messiah is an oxymoron, a Christian koan that shatters conventional ways of thinking and expectations. In Paul's words, it is "a stumbling block to Jews and foolishness to Gentiles."[77]

For Paul, "Christ crucified" is also the revelation of God's love for us. The death of God's son on the cross discloses the depth of God's love for us: "While we were still sinners, Christ died for us."[78] For Paul, the cross of Jesus is the sacrifice provided by God.[79] It is thus both the fulfillment of the law and the end of the law as a system of requirements.[80]

Finally, as we have seen, "Christ crucified" is also for Paul a symbol of the path of transformation. At the center of Paul's life was not only the proclamation of "Christ crucified," but also his own experience of dying and rising with Christ: "I have been crucified with Christ; it is no longer I who live, but Christ who lives in me."

Paul's metaphorical dying with Christ was to become actual. And his death, like his message and mission, brought together the spiritual and the political. The New Testament does not tell us about Paul's death, but according to early and reliable church tradition, he was executed in Rome in the 60s during the reign of the emperor Nero. The empire of which he was a citizen, and to which he had carried his message of a crucified messiah now exalted as Lord, put him to death. As a citizen, he was exempt from crucifixion, and so, perhaps observing the fine points of Roman law, imperial Rome beheaded him.

Thus Paul, in his death, embodied the path of dying that he had taught. The metaphor of "dying with Christ" became flesh. Like Jesus before and martyrs since, he became an incarnation of "the way" that lies at the center of the Christian life.

Paul's execution by Rome merits pondering. Was Rome simply mistaken in killing him? Was the execution based on a misunderstanding? Was it due to the decree of a crazed and callous emperor? Were Paul and his message actually harmless to the empire that killed him? Was it all about words—about calling

Jesus "Lord" and refusing to give Caesar the same honor? *Or was it about something much deeper and much more important?*

Certainly Paul and his small communities scattered through Greece and Asia Minor posed no immediate political threat to Rome. But did Paul's proclamation of a rival Lord and a rival social vision genuinely and ultimately threaten the imperial vision of life?

We who live after centuries of Christian accommodation with imperial systems are inclined to think that Rome simply made a mistake—that Rome failed to recognize that Christianity is harmless to empire (and maybe even helpful). But what happened to Jesus and Paul should give us pause. Christianity is the only major religion whose two most formative figures were executed by established authority. Accident? Plan of God? Or is there in Jesus and Paul a vision and a program, a message and a mission, that should cause systems of domination, ancient and modern, to tremble?

NOTES

1. I Tim. 2.8–15. Passages about wives submitting to husbands: Eph. 5.22–24, Col. 3.18–19. As I will soon note, these letters are among those that scholars think were probably written not by him but in his name sometime after his death.
2. These charges against Paul are, at most, only partially fair. Many of the offensive passages come from letters written by others in his name, and at least some of the rest can be read more than one way.
3. Acts 9.1–19, 22.3–21, 26.4–18. In his letters, Paul does not provide a detailed description of this experience, though he does allude to it, most clearly in Gal. 1.13–17. He also speaks of having "seen the Lord" in I Cor. 9.1 and includes himself in the list of those to whom the risen Christ "appeared" in I Cor. 15.3–8. Whether these two texts refer specifically to his Damascus experience or also to additional experiences of the risen Christ is impossible to know.
4. Acts 9.3–5.
5. These differences need not suggest either carelessness or historical inaccuracy on the part of Luke; rather, they may reflect the nature of such experiences: they are on the edge of the ineffable, and thus language about them is necessarily imprecise.
6. Acts 9.10–18.
7. Acts 9.15, 22.15, 26.17–19; Gal. 1.16.
8. The other candidate is the author of Revelation. As I will say in the next chapter, he seems to have had visions. But whether some of the accounts of

visions in Revelation are "vision reports" or whether they are all literary creations is a difficult question. Though I think it likely that other New Testament authors had dramatic religious experiences, and though they report the experiences of other people, they do not write about their own religious experiences.

9. In what follows, I will report what is generally accepted by scholars without reporting the arguments. When a point is quite uncertain, I will indicate that.

10. The New Testament provides no indication of when Paul was born or his age at his conversion (or at any other point in his life). The basis for the guess: he was vigorously active into the 60s of the first century, suggesting that he was probably not born before the beginning of the current era. If he was born in the first decade, his conversion experience would have happened when he was twenty-five or thirty years old.

11. On Tarsus, see Jerome Murphy-O'Connor, *Paul: A Critical Life* (Oxford: Clarendon Press, 1996), pp. 33–35.

12. Strabo and Philostratus, cited by Murphy-O'Connor, *Paul,* pp. 34–35.

13. Günther Bornkamm, *Paul* (New York: Harper & Row, 1971), trans. by D.M.G. Stalker, p. xxvi.

14. Wilamowitz-Moellendorf, cited by Bornkamm and described as "the great Greek scholar," pp. 9–10.

15. My impression is that at least a slight majority of Pauline scholars accept the tradition that Paul studied in Jerusalem.

16. Gal. 1.14, 13.

17. Phil. 3.5–6.

18. Emphasized by Alan Segal, a Jewish scholar, in his *Paul the Convert: The Apostolate and Apostasy of Saul the Pharisee* (New Haven: Yale University Press, 1990), chap. 2.

19. II Cor. 12.2–4.

20. It is difficult to know whether Paul's language refers to the ineffability of mystical experience or to the Jewish prohibition against talking about such experience to all but a very few mature people.

21. II Cor. 12.7.

22. I Cor. 15.5–8.

23. Gal. 2.19–20.

24. II Cor. 3.18. A few verses later we find another passage reflecting mystical consciousness: II Cor. 4.6.

25. See the interesting article by Jerome Murphy-O'Connor, "On the Road and On the Sea with St. Paul," *Bible Review* 1 (1985), pp. 38–47.

26. I and II Corinthians are two of his longest letters; together, they are longer than Romans, his longest letter. Moreover, he clearly wrote a letter (two?) to Corinth that we no longer have, and II Corinthians is a combination of two letters. Thus he wrote at least four and maybe five letters to Corinth.

27. II Cor. 11.23–28.

28. As I will mention at the end of this chapter, early and probably reliable tradition reports that Paul was executed in Rome in the 60s. Because Acts ends without reporting his death, readers have often thought that Acts must have

been written before his death: If the author knew about it, how could he omit it? However, most scholars think that the purpose of the author of Acts was not to write a biography of Paul but to report the spread of the gospel from Jerusalem to Rome. For this purpose, the end of Acts is perfect. Indeed, the author's purpose would have been poorly served if, after reporting Paul's preaching in Rome, he had then written, "And then they killed him."

29. There is no uniform term in the New Testament for Gentiles associated with the synagogue. Acts refers to such Gentiles as people who "feared God" (10.2, 13.16, 13.26), "devout persons" (17.4, 17), and "worshipers of God" (16.14, 18.7).

30. This estimate comes from Rodney Stark, *The Rise of Christianity* (San Francisco: HarperSanFrancisco, 1997). Stark's estimates are based on a growth rate of forty percent per decade, matching the most rapid rate of growth known for a new religious movement in the modern period (the Mormons).

31. For the distinction between "villa house churches" in the home of a wealthy patron and "shop or tenement house churches," and the distinction between "patronal share-meals" and "communal share-meals," see John Dominic Crossan, *The Birth of Christianity* (San Francisco: HarperSanFrancisco, 1998), pp. 424–30. See also Robert Jewett, "Tenement Churches and Communal Meals in the Early Church: The Implications of a Form-Critical Analysis of 2 Thessalonians 3.10," *Biblical Research* 38 (1993), pp. 23–43, cited by Crossan.

32. It is illuminating to see the typical form of an ancient letter reflected in Paul's letters. To illustrate, I use I Thessalonians. Letters began by identifying the sender (1.1a) and the recipient (1.1b), then moved on to a greeting (1.1c), a thanksgiving (1.2–10), the body (2.1–5.22), and a closing. The latter was typically made up of greetings, a close, an exhortation, and a benediction (5.23–28).

33. I owe the phrase to the subtitle of Calvin Roetzel's helpful introduction to Paul's letters, *The Letters of Paul: Conversations in Context*, 4th ed. (Louisville: Westminster/Knox, 1998; first edition published 1974).

34. I Cor. 11.2–16 and I Cor. 8. Much of the meat for sale in butcher shops in Corinth was left over from sacrifices to the gods. Thus the question was a very practical one: Is it all right to eat such meat?

35. I Cor. 7.1–3.

36. And thus the NRSV puts the sentence in quotation marks.

37. The brief story is found in Acts 16.13–15. Paul and his companions Timothy and Silas then stay at her house, which apparently became the location of the "house church" in Philippi. See also 16.40.

38. This is not taken for granted by New Testament scholars. Some (perhaps even a slight majority) assume, simply because Paul says little about Jesus in his letters, that the historical Jesus did not matter very much to him. This strikes me as incredible.

39. That Paul expected the return of Jesus soon is mentioned often in his letters, most clearly in I Thess. 4.13–18 and I Cor. 15.51–52.

40. See the comment of Joseph Fitzmyer in Raymond Brown, Joseph Fitzmyer, and Roland Murphy, eds., *The New Jerome Biblical Commentary* (Engle-

wood Cliffs, NJ: Prentice-Hall, 1990), p. 1394: "Lord" is "perhaps an even more important Pauline title for Jesus" than "Christ," which Paul clearly uses in a "titular sense" only once. See also, among others, James D. G. Dunn, *Unity and Diversity in the New Testament*, 2nd ed. (Valley Forge, PA: Trinity Press International, 1990), p. 50: Jesus is Lord "is undoubtedly *the principal confession of faith for Paul and his churches*" (italics in original).

41. Phil. 2.9–11. The passage begins in v. 5.

42. The quoted phrase is from Dunn, *Unity and Diversity*, p. 50.

43. Gal. 3.28.

44. Even as Paul refers to Jesus as "Lord," he remains a Jewish monotheist. The notion of the Trinity was still in the future, and it is best understood as the Christian way of affirming the divinity of the risen Christ within the framework of monotheism.

45. See, for example, Dieter Georgi, *Theocracy in Paul's Praxis and Theology* (Minneapolis: Fortress, 1991); Neil Elliott, *Liberating Paul: The Justice of God and the Politics of the Apostle* (Maryknoll, NY: Orbis, 1994); and Richard Horsley, ed., *Paul and Empire* (Harrisburg, PA: Trinity Press International, 1997).

46. Phil. 2.6, where Paul contrasts Christ with Adam; Adam did regard equality with God as something to be grasped or seized, building on the serpent's temptation in Gen. 3.5: "You shall be like God."

47. Rom. 5.12–21. Note the language of death exercising "dominion" in vv. 14 and 17 and sin exercising "dominion" in v. 21. This passage is sometimes associated with the doctrine of original sin, but that doctrine was not developed until centuries later. Paul is referring here to a universal way of being.

48. The whole passage is found in Rom. 7.7–24; quoted verses are 15–17. A formerly common interpretation of this powerful passage (especially among Protestants) saw it as Paul's description of his pre-Damascus life under the (Jewish) law. But other passages in Paul (esp. Phil. 3.6) suggest that Paul did not experience life under the Torah this way. Rather, the passage describes life in "the Adamic epoch," to quote a footnote in *The HarperCollins Study Bible: New Revised Standard Version* (New York: HarperCollins, 1993), p. 2125.

49. See Virginia Wiles, *Making Sense of Paul* (Peabody, MA: Hendrickson, 2000), p. 57: "The problem is not that people are sinners because they do wrong things. Rather, people do wrong things because they are sinners." In my judgment, Wiles's book is one of the two or three best contemporary introductions to Paul.

50. The entire passage is found in Rom. 7.7–24. Quoted words are from vv. 15, 18–20, 23, 24.

51. See, for example, Rom. 6.6–7, 18, 22; 8.2; Gal. 5.1.

52. II Cor. 5.18–19. See also Rom. 8.35–39, whose theme is that nothing can separate us from the love of God in Christ.

53. II Cor. 5.17–18. See also Gal. 6.15. New-creation imagery connects not only to Genesis but also to Second Isaiah and the return from exile. See also Rom. 6.4, 7.6

54. For the contrast, see Gal. 5.16–26 and Rom. 8.4–17.

55. Gal. 5.19–21.
56. "Freedom" is emphasized earlier in Gal. 5 (vv. 1, 13–14); the list is found in 5.22–23.
57. I Cor. 13.13. The extended context of 12.1–14.40 is important, for it puts Paul's oft-quoted and romanticized tribute to love in the framework of spiritual gifts, thus making it clear that Paul is talking not *simply* about ethics and not *at all* about romantic love. Love as Paul writes about it cannot be willed but flows out of a new way of being.
58. Gal. 2.19–20.
59. Rom. 6.3–4. The whole of 6.1–14 is relevant.
60. Rom. 12.1–2.
61. Phil. 2.5–11.
62. I Cor. 12.12–13; Rom. 12.4–5.
63. Gal. 3.26–28.
64. Passages speaking of the subordination of women and wives are all found in letters most likely not written by Paul. The possible exceptions are I Cor. 14.34–35 and I Cor. 11.2–16. The first text says that women should not speak in church but should ask their husbands about matters after they get home; many scholars think that these verses are a later, non-Pauline addition to the letter. In the second text, Paul says that women should not pray or prophesy in church with their heads unveiled and their hair therefore exposed. Whether this text speaks of subordination depends upon the translation of the Greek word *kephale* (pronounced "kefalay") in v. 3: the husband/man is the *kephale* of the wife/woman. Often translated "head," here it almost certainly means "source"; if so, it echoes the Genesis creation story in which the man *(adham)* is the source of the woman (who is made from his rib) and does not mean subordination. Strikingly, v. 12 affirms the equality of man and woman: "just as woman came from man [in the creation story], so man comes through woman [in birth]." But whatever the judgment about the correct translation of *kephale,* it is important to underline that Paul does not say that women should not pray or prophesy in church, only that they should be veiled when doing so. Finally, it is interesting to note that Paul grew up in a city (Tarsus) in which women wore the complete *chador* in public, completely covering them from head to foot (including their faces). Thus it is possible that Paul found unveiled women rather shocking.
65. I Cor. 11.17–34. Quoted words are from vv. 17, 20–22, 27, 29. The "words of institution" of the Lord's supper are in vv. 23–26. Because Paul reminds the Corinthian church of them in this context, it is tempting to think that he is also calling to mind the egalitarian quality of Jesus' open meal practice. If not, why mention these words here?
66. Rom. 8.35, 38–39.
67. Gal. 2.16, 3.10–11, 2.21.
68. Gal. 5.4, 12. Paul's language could get hot. Earlier in the letter, he accuses his Christian opponents of "perverting the gospel" and pronounces a curse on them (1.7–9), addressing his audience as "you foolish Galatians!" (3.1, 3).

69. Rom. 3.9, 19–20, 23. The argument begins in 1.16 and continues through 5.11.
70. Rom. 3.24–25.
71. Abraham is the topic of Rom. 4; quoted verses are 4.3 and 9.
72. Rom. 4.5; 5.8, 10.
73. Rom. 7.12.
74. Robin Scroggs, *Paul for a New Day* (Philadelphia: Fortress, 1977), p. 10. Along with the book by Virginia Wiles mentioned in note 49, it is one of the most accessible introductions to this aspect of Paul's message.
75. I Cor. 2.2, 1.23.
76. I Cor. 2.6–8.
77. I Cor. 1.24 in the context of 1.18–31. Because the wisdom of God is the opposite of the wisdom of the world, Paul can also refer to the wisdom of God as "the foolishness of God."
78. Rom. 5.8.
79. Rom. 3.25. Because a literal interpretation of this notion leads to unacceptable and indeed incredible implications, I stress that it must be read metaphorically. As a metaphor, its meaning is clear: if God has provided the atoning sacrifice, then nothing can separate us from the love of God in Christ.
80. Echoing Rom. 10.4: "Christ is the end of the law." There is a scholarly debate about the meaning of "end" in this verse. Does it mean "end" as in "finished," or "end" as in *telos* (meaning "goal" or "fulfillment")? And does "law" here mean Torah (the Jewish law) or law as a system of requirements? The debate is difficult to resolve. My use of it reads "law" not as Torah but as "system of requirements," and "end" can thus mean both "fulfilled" and "finished."

10

Reading Revelation Again

"Revelation is widely popular for the wrong reasons," says biblical scholar Raymond Brown, "for a great number of people read it as a guide to how the world will end, assuming that the author was given by Christ detailed knowledge of the future that he communicated in coded symbols."[1] Indeed, a substantial percentage of fundamentalist and conservative-evangelical Christians read Revelation as forecasting the imminent "end of the world" and second coming of Christ.

The conviction that Jesus is coming soon, or at least that he *may* be, is widespread. According to one national public-opinion poll, sixty-two percent of Americans (not just American *Christians,* mind you) have "no doubts" that Jesus will come again.[2] Another poll reports that one-third believe the world will end soon.[3]

I call a reading of Revelation that emphasizes the imminent second coming of Christ a "millennialist" interpretation. That view has flourished in the last half-century. During the last thirty years, books by Hal Lindsey, beginning with *The Late Great*

Planet Earth, have sold over forty million copies. During the decade of the 1970s, Lindsey was the best-selling nonfiction(?) author in the English-speaking world. In the last several years, a series of novels on "the rapture" by Tim LaHaye and Jerry B. Jenkins have been on the best-seller lists. A millennialist reading of Revelation is a frequent theme of television and radio evangelists and "prophecy conferences" throughout the world. Recently, as I surfed through my viewing options on TV, I saw one of the best-known television evangelists standing in front of a chalkboard displaying biblical "signs of the end" and suggesting that 2007 may be the year of the second coming. Speaking in the context of a fund-raising drive, he sent this message: "You don't want to be burdened when Jesus comes again."

The millennialist interpretation is not universally accepted, however. In fact, the interpretation of Revelation divides the contemporary church. But those Christians who reject the millennialist view often lack an alternate interpretation, choosing instead to ignore Revelation. The majority of mainline Christians have little familiarity with this troubling text; they avoid it in personal devotions and seldom hear it preached about (for there are few texts from Revelation in the lectionary, which sets out the portions of the Bible assigned for reading in public worship). Readers are puzzled by Revelation's difficult and bizarre imagery, perplexed by its scenes of destruction and divine violence, and put off by the message, "Jesus is coming soon and you'd better be ready, or you'll be in big trouble." To them, the God of Revelation and the message of Revelation seem to have little to do with the gospel of Jesus. They are willing (even if not happy) to leave Revelation to others.

Introduction

Revelation stands at the end of the New Testament and thus at the end of the Christian Bible. However, it was not the last document of the New Testament to be written, nor did its author know that it would someday conclude the Christian Bible. Its placement at the end of the New Testament canon is due to its subject matter: "the end"—judgment upon the world, the second coming of Christ, the destruction of Satan, and the advent of the New Jerusalem, described in language that echoes the portrait of Eden at the beginning of Genesis. With Revelation at its end, the Bible moves from "paradise lost" to "paradise restored."

Revelation has been controversial from Christian antiquity to the present. In fact, it almost failed to make it into the Bible. Though generally accepted in the Latin-speaking church of the West from the second century onward, Revelation took much longer to be accepted as scripture in the Greek-speaking Eastern church. In the fourth century, the Christian historian Eusebius listed it as one of the disputed books. At about the same time, the early church father Cyril of Jerusalem not only omitted it from his list of canonical books, but forbade its public or private use.[4] Though gradually accepted in the East, as late as 810 CE a Byzantine (Eastern) list of canonical writings did not include it. In the tenth and eleventh centuries, it began to be routinely included in Greek manuscripts of the New Testament.[5]

Much later, leaders of the Protestant Reformation of the sixteenth century had doubts about Revelation. Martin Luther included it in the New Testament only reluctantly and gave it secondary stature (even as he wished it would be thrown into the Elbe River); Ulrich Zwingli denied it scriptural status; and John Calvin largely ignored it (writing commentaries on the other twenty-six books of the New Testament but not on Revelation).

Thus what to do with Revelation has been an issue for Christians for a very long time. In this chapter I will describe two very different ways of reading the book and look at the larger issues it raises. First, though, I will introduce it and provide a compact summary of its content.

A Christian Apocalypse

The book of Revelation is an apocalypse. Indeed, the two words—"Revelation" and "apocalypse"—are synonyms, for both translate the same Greek word, *apokalypsis*. Thus Revelation in some Christian circles is called "The Apocalypse." Because Revelation was written by a person named John, the book is often known more fully as "The Revelation of John" or "The Apocalypse of John." (Note that the singular is used, not the plural; the name of the book is not "Revelations.")

The word "apocalypse" means an "unveiling" or a "disclosure" or a "revelation." It also names a type of literature. As a literary genre, an apocalypse is defined by both content and style. Its subject matter is one or more visions disclosing or unveiling either the future or the heavenly world or both. Commonly, the present age is seen to be under the rule of evil powers who will soon be overthrown and destroyed by God, ushering in an age of blessedness for the faithful. The coming of the new age is typically marked by intense suffering and cosmic catastrophes. The stylistic features of apocalyptic literature include luxuriant imagery, fabulous beasts, and symbolic numbers.[6] Apocalyptic writings flourished in Judaism from about 200 BCE to 100 CE. In the Hebrew Bible, the second half of the book of Daniel, written around 165 BCE, is the most sustained example.[7]

Revelation was written late in the first century by a man named John living on the island of Patmos off the coast of Asia Minor. Some have thought that John of Patmos was the disciple John, who also wrote the Fourth Gospel and the three letters of John, though virtually all modern scholars reject this identification.[8] A few scholars have argued that Revelation was written in the time of the Roman emperor Nero in the 60s of the first century, though most affirm a date around the year 95, near the end of the rule of the emperor Domitian.

Though Revelation is an apocalypse, it is also a letter addressed to seven Christian communities in seven cities in Asia Minor. John of Patmos was apparently known in these communities and may have been an itinerant Christian prophet and charismatic authority figure. He knew the Hebrew Bible very well. Though he never formally quotes a single verse, as many as sixty-five percent of the verses in Revelation echo or allude to passages from the Hebrew Bible.[9] John's frequent use of the Hebrew Bible led one scholar to speak of the book as "a rebirth of images."[10]

Like the letters of Paul, Revelation would have been read aloud to its recipients at a community gathering, most likely in the context of worship. It was thus *heard* by its original audience (not read silently by individuals), and the listeners would have heard it all at once at a single sitting.[11] This in itself has implications for interpretation: *hearing* Revelation *all at once* would convey the cumulative effect of John's visions in a way that the private reading of individual texts in isolation from the broad sweep of the book does not.

Summary of Content

After a brief introduction, John of Patmos speaks of the visionary experience in which he is commanded to write the book. Because the vision illustrates a number of characteristics of Revelation, I quote it at length:

> I was in the spirit on the Lord's day, and I heard behind me a
> loud voice like a trumpet saying, "Write in a book what you
> see and send it to the seven churches, to Ephesus, to
> Smyrna, to Pergamum, to Thyatira, to Sardis, to Philadel-
> phia, and to Laodicea.

John then turns to see who is speaking to him. In his visionary state, he sees the risen Christ:

> Then I turned to see whose voice it was that spoke to me, and
> on turning I saw seven golden lampstands, and in the midst
> of the lampstands I saw one like the Son of Man, clothed
> with a long robe and with a golden sash across his chest.
> His head and his hair were white as white wool, white as
> snow; his eyes were like a flame of fire, his feet were like
> burnished bronze, refined as in a furnace, and his voice was
> like the sound of many waters. In his right hand he held

seven stars, and from his mouth came a sharp two-edged
sword, and his face was like the sun shining with full force.

John then "fell at his feet as though dead." But the figure
"placed his right hand on me, saying 'Do not be afraid,'" and
then identified himself: "I am the first and the last, and the living
one. I was dead, and see, I am alive for ever and ever; and I have
the keys of Death and of Hades." The vision then concludes
with the command of the risen Christ:

> Now write what you have seen, what is, and what is to take
> place after this. As for the mystery of the seven stars that
> you saw in my right hand, and the seven golden lampstands:
> the seven stars are the angels of the seven churches, and the
> seven lampstands are the seven churches.[12]

John's inaugural vision illustrates several features of Revelation: emphasis upon visions and "seeing," use of luxuriant imagery, allusion to the Hebrew Bible, and frequent use of
symbolic numbers. Most of the book is narrated as a series of visions; in the book as a whole, "I saw" is used about fifty-five
times. The luxuriant imagery in John's initial vision speaks for itself, much of it drawn from the Hebrew Bible; there are no fewer
than twelve allusions to that older document in this passage. The
number seven recurs frequently throughout the book. Here,
there are seven stars, seven lampstands, and seven churches; in
subsequent chapters, there will be seven letters, seven seals,
seven trumpets, and seven bowls. Even when the number seven
is not explicitly used, there are series of sevens: seven beatitudes,
seven hymns of praise, seven categories of people, seven references to the altar, and seven prophetic affirmations of the second
coming of Jesus.[13]
Chapters two and three contain the letters to the seven
churches. They include an evaluation of each community, threats
and/or encouragement, and a promise. Nothing bad is said
about Smyrna and Philadelphia; nothing good is said about

Sardis and Laodicea; Ephesus, Pergamum, and Thyatira receive mixed verdicts.[14] The issues facing the communities are persecution, false teaching, and accommodation to the larger culture.

Chapters four through twenty-two contain the long series of visions that fills virtually the rest of the book.[15] As chapter four begins, John exclaims, "I looked, and behold, in heaven, an open door!" He then looks through that door into another level of reality. There is no substitute for reading these chapters themselves, preferably at a single sitting. Nevertheless, I provide a summary.

The section begins with a vision of God enthroned in heaven, surrounded by twenty-four elders clothed in white with crowns of gold on their heads. Four beasts are around the throne, each with six wings and eyes in the wings—strange creatures from another world. From the throne itself come lightning and thunder and voices.

It continues with a vision of the Lamb that was slain but that now lives and is worthy to open the seven seals of the scroll of judgment. As the seven seals are opened, we see the four horsemen of the apocalypse riding forth upon the earth, bringing war, famine, pestilence, and death. Then there is a great earthquake, the sky blackens, the stars fall from the heavens, and the sky rolls up like a scroll. The seventh seal is opened, and it introduces another series of seven judgments: seven angels begin to blow seven trumpets in succession. The blowing of the trumpets unleashes another series of plagues and catastrophes on the earth, including giant locusts that look like horses equipped for battle (bearing tails like scorpions and making a noise like many chariots) and an immense army of two hundred million invading from the east.

At the start of chapter twelve, we see a vision of a woman clothed with the sun, a crown of twelve stars on her head and the moon under her feet. She is giving birth to a child whom a great red dragon immediately tries to devour. At the same time, war breaks out in heaven: the archangel Michael and his angels battle against the great dragon, who loses and is cast down to earth. In chapter thirteen, a beast with seven heads and ten horns to whom the dragon has given authority rises out of the sea and takes control of the earth. The number of the beast, we are told, is 666.

Then seven angels pour out upon the earth the seven bowls of the wrath of God, and we are shown the judgment and destruction of the "great harlot" or "great whore" who rides upon the beast and whose name is "Babylon the Great." This is soon followed by the battle of Armageddon and the second coming of Christ on a white horse. Christ leads an army clad in white robes against the armies of the beast and destroys them, their bodies becoming food for carrion birds that gorge themselves with their flesh. The dragon, now named "the devil" and "Satan," is cast into a bottomless pit for a thousand years, during which Christ and the saints rule. After a thousand years, Satan is released, and with Gog and Magog he fights a final battle and is again defeated. Then the last judgment occurs: all the dead, great and small, are raised, the book of life is opened, and all whose names are not in it are cast into the lake of fire, along with the devil, the beast, death, and Hades.

After all of this, at the beginning of chapter twenty-one, comes the magnificent concluding vision. The New Jerusalem, adorned as a bride for her husband, descends from the sky—a city in which there will be no more tears, no pain, no death. The city has no need of a temple, for its temple is the Lord God The Almighty and the Lamb. Nor does the city have need of sun or moon, for the glory of God will be its light, and its lamp the Lamb of God. Through it flows the river of the water of life, and in it grows the tree of life whose leaves are for the healing of the nations. There, the servants of God will worship God and the Lamb:

> They will see God's face, and God's name will be on their foreheads. And there will be no more night; they need no light of lamp or sun, for the Lord God will be their light, and they will reign forever and ever.[16]

Two Ways of Reading Revelation

How are we to read all this? How are we to interpret the visions and images of this strange, violent, unsettling, and yet magnificent book? In this section, I will describe two very different ways of reading the Apocalypse of John in our time.

The Futurist Interpretation

The central claim of a futurist reading is simple: Revelation tells us about what will happen some time in the future. It has three premises:

- What Revelation describes has not yet happened.
- As the inspired Word of God, the Bible cannot be wrong.
- Therefore, what Revelation describes must still be future.

These premises are the foundation of the millennialist reading of Revelation mentioned in the introduction to this chapter. This way of reading the book sees it as a cryptogram, a message encoded in symbols about the signs of the end that will precede the second coming of Christ.

To illustrate this way of reading Revelation, I will use the work of the popular millennialist author Hal Lindsey. In his book *The Late Great Planet Earth,* Lindsey argues that the events foretold by Revelation are unfolding in our time. For him (as well as for other contemporary millennialists), the establishment of the modern state of Israel in 1948 is a key sign that the end may be near. The reason is that some biblical passages speak of Israel as a nation living in her own land in the time of the end. Only since 1948 has this been true.

Lindsey then "decodes" much of the language of Revelation to refer to phenomena of our time. For example, he speculates that the opening of the sixth seal in Revelation 6.12–17 refers to a thermonuclear exchange. The "stars of the sky falling to earth" are orbiting nuclear bombs reentering the atmosphere. The sky vanishing "like a scroll rolling itself up" refers to what happens to the atmosphere in a nuclear explosion.

When the sixth angel blows the sixth trumpet in Revelation 9.13–16 and unleashes an army from the east that numbers two hundred million, Lindsey deduces that the reference is to Communist China. Only China, he says, has a large enough population to put so huge an army in the field. So also he speculates that the giant locusts with tails like scorpions and wings that make a noise like many chariots (Rev. 9.7–10) may be a particular kind of attack helicopter.

The ten-horned beast from the sea in Revelation 13 is central to Lindsey's interpretation. Recognizing that it has some connection to Rome, he suggests that it refers to a revived Roman Empire composed of a ten-nation confederacy. This confederacy, he suggests, is the European Economic Community, whose membership was nearing ten nations when he wrote, and which was formed by the Treaty of Rome. The horn that received a mortal wound but recovered refers to a future ruler of the ten-nation confederacy who will also become the ruler of the world. Lindsey speaks of this person as "the future Führer" and claims that he is already alive, even though we do not yet know who he is.

Thus, according to Lindsey, the time of "the rapture," the final "tribulation," the battle of Armageddon, the second coming of Christ, and the last judgment is near. The rapture is the notion that "true-believing Christians" will be taken up from the earth "to meet the Lord in the air" and thus be spared the intense suffering that will precede the end.[17] That period of suffering is known as the "tribulation" and is signified in Revelation by the opening of the seven seals, the blowing of the seven trumpets, the pouring out of the seven bowls, all of them unleashing the destructive wrath of God upon the world. The tribulation comes to an end with the battle of Armageddon and the defeat of the armies of the beast by the returning warrior Christ.

The futurist reading in its millennialist form has striking effects on the meaning of the Christian message. The gospel (if it can be called that in this context) becomes "the good news" that you can be saved from the soon-to-come wrath of God by believing strongly in Jesus. The focus is on saving yourself and those whom you love (and as many others as you can get to listen to you) from the fate that awaits most of humankind. The message also has striking effects on our attitude toward life on earth, including issues of social justice and the environment. If the world is going to end soon, why worry about improving conditions here? Why worry about preserving the environment? It's all going to end soon anyway.

Though Lindsey's approach has attracted millions of Christians, many other Christians (and, I suspect, most readers of this book) find his reading of Revelation to be bizarre and perhaps even amusing. But the central claim of a futurist reading—that Revelation speaks about what will happen some time in the future—is shared by a broad spectrum of Christians, including many who reject a millennialist reading. The latter group of Christians are doubtful, however, that the images of Revelation can be decoded in a highly specific way. They see the book as speaking in vague, general terms about the end of the world and regard attempts to figure out whether we are living in the last days as misguided interpretations or even as manifestations of human pride. They are content to leave the future up to God, even as they affirm with varying degrees of conviction and in a general way that God will bring history to a conclusion consistent with the overall message of Revelation. Indeed, this has probably been the conventional and commonsense way of reading Revelation throughout most of Christian history: it tells us about the future, but we should not become too fascinated with it or too confident that we have discerned the meanings of its symbolic language.

But if we think that Lindsey's approach is farfetched at best, what is wrong with it? Is it simply that Lindsey has got the details wrong? That, in his enthusiasm, he has become too specific? Or does he perhaps simply have the timing wrong? Is it the case that Revelation does describe what will happen sometime, in however general a way, even if that time is hundreds or thousands or even millions of years in the future? Or is the futurist approach itself—not just Lindsey's version of it—mistaken? These questions lead us to a second way of reading Revelation.

The Past-Historical Interpretation

The past-historical reading, which grows out of the belief that we understand the message of Revelation only by setting the text in the *historical context* in which it was written, emphasizes what Revelation would have meant *in the past*.[18] In this reading, Revelation tells us what the author believed would happen in his time. This approach takes seriously that the visions of Revelation are found in a letter addressed to specific Christian communities in Asia Minor late in the first century. As such, the text was meant to be a message to *them*, not a message to people thousands of years later.

The book itself indicates that John was thinking of his own time. Seven times in his prologue and epilogue, he tells his audience that he is writing about the near future. His first sentence begins, "The revelation of Jesus Christ, which God gave him to show his servants *what must soon take place.*" Two verses later, he says, "Blessed is the one who reads aloud the words of the prophecy, and blessed are those who hear and who keep what is written in it; *for the time is near.*" In his epilogue, the emphasis upon nearness occurs five times. The italicized phrases above are repeated once each, and three times the author attributes to the risen Christ the words, "I am coming *soon.*"[19]

Christians in subsequent centuries have often sought to avoid the implications of "soon" and "near" by saying that God's time is not our time. As the latest book in the New Testament puts it, "With the Lord, one day is like a thousand years, and a thousand years are like one day."[20] But the original hearers of Revelation would not have thought of hearing the language of "soon" with this qualification. It would not have occurred to them to think, "Maybe soon, maybe thousands of years from now."

In addition to John's prologue and epilogue, there is also compelling evidence in the main body of the book that the author was writing about realities of his own day. This evidence is most visible in chapters thirteen and seventeen. In chapter thirteen, the ten-horned beast from the sea rules the world and demands worship, just as the Roman Empire ruled the world known to John. Its emperors were hailed as lord and god in temples honoring them throughout the empire. At the end of chapter thirteen, we are told that the "the beast" is a person whose "number is 666." In antiquity, letters of the alphabet had numerical values, and the technique for encoding and decoding a name into a number was called *gematria*. Using the rules of *gematria*, the number 666 decodes into "Caesar Nero."[21]

That John intended to identify the beast of chapter thirteen with the Roman Empire of his day is confirmed in the vision of "the great whore" in chapter seventeen. This woman, dressed in royal attire, rides upon the beast of chapter thirteen, and her name is "Babylon the Great." The Babylonian Empire had vanished some six hundred years earlier, so why would John name this creature Babylon? Historical context provides the answer: just as Babylon had destroyed Jerusalem and the temple in 586 BCE, so Rome had destroyed Jerusalem and the temple in 70 CE. In some Jewish and Christian circles, Babylon had become a symbolic name for Rome.[22]

The identification of this woman whose name is Babylon with the Roman Empire is made complete by two more details in chapter seventeen. The woman is seated on "seven mountains"; from antiquity, Rome has been known as the city built on seven hills or mountains. The identification becomes explicit in the last verse of the chapter: "The woman you saw is the great city that rules over the kings of the earth."[23] In the first century, this could only have meant Rome. For John, the beast and the person whose number was 666 were not figures of the future, but realities of his present.

In addition to this evidence in the book, there is a further reason why the past-historical reading supplants the futurist reading. If John was in fact writing about events thousands of years in the future, then the communities to which he wrote had no chance whatsoever of understanding his letter. If the ten-horned beast is really the European Economic Community (or some other future empire), if the giant locusts are really attack helicopters (or symbolize some other future death-dealing machines), and if the army of two hundred million refers to some future army, then the message of Revelation had no significance for the people to whom it was addressed. Though John wrote the letter and apocalypse to a specific audience, its message could not have been intended for them.

For all of these reasons, the past-historical reading of Revelation affirms that John was writing about realities of his time. Of course, John was also writing about the future, but it was a future that he expected to happen soon, not a future that is still future from our point in time. His message to the communities to which he was writing was a mixture of warning (especially in the letters in chapters two and three) and encouragement. About his message, I will soon say more. For now, I summarize it very compactly as threefold:

- Despite appearances to the contrary, Christ is Lord; Caesar and the beast are not.
- God will soon act to overthrow the rule of the beast and its incarnation in Caesar.
- Therefore, persevere, endure, be confident, take heart, have faith.

The past-historical reading of Revelation has an important implication. To make the implication explicit: to the extent that Revelation is seen as foretelling the future, as prediction, it is mistaken prediction. What the author expected to happen soon did not happen. The Roman Empire continued for another three hundred years, more or less; and when it did fall, the events leading up to its collapse were not like those spoken of in John's visions. Furthermore, Jesus did not return soon.

In other words, the past-historical interpretation takes seriously that the Bible is a human product, not a divine product with a divine guarantee. It acknowledges that the Bible can be mistaken.

This realization raises the question of what it means to take the Apocalypse of John seriously. Do we take it seriously if we project John's symbols, visions, and end-times scenario from the first century to our time or some still-future time? Do we honor the message of the book by affirming that what it says will still come to pass? Which reading of the book—the futurist or the past-historical—takes the text more seriously? Ironically, though the millennialist reading claims to take Revelation very seriously indeed, it does not, because it ignores what John was saying to the people to whom he was writing.[24]

The past-historical reading of Revelation also raises the question of what to think about the second coming of Jesus. Not just John of Patmos, but other early Christians as well, believed that it would be soon. The authors of Mark and Matthew, for example, refer to the imminent coming of "the Son of Man," presumably referring to the second coming of Jesus. The gospel of John also refers to the imminent second coming, though it is not clear that the author accepts the notion literally. Passages in Paul point to the same expectation.

Obviously, these early Christians were wrong. What are we to do with this? Do we say that they got the expectation right and that Jesus really will come again, but their timing was off? For a variety of reasons, I do not think that it makes sense to expect a visible future second coming of Christ. The belief can be understood metaphorically, however, as an affirmation that Jesus comes again and again in the lives of Christians: in the eucharist, in the celebration of Christmas each year, in the experience of the Spirit as the presence of Christ, and perhaps in other ways as well.[25]

The Larger Themes

But Revelation is more than mistaken prediction. The book has power.[26] Its numinous language about God and Christ has been integrated into Christian worship, liturgy, and art. Its affirmation of another reality that transcends the visible world has been a source of inspiration, hope, and courage. Its archetypal imagery speaks to both the political and spiritual realms of life; indeed, it integrates rather than separates those realms.

A Tale of Two Lordships

John portrays the central conflict of the book of Revelation in a number of ways. One of the most important is the conflict between competing lordships: Christ's and Caesar's. Is Caesar lord, or is God as known in Jesus lord? John's answer, of course, is clear. But to appreciate it fully, we must know the claims being made for Caesar.

Ever since the emperor Augustus had brought the devastating civil wars that followed the assassination of Julius Caesar to an end, ushering in the Pax Romana (the peace of Rome) and a "golden age," the emperors of Rome had been given divine titles. They were known as *filius deus* (son of god), *dominus* (lord), and even *deus* (god). Augustus was heralded as the savior who had brought peace on earth. As an inscription from 9 BCE in Asia Minor puts it:

> The *most divine Caesar* . . . we should consider equal to *the Beginning of all things*. . . . Whereas the Providence which has regulated our whole existence . . . has brought our life to the climax of perfection in giving to us the emperor Augustus . . . who being sent to us *as a Savior*, has put *an end to war*. . . . The birthday of *the god Augustus* has been for the whole world the beginning of *good news* (the Greek word is *euaggelion*, commonly translated "gospel").[27]

Throughout the empire, in temples of the imperial cult, worship was offered to the emperors. Such worship did not preclude the inhabitants from following their own religion as well. But it did have the effect of providing religious legitimation to the rule of Caesar and empire.

Against this, John proclaims the exclusive lordship of God and "the Lamb"—that is, God as known in Jesus. John's first description of Jesus speaks of him as "the faithful witness, the firstborn of the dead, and *the ruler of the kings of the earth*."[28] As "the faithful witness," he is the Lamb that was slain, executed by the power of Rome. As "the firstborn of the dead," he has been vindicated and exalted by God, disclosing Rome as a false pretender lord. Now he rules upon the throne with God and has become *"the ruler of the kings of the earth."*

Throughout the book, the honor and praise demanded by Caesar is offered to God and Jesus instead. Much of Revelation is doxology, and its hymns of praise have been a fountainhead for Christian hymn-writers ever since:

> Holy, holy, holy, Lord God Almighty.
>
> Worthy is the Lamb that was slain
> to receive power and wealth and wisdom
> and might and honor and glory and blessing.
>
> Blessing and glory and wisdom
> and thanksgiving and honor
> and power and might
> be to our God forever and ever.
>
> The kingdom of the world has
> become the kingdom of our Lord
> and of his Christ,
> and he will reign forever and ever.
>
> Hallelujah!
> For the Lord our God
> the Almighty reigns.[29]

Jesus is Lord; Caesar is not. John shares this affirmation in common with the whole of the New Testament.

The Ancient Cosmic Combat Myth

Among the reasons for the power of the Apocalypse is John's use of one of humankind's most widespread archetypal stories: the ancient cosmic combat myth. John draws on that myth to continue the theme of two lordships and to deepen and amplify his indictment of empire.

The cosmic combat myth appears in many cultures, ancient and modern, and it takes many forms.[30] The archetypal plot is a story of cosmic conflict between good and evil. In the ancient world, the conflict was between a god (or gods) of light, order, and life against an evil power of darkness, disorder, and death. Commonly the evil power was imaged as a dragon or sea monster or primeval serpent.

In the ancient Near East, the cosmic combat myth is found in one of the world's oldest creation stories, the *Enuma Elish*. In that story, the god Marduk creates the world by slaying Tiamat, a seven-headed monster of chaos associated with the sea. In Babylon, that primordial battle was ritually reenacted each year.

Traces of the ancient cosmic combat myth are found in the Hebrew Bible. According to Psalm 74, God "broke the heads of the dragons in the waters and crushed the heads of Leviathan."[31] Passages in Isaiah echo the myth: "On that day the LORD with his cruel and great and strong sword will punish Leviathan the fleeing serpent, Leviathan the twisting serpent, and will kill the dragon that is in the sea."[32] The book of Job refers several times to the dragon or sea monster, naming it Rahab and Leviathan.[33]

In the New Testament, the cosmic combat myth lies behind one of the most central interpretations of the death and resurrection of Jesus. Often called the "Christus Victor" understanding of Good Friday and Easter, it portrays Jesus' death and resurrection as the means whereby God defeated the principalities and powers that hold humankind in bondage.[34] In the postbiblical Christian tradition, the cosmic combat myth is reflected in two of the most popular Christian icons: St. George slaying the dragon, and the archangel Michael warring with the dragon.

In our own time, this ancient myth is the central plot element of the *Star Wars* movies: the battle between good and evil symbolized in the conflict between Jedi knights wielding light-sabers against an empire of darkness whose most vivid representative is Lord Darth Vader, commander of the "Death Star." The popularity of the *Star Wars* saga is due not simply to the stunning special effects, but also to the re-presentation of this ancient story.

The series taps into something deep within human memory and consciousness: the awareness of conflict between good and evil and the yearning that good will triumph. Thus Revelation and *Star Wars* are powerful for the same reason.

The myth was also well known in Greco-Roman culture. Its most common form in that context was the story of the god Apollo (son of Zeus and thus son of god) and Python, the ancient monster. When Apollo's mother, Leto, was about to give birth to her child, Python looked for his chance to devour the infant. Apollo was delivered safely, however; and after he had grown up, he battled and killed Python. It is the same story, appearing again and again.

John of Patmos obviously knew this version of the ancient myth, and it shapes much of the Apocalypse.[35] Now the battle is between, on one side, God and "the Lamb that was slain," and, on the other, the dragon, the ancient serpent, the beast from the abyss, who is also Satan and the devil. Like ancient Tiamat and Leviathan, the beast of Revelation 13 has seven heads. The battle climaxes with an army dressed in white defeating the armies of the beast and Satan cast into a bottomless pit and then into a lake of fire. John is telling one of the most powerful stories known.

Revelation and Empire

But it is John's identification of the dragon that gives to the Apocalypse a stunning political dimension. John is not simply speaking about a mythological battle between gods in primordial time; he is also talking about a conflict going on in his own time. For John, the present incarnation of the dragon is the Roman Empire. As already noted, the identification of the beast with the Roman Empire is most clearly made in chapters thirteen and seventeen.

Moreover, John pointedly reverses the Roman Empire's version of the story of Apollo and Python. Both Caesar Augustus and Nero styled themselves as Apollo, the son of a god and himself the god of light, who had brought in a golden age of order and peace by slaying Python, the mythical power of disorder, darkness, and death.

John echoes the story of Apollo's birth and reverses the imperial version of it in the vision found in Revelation 12. There a woman is about to give birth to a son who will rule the nations. A great dragon waits to devour the son, but the child is delivered by being taken up to the throne of God. For John, the child is Jesus, of course. Then we are shown a scene in heaven in which Michael and his angels fight against the dragon and defeat him. Though the war occurs in heaven, the means of the dragon's defeat is an event that happened on earth: he has been conquered "by the blood of the Lamb"—that is, by the death of Jesus. The result: the dragon is cast down to earth and gives his authority, power, and throne to the seven-headed "beast from the sea" who appears at the beginning of Revelation 13.

This is a remarkable subversion of the Roman story of Apollo's birth. Jesus, not Caesar, is Apollo, the light of the world who brings in the true golden age of peace on earth. Caesar and the Roman Empire are not Apollo, slaying the beast; they are the incarnation of the dragon, the beast, the ancient serpent. Rome is the opposite of what it claimed to be: the empire that claimed to bring peace on earth, and whose emperors were spoken of as lord, savior, son of god, and even god, was in fact the incarnation of disorder, violence, and death.

What's Wrong with Rome?

That the book of Revelation indicts the Roman Empire in the strongest terms is thus clear. But why? What was wrong with Rome? Why did John call it "the beast"?

An earlier generation of scholars identified the reason as Roman persecution of Christians. In particular, these scholars thought that John's communities were facing a major outbreak of persecution ordered by the emperor Domitian around the year 95. According to this earlier view, Domitian demanded that he be acknowledged as "lord" and "god" in temples to the emperor. Refusal to do so meant possible arrest and even execution.

More recently, however, scholars have concluded that there is little historical evidence to support the claim that there was major persecution in the time of Domitian. While some scholars argue that there was no persecution and others argue that there was only minor, limited persecution, most agree that there was no massive persecution of Christians at that time.[36]

What John says in his letters to the seven churches is consistent with minor rather than massive persecution. He mentions only one martyr in the communities to which he writes—a person named Antipas; and though he does warn of persecutions and trials to come, it is not clear that these have begun.[37] In the body of the book, he mentions martyrs several times, but these may well be martyrs from the time of Nero some thirty years earlier.

Why does the level of persecution matter? It affects our perception of why John called Rome "the beast." If there was massive Roman persecution of Christians in John's day, then Rome was "the beast" because of what it was doing to Christians. *This* was why Rome faced God's wrath and destruction. John's message would be, in effect, "Rome has been giving us a hard time, so God's going to destroy her."

Seeing the issue this way has an important corollary. It implies that if Caesar had not called himself "lord" and "god," if he had not demanded worship in imperial shrines, if he had left Christians alone, then Caesar would have been okay and imperial Rome would have been okay. In short, this reading makes the issue narrowly religious, domesticating John's indictment of Rome. It suggests that if Rome had allowed "religious freedom" to Christians, then Christians would have had no issue with Rome.

The persecution of Christians cannot be eliminated from the passion that drives the Apocalypse. Nevertheless, there are clear indications that it is not simply Rome-as-persecutor but Rome-as-*empire* that accounts for John's indictment of Rome as the incarnation of the dragon, the ancient seven-headed monster that plunges the world into chaos.

Recent scholarship has moved in this direction. It sees the book of Revelation as a powerful indictment of the Roman Empire not simply because of its persecution of Christians, but also because that empire was the then-contemporary incarnation of the "domination system" that has marked so much of human history.[38]

The Indictment of Empire

Earlier in this book, the ancient domination system was described as a web of political oppression, economic exploitation, and religious legitimation.[39] Elites of power and wealth controlled societies in their own interests and declared the order they imposed to be the will of God. In his indictment of the Roman Empire, John names all of these features.[40]

Political Oppression Rome controlled the world of the first century through a combination of seduction, intimidation, and violence. The Roman Empire personified itself as a woman in the form of the goddess Roma. So also John personifies Rome as a woman, but as "the great whore" dressed in finery, the appealing seductress "with whom the kings of the earth have committed fornication."[41] She practices not only seduction but sorcery, bewitching the inhabitants of earth to follow the ways of empire.[42]

Rome is not only a seductive sorceress; it is also a ferocious beast ruling through intimidation and violence. The inhabitants of "the whole earth followed the beast," for they said, "Who is like the beast, and who can fight against it?"[43] When intimidation was not adequate, the empire used brutal violence. John knew of Rome's reconquest of the Jewish homeland some twenty-five years earlier, the mass crucifixions, and the destruction of Jerusalem and the temple. John knew also of Rome's execution of Christian martyrs, including Peter and Paul. But the beast incarnate in the empire of John's day is the slayer not only of Christian martyrs but also of prophets and countless others: "In you was found the blood of *prophets and saints,* and of *all who have been slaughtered on earth.*"[44] Above all, John knew of the murderous power of the empire in its killing of Jesus, "the Lamb." In its execution of Jesus, the empire exposed itself as the beast as well as sealed its doom, for God had vindicated "the Lamb that was slain" against the power of empire.

Economic Exploitation It is striking how much of John's picture of "Roma" personified as "the great whore" and "Babylon the Great" emphasizes the wealth of Rome. Chapter eighteen imaginatively celebrates her fall. As it does so, it describes the luxury of empire: "She glorified herself and lived luxuriously . . . clothed in fine linen, in purple and scarlet, adorned with gold, with jewels and with pearls." Her "merchants were the magnates of the earth," and "the kings of the earth lived in luxury with her."[45]

John provides a vivid picture of cargo ships carrying the wealth of the world to Rome as the center of the domination system. His list of cargo includes luxury items, agricultural products, and human slaves:

> . . . gold, silver, jewels and pearls, fine linen, purple, silk and scarlet, all kinds of scented wood, all articles of ivory, all articles of costly wood, bronze, iron and marble, cinnamon, spice, incense, myrrh, frankincense, wine, olive oil, choice flour and wheat, cattle and sheep, horses and chariots, slaves, and human lives.[46]

But all of this will end: "All your dainties and your splendors are lost to you." Those who had grown wealthy from her exploitation will mourn: "Alas, alas the great city, where all who had ships at sea grew rich by her wealth."[47]

Religious Legitimation Little more needs to be said about religious legitimation. The Roman Empire's claim that its domination reflected the will of the gods has already been emphasized. John refers to this in the second half of Revelation 13, in his portrait of "the false prophet" who leads people to worship "the beast."[48]

Thus, as we have seen, Rome is indicted by John not simply for its persecution of Christians but because it incarnates the domination system. That same system, in different incarnations, was known in Egypt in the time of Moses and in Israel in the time of the predestruction prophets of the Hebrew Bible. Rome and the beast have an ancient lineage. "Babylon the Great" is not a code name simply for Rome; it designates all domination systems organized around power, wealth, seduction, intimidation, and violence. In whatever historical form it takes, ancient or modern, empire is the opposite of the kingdom of God as disclosed in Jesus.

This analysis is consistent with the content of John's letters to the seven churches. Some (and perhaps all) of these communities had been established a generation earlier. We should imagine them as having been similar to the communities of Paul: initially remarkably egalitarian communities living by an alternative social vision. Now, a generation later, some are beginning to fall away from the power and passion of the founding vision.

John does warn some of his communities of the possibility of persecution, but that is not his focus. His messages to the individual groups commend some for their faithfulness to Jesus and reprove others for their accommodation to the culture and values of empire, calling them back to what they first heard. The communities in Smyrna and Philadelphia, to whom nothing negative is said, are commended for being rich even though poor and for being faithful to Jesus' word even though they have little power.

The community in Ephesus is reproached for having abandoned the love its members had at first and is urged to repent "and do the works you did at first." The communities in Pergamum and Thyatira are charged with eating food that has been sacrificed to idols, a symptom of accommodation. To those in Sardis, John says, "You have a name of being alive, but you are dead." That community is urged to "strengthen what remains and is on the point of death" and "to remember what you received and heard." The community at Laodicea, which has become rich and prosperous, is indicted for being "lukewarm, neither hot nor cold." Cumulatively, John's negative indictments portray communities that no longer differentiate themselves from the world of empire.

In this context, John's portrait of Rome means, Do not betray the vision of Jesus and accommodate yourself to empire, for it is the beast. In his own words, as he writes about Babylon the Great, the world of empire: "Come out of her, my people, so that you do not take part in her sins, and so that you do not share in her plagues, for her sins are heaped high as heaven."[49]

A Tale of Two Cities

The tale of two lordships concludes with a tale of two cities. The climax of the Apocalypse is a vision of a very different kind of city. After John's vision of Babylon the Great and its fall, he sees "a new heaven and a new earth" and "the New Jerusalem" descending out of the sky. Babylon the Great, just described, is the city of Rome as well as the Roman Empire. The New Jerusalem is the city of God as well as the kingdom of God. Revelation is thus a tale of two cities: one city comes from the abyss, the other from God.[50]

John's vision of the New Jerusalem is highly symbolic, with virtually every one of its details based on imagery from the Hebrew Bible. His symbolism echoes the story of creation and paradise even as it moves beyond and speaks of the deepest yearnings of humankind.

John sees a "new heaven [sky] and new earth."[51] It is a new creation, and in the new creation "the sea was no more." The sea as the home of the ancient monster, from which empire after empire ascended, is gone. Then he sees the New Jerusalem descending out of the sky "prepared as a bride adorned for her husband," and he hears a loud voice proclaiming that God now dwells with humankind:

See, the home of God is among mortals.
God will dwell with them.
They will be God's peoples,
And God will be with them.

In the New Jerusalem, the ancient afflictions of humankind are all gone: grief, pain, and death are no more. "God will wipe every tear from their eyes. Death will be no more; mourning and crying and pain will be no more."

The size and construction of the New Jerusalem are fantastic. It is huge. It is a square, fifteen hundred miles on each side. Indeed, its height is equal to its width and length, so it is a cube, like the holy of holies in the temple in Jerusalem. But the city has no need of a temple, "for its temple is the Lord God the Almighty and the Lamb." The city is made of transparent gold, "pure gold, clear as glass." So also its streets are "pure gold, transparent as glass." It is Jerusalem the Golden.[52] Its walls are pure jasper, and its foundations are adorned with every kind of jewel. Its twelve gates are twelve pearls, and they are never shut by day—and there is no night.

The significance of the New Jerusalem is universal. Not only is it huge, with open gates, but "the nations will walk by its light, and the kings of the earth will bring their glory into it." In this great city, next to "the river of the water of life" is "the tree of life" whose "leaves are for the healing of the nations." It is the city of light, in which there is no more night. It is the city of God, in which God and the Lamb dwell with humankind.

But what are we to make of this vision of the New Jerusalem? The city that John contrasts to Babylon and the world of empire is clearly no *actual* city. One cannot imagine it ever existing, whether in this world or another. So has John left the world of history? Is he, as one might imagine, speaking of "heaven" in his highly symbolic language?

We must not too quickly assume so. For it is impossible to reconcile all of what he says with the supposition that he is speaking of heaven. Many of the details John mentions are specific to earthly life:

- The new Jerusalem is "on earth," though it is a new earth and heaven.
- Kings and nations remain in John's vision, for they come streaming to the light of the New Jerusalem.
- The city's tree of life is for the healing of the nations.
- The gates of the city are open to the world.

Though John's vision recalls the language of paradise (and is in that sense paradise restored), it is not a vision of individuals communing with God in an idyllic garden. It is a vision of humans living together *in a city*. And it is the opposite of life in the other city, the world of empire.

Thus John's vision has historical elements. We need to remember that this is the language of apocalyptic. As such, it is enigmatic, metaphorical, parabolic. John's concluding vision is perhaps best understood as "the dream of God"—God's dream for humankind.[53] Throughout the Bible, God's dream is a dream for this earth, and not for another world. For John, it is the only dream worth dreaming.

Concluding Reflections

The book of Revelation is not without its flaws. John's portrait of Rome as "the great whore" and of 144,000 men "who have not defiled themselves with women" reflects a misogynistic attitude.[54] His portrait of God as sending massive destruction upon the inhabitants of earth is extreme. In one scene, blood flows "as high as a horse's bridle for a distance of about two hundred miles."[55] The God of Revelation sometimes has more to do with vengeance than justice, and the difference is crucial.[56] Though John cannot be blamed for all the meanings that Christians have sometimes seen in his book, Revelation supports a picture of God as an angry tyrant who plans to destroy the earth and most of its people.

Nevertheless, in this final book of the Christian Bible, we find the same twofold focus that marks so much of the Bible as a whole: radical affirmation of the sovereignty and justice of God, and radi-

cal criticism of an oppressive domination system pretending to be
the will of God. The domination system that John indicts is a subsequent incarnation of the domination system that existed in Egypt
in the time of Moses and then within Israel itself in the time of the
classical prophets. It is the same domination system that Jesus and
Paul and the early Christian movement challenged.

Rome and the beast have an ancient lineage. "Babylon the
Great" is not simply a symbolic name for Rome, but for domination systems organized around power, wealth, seduction, intimidation, and violence. In whatever ancient or modern forms they
take, domination systems are the opposite of the lordship and
kingdom of God as disclosed in Jesus. Thus John's indictment of
empire sounds the same theme as the central voices of the biblical tradition. As with Moses, the prophets, Jesus, the gospel writers, and Paul, his claim is stark and compelling: God is Lord; the
kingdoms and cultures of this world are not.

John's vision of the New Jerusalem has both historical and
trans-historical elements. Indeed, its power as a trans-historical
vision may be the primary reason that Revelation ultimately
made it into the Bible. Its speaks of the reunion of God with humankind, thereby overcoming the exile that began in Eden.
There every tear shall be wiped away. The river of life flows
through it and the tree of life is in it. There we will see God. It is
difficult to imagine a more powerful ending to the Bible.

NOTES

1. Raymond Brown, *An Introduction to the New Testament* (New York: Doubleday, 1997), p. 773. Two excellent accessible commentaries on Revelation are
Adela Yarbro Collins, *The Apocalypse* (Wilmington: Michael Glazier, 1979),
and Eugene Boring, *Revelation* (Louisville:Knox, 1989). See also the earlier
work by George B. Caird, *A Commentary on the Revelation of St. John the Divine* (London: Adam and Charles Black, 1966). An excellent highly readable
introduction to various ways "the end of the world" has been understood in
prophetic and apocalyptic literature and in the history of the church is Regi-
nald Stackhouse, *The End of the World? A New Look at an Old Belief* (New
York: Paulist, 1997).
2. A 1980 Gallup poll cited by Wes Howard-Brook and Anthony Gwyther,
Unveiling Empire: Reading Revelation Then and Now (Maryknoll, NY:
Orbis, 1999), p. 16.

3. A *U.S. News & World Report* survey cited by Stackhouse, *The End of the World*, pp. 1–2.

4. Boring, *Revelation* p. 3.

5. Adela Yarbro Collins, *The Anchor Bible Dictionary*, ed. David Noel Freedman (New York: Doubleday, 1992), vol. 5, p. 695.

6. I owe the phrase "fabulous beasts" to Luke Timothy Johnson, *The Writings of the New Testament* (Philadelphia: Fortress, 1986), p. 514. On p. 515, he refers to the "apocalyptic menagerie."

7. For a study of Jewish apocalypses not included in the Hebrew Bible, see John Collins, *The Apocalyptic Imagination* (New York: Crossroad, 1984). Apocalyptic literature has antecedents in portions of exilic and postexilic books of the Hebrew Bible, including Ezekiel, Joel, Zechariah, and Isaiah (24–27).

8. The argument that the author of the Fourth Gospel and the author of Revelation are two different people is also ancient, made by an early Christian writer named Dionysius, bishop of Alexandria in the middle of the third century. Dionysius's denial of apostolic authorship of Revelation was among the reasons for the book's slow acceptance as scripture in the Eastern church.

9. Brown, *An Introduction to the New Testament*, p. 775. Boring, *Revelation*, p. 27, notes that there are over five hundred allusions to the Hebrew Bible.

10. Austin Farrer, *A Re-Birth of Images* (Westminster: Dacre Press, 1949).

11. About two hours are required to read Revelation aloud. For a contemporary dramatic reading of Revelation that seeks to convey what it was like to hear it at a single sitting, see a videotape featuring David Rhoads, professor of New Testament at the Lutheran School of Theology in Chicago, The video is available from SELECT, Trinity Lutheran Seminary, Columbus, Ohio.

12. Rev. 1.10–20.

13. For the series of sevens and chapter and verse references, see Boring, *Revelation*, p. 31.

14. See the useful two-page tabulation in Brown, *An Introduction to the New Testament*, pp. 784–85.

15. Are the vision narratives in these chapters based on actual visionary experiences? Did John "see" all of this in a visionary state of consciousness? Or are the vision narratives literary constructions? It is, I think, impossible to make a discerning judgment. Although I think that John did have visions, the use of repeating structural elements (seven seals, seven trumpets, seven bowls, and so forth) and the frequent echoing of the Hebrew Bible suggest literary construction. But literary construction can be based on real experiences, of course.

16. Rev. 22.4–5.

17. The "proof text" for the rapture is I Thess. 4.13–18, in which Paul speaks of followers of Jesus "being caught up in the clouds . . . to meet the Lord in the air." It is difficult to know how literally Paul meant this language. In any case, he seems (like the author of Revelation) to have believed that the second coming of Christ was near, for he imagines that some of those to whom he is writing (and perhaps he himself) will still be alive when it happens.

18. This approach to Revelation is the foundation of modern scholarly study of the book and is affirmed by virtually all mainline scholars. Many scholars move beyond this approach and also emphasize the literary and/or aesthetic and/or political meanings of the book, but the past-historical reading is their common foundation.

19. Rev. 1.1, 3; 22.6, 10, 7, 12, 20.

20. II Pet. 3.8, echoing Ps. 90.4. It is interesting to note that the context is the delay of the second coming of Christ: II Pet. 3.1–10.

21. Rev. 13.18. Nero was caesar (emperor) from 54 until the time of his suicide in 68 CE, when he was still only about thirty years old. Because "666" refers to Nero, some have thought that Revelation must have been written during his reign rather than some thirty years later, near the end of the reign of the emperor Domitian. However, for two different reasons, the name of the beast as Nero need not conflict with a late-first-century date. On the one hand, there was a rumor that Nero had survived and would return to claim the imperial throne. On the other hand, Nero was the first Roman emperor to persecute Christians, and thus the name Nero could refer to the empire in its role as persecutor of the Christian movement.

22. In the New Testament, see I Pet. 5.13.

23. Rev. 17.9, 18.

24. In what he calls a "strong clarifying statement," Raymond Brown writes, "God has not revealed to human beings details about how the world began or how the world will end, and failing to recognize that, one is likely to mis-read both the first book and the last book of the Bible. The author of Revelation did not know how or when the world will end, and neither does anybody else." *An Introduction to the New Testament*, p. 810.

25. For further exposition, Marcus Borg and N. T. Wright, *The Meaning of Jesus: Two Visions* (San Francisco: HarperSanFrancisco, 1998), chap. 13, esp. pp. 194–96.

26. In *The Writings of the New Testament*, p. 513, Luke Timothy Johnson comments, "[T]he book of Revelation is one of those rare compositions that speak to something deep and disturbed in the human spirit with a potency never diminished by fact or disconfirmation."

27. Excerpted from Richard Horsley, *The Liberation of Christmas* (New York: Crossroad, 1989), p. 27. Italics added. See also pp. 25–33.

28. Rev. 1.5.

29. In sequence, Rev. 4.8, 5.12, 7.12, 11.15, 19.6.

30. See Walter Wink's compelling analysis of its presence in comic strips, television cartoons, spy thrillers, and movies, as well as in the policies of contemporary national-security states, in his *Engaging the Powers* (Minneapolis: Fortress, 1992), pp. 13–31. I am impressed again and again with the brilliance of this book and commend it to everybody. See also Robert Jewett, *The Captain America Complex*, rev. ed. (Santa Fe: Bear, 1984); and Robert Jewett and John Sheldon Lawrence, *The American Monomyth* (Garden City: Doubleday, 1977).

31. Ps. 74.12–13; see also Ps. 89.9–10, where the primordial monster is named Rahab.

32. Isa. 27.1. See also 51.9: "Was it not you who cut Rahab in pieces, who pierced the dragon?" In Isa. 30.7, Egypt is referred to as "Rahab"; see also Ezek. 29.3, which identifies Pharaoh "as the great dragon."

33. Job 7.12, 9.13, 26.12–13, and all of chap. 41.

34. See especially Gustav Aulen's classic study of Christian understandings of Jesus' death and resurrection: *Christus Victor,* trans. A. F. Hebert (New York: Macmillan, 1969; first published in 1931).

35. For the way the ancient cosmic combat myth shapes Revelation, see Adela Yarbro Collins, *The Combat Myth in the Book of Revelation* (Missoula: Scholars Press, 1976). See also compact expositions in Boring, *Revelation,* p. 151; Wink, *Engaging the Powers,* pp. 90–93; Collins, *Crisis and Catharsis: The Power of the Apocalypse* (Philadelphia: Westminster, 1984), pp. 148–50. On p. 148, Collins writes, "This basic plot or pattern is found *in every series of visions in Revelation,* beginning with the seven seals (in Rev. 6) . . . and in more elaborate form, for example, in the passage that extends from 19.11–22.5" (italics added).

36. Some scholars deny that there was any official Roman persecution of Christians in the time of Domitian. For a persuasive argument that there was minor (but not massive) persecution, see Raymond Brown, *An Introduction to the New Testament,* pp. 807–9.

37. Antipas is mentioned in Rev. 2.13; references in the letters to persecutions to come are found in 2.10 and 3.10. See also 1.9.

38. The most sustained recent study arguing for this point of view is Howard Brook and Gwyther, *Unveiling Empire.* See also Ward Ewing, *The Power of the Lamb* (Cambridge, MA: Cowley, 1990); and Wink, *Engaging the Powers,* pp. 89–104. See also earlier books by William Stringfellow, *Conscience and Obedience* (Waco: Word Books, 1977), and Daniel Berrigan, *Beside the Sea of Glass: The Song of the Lamb* (New York: Seabury, 1978), and *The Nightmare of God* (Portland, OR: Sunburst, 1983).

39. See chap. 5 above.

40. Wink, *Engaging the Powers,* p. 99: "Never has a more withering political and economic criticism of empire been penned."

41. Rev. 17.3, 18.3.

42. Rev. 18.23. See Wink's comment, *Engaging the Powers,* p. 93: "People must be made to believe that they benefit from a system that is in fact harmful to them."

43. Rev. 13.3–4.

44. Rev. 18.24.

45. Rev. 18.7, 16; 18.23, 9.

46. Rev. 18.12–13.

47. Rev. 18.14, 19.

48. Wink, *Engaging the Powers,* p. 93: it "proselytizes by means of a civil religion that declares the state and its leaders divine."

49. Rev. 18.4. See the comment of Gerd Theissen, *The Religion of the Earliest Churches,* trans. John Bowden (Minneapolis: Fortress, 1999), p. 244: John drives a wedge "between the community and the world. It was not the emperor cult that was the great problem, but the lack of demarcation between

many Christians in the churches and the pagan world, its affairs, and its society." John seeks to resist "tendencies in the community to assimilate to this world. ... The Roman empire did not declare war on the Christians; a Christian prophet declared war on the Roman empire."

50. For a striking tabulation of the symmetrical contrasts between the two cities, see Howard-Brook and Gwyther, *Unveiling Empire,* p. 160, and their chapter on "Babylon or New Jerusalem?" pp. 157–96.

51. The paragraphs that follow are all based on Rev. 21.1–22.5.

52. The phrase "gold transparent as glass" makes me wonder if John perhaps did see the New Jerusalem in a visionary state (in contrast to the whole of the vision being a literary creation). Mystical experiences are frequently marked by golden light, so much so that the historian of religions Mircea Eliade refers to such experiences as "experiences of the golden world." Cited by Robert A. Johnson (with Jerry M. Ruhl) in *Balancing Heaven and Earth* (San Francisco: HarperSanFrancisco, 1998), p. 2.

53. As noted in chap. 6, I owe the phrase "the dream of God" to the title of Verna Dozier's book, *The Dream of God* (Cambridge, MA: Cowley, 1991).

54. Rev. 14.4. For critiques of his misogynistic language and two different ways of dealing with it, see Elisabeth Schüssler Fiorenza, *Revelation: Vision of a Just World* (Minneapolis: Augsburg Fortress, 1991) and Tina Pippin, *Death and Desire: The Rhetoric of Gender in the Apocalypse of John* (Louisville: Westminster John Knox, 1992).

55. Rev. 14.20.

56. See John Dominic Crossan, *The Birth of Christianity* (San Francisco: HarperSanFrancisco, 1998), p. 586

Epilogue

I close with some personal reflections. Of course, the whole book reflects my personal perceptions. I do not have an objective vantage point outside of my own history. All any of us can do is to say, "Here's how I see it." We can muster our reasons for seeing in a certain way, of course. But ultimately it is always personal. For me, this book comes down to what I have been able to see thus far about how to read the Bible.

So the whole book has been personal. Nevertheless, in this epilogue, I give myself permission to speak about how it all comes together for me—about how I see "the whole" of the Bible and "the whole" of the Christian life at a very elemental level. And if what I say perhaps has application to other religions as well, that is *lagniappe*, a bonus.

It is clear to me that the Bible speaks with more than one voice. I do not mean simply that many authors, communities, and storytellers speak in it, though this is true. Nor do I mean simply that in, with, and under these human voices the voice of the Spirit sometimes speaks to us, though this is also true. In addition to all of that, I mean that the Bible contains different voices (and thus different visions) of what life is about. And for each of the speakers, "what life is about" meant "what life with God" is about. Thus the Bible contains different voices responding to this central question.

These different voices are found throughout the history of the biblical period, as well as in the postbiblical history of Christianity. The conflict between them shapes both testaments. We hear the different voices in the conflict between the royal theology of pharaohs and kings and caesars, and prophetic protest against it by Moses, the prophets, Jesus, and in their own ways Paul and John of Patmos. Royal theology, whether in biblical or postbiblical forms, legitimates domination systems. Prophetic theology opposes them.

The tension between these voices continues into the present day in both religious and secular forms. Within Christianity, we see an acceptance of royal theology in the alliance between some forms of Christianity and a politics of radical individualism. The emphasis of these belief-forms upon individual responsibility and accountability, though good in itself, ignores the way that systems affect people's lives and leaves the domination systems of our day intact. Secular forms of individualism perform the same legitimation. Other Christians, especially (though not only) in marginalized communities, hear the voice of radical critique of domination systems that sounds through so much of the biblical tradition.

We also hear the different voices in the central conflict within the wisdom tradition. Some voices affirm a confident conventional wisdom that makes life "safe" by domesticating it. Other voices subvert the easy confidence of convention and affirm an alternative wisdom much more in touch with the wildness of life.

The tension between these voices also continues into the present day. Systems of conventional wisdom, both secular and religious, not only domesticate reality but put us in bondage to the internalized messages we acquire in our socialization. But does convention—even religious convention—come from God? Or is it like a grid that we lay over reality—a grid that in fact estranges us from "what is"? Is conventional wisdom to be blessed? Or is it to be let go of for the sake of following the road not taken? Is conventional wisdom an accurate map of how things are? Or is it a rough guide and a pointer to a sacred Mystery that lies right behind it?

Affirmations of both ways of seeing life are found in the Bible and in postbiblical Christianity. Much of Christianity through the centuries and into the present has simply been conventional wisdom in Christian form: a domestication of reality with Christian language and directives for how to live one's life—"Follow this way and all will go well." The second way is the common voice of Job, Ecclesiastes, Jesus, and Paul. It surfaces again and again in the more experiential and spiritual stream of the Bible. Experience, and the experience of the Spirit, make it clear that convention is just that: convention.

From these paragraphs and this book as a whole, it is clear that among these voices I have favorites. I think I can make a decent case that the voices I favor are the major voices of the Bible, and that I am "hearing" them reasonably accurately (at least at a very general level).

Nevertheless, as I now suggest what I think I hear these voices saying, I want to acknowledge again that I am aware of how subjective all this is. But subjectivity in this arena is unavoidable.

The major voices of the biblical tradition, as I hear them, share three primary convictions in common:

First, there is a deep sense of the reality of the sacred. God is not only real, but knowable. Moreover, the sacred is known not in a set of statements about God, but experientially, as a Mystery beyond all language. This Mystery— God—transcends all of our domestications of reality, including those generated by theology and even the Bible itself. God also transcends empires and emperors, nations and kings. These humans and their creations are not lords; God alone is. God also transcends peoples and religions, and thus a unity is possible in the God who made heaven and earth that is not possible when lesser lords of cultures and religions rule.

Second, there is a strong conviction that our lives are made "whole" and "right" by living in a conscious relationship with the Mystery who is alone Lord. Life with God is not about believing certain teachings about God. It is about a covenant—a relationship. More specifically, it is about becoming conscious of a relationship that already exists, for the God of the Bible has been in relationship with us from our beginning, whether we know it or not, believe it or not. And we are not simply to become conscious of it; we are to become intentional about deepening the relationship. Christian faith is not about believing, but about faithfulness—fidelity—to the relationship. To use the rela-

tional metaphor at the center of both the Hebrew Bible and the
New Testament: we are in a covenant with the sacred. Taking
that covenant seriously is the path of life.

As the path of life, this relationship is the path of personal
transformation. It is the path of liberation from existential, psychological, and spiritual bondage to the lords of convention and
culture. It involves dying to an old way of being and being born
into a new way of being. It is life lived in accord with radical
monotheism: centering one's life in God rather than in the rival
lords of culture and convention.

Third, these voices are convinced that God is a God of justice
and compassion. The God of the Bible is full of compassion and
passionate about justice. God's passion for justice flows out of the
very character of God. God cares about suffering, and the single
greatest source of unnecessary human misery is unjust and
oppressive cultural systems. These systems range from a few that
have been relatively benign and humane to more that have been
demonically destructive, with many in the middle range of mildly
to severely oppressive. The God about whom these voices speak
wills human well-being and rages against all humanly constructed
systems that inflict unnecessary wounds. They speak about God's
passion for life on earth—for the dream of God in the world of
the everyday.

God's passion is the ground of a biblical ethic centered in justice
and compassion. Both words—"justice" and "compassion"—are
needed. Justice without compassion easily sounds like "just politics"; compassion without justice too easily becomes individual-
ized and systemically acquiescent.

By justice, as mentioned earlier in this book, I do not mean
primarily criminal justice or procedural justice, but substantive or
systemic justice: a justice judged by its results. But to emphasize
God's passion for systemic and structural justice alone, as some
theologies do, makes it sound as if the biblical message is primarily about politics and public morality and not very much about
individuals at all. The message of the Bible's passion for social
justice should always be grounded in the reality of God and ac-
companied by the message of personal liberation.

Yet the word "justice" is utterly essential, for to speak of compassion without justice easily turns the Bible's passion for the victims of systems into the importance of individual kind deeds and charity. Charity and kind deeds are always good; there will always be need for help. But the individualization of compassion means that one does not ask how many of the suffering are in fact victims. Compassion without justice can mean caring for victims while quietly acquiescing to a system that creates ever more victims. Justice means asking why there are so many victims and then doing something about it.

So these three, I am suggesting, are at the core of the biblical vision of life with God: a sacred Mystery at the center of life, with whom we are to be in a conscious relationship and who is passionate about the well-being of the whole creation. We are called to participate in the passion of God. This is what I perceive when I use the Bible as a lens for seeing life with God, when I think of it as a finger pointing to the moon, when I hear it as the foundation of the Christian cultural-linguistic world, and when I listen to it as a sacrament of the sacred.

From these three core elements flows a remarkably simple vision of the Christian life. It is not complicated, though it is challenging. It is crystallized in the very familiar twofold "great commandment" attributed to Jesus. I prefer to think of it as the "great relationship," and I thus paraphrase it as follows:[1]

> The first relationship is, "Hear, O Israel: the Lord our God, the Lord is one; and you shall love the Lord your God with all your heart, and with all your soul, and with all your mind, and with all your strength." This is the great and first relationship. And a second relationship is like it: "You shall love your neighbor as yourself." On these two relationships depend all theLaw and the Prophets.

The two primary relationships are common to Judaism and Christianity. Central to the Christian tradition and spoken by Jesus, they are also both quotations from and central to the Hebrew Bible. The first is the *Shema*, the classic Jewish expression of faith through the centuries; the second is from the book of Leviticus.[2] Judaism and Christianity share this elemental core in common.

Thus at the center of a life grounded in the Bible is the twofold focus of the great relationship. Of course, being Christian means more than this. It means living within Christian community and letting one's life be shaped by that community's scriptures, stories, songs, rituals, and practices. Community is not only central to the biblical vision (the New Jerusalem, after all, is a *city*); it also mediates the internalization of a new identity and vision. At its best, Christian community nourishes the alternative life of centering in God and instills a passion for compassion and justice for the whole creation.

In this process of shaping Christian identity and vision in community, the Bible has a central role, perhaps second only to that of the Spirit. As the foundation of the Christian tradition, the Bible is the source of our images and stories for speaking of God's passion. Thus its interpretation shapes our vision of what it means to take the God of the Bible seriously. The Bible is also a sacrament of the same sacred Mystery, a means whereby God speaks to us still today. Through and within the Bible's many voices, we are called to discern *the voice* that addresses us in our time. And listen: what we hear matters greatly. It makes all the difference.

NOTES

1. Matt. 22.37–40; see also Mark 12.29–31. I owe the relational readings of this passage to the Rev. Dr. Fred Burnham of Trinity Institute, New York City.
2. Deut. 6.4–5; Lev. 19.18.

Subject Index

Abraham, 253, 263n.71, and
Sarah, 62, 81n.9, 85, 89–90,
106n.4, 106n.5
Acts, 199–202, 229–31
Adam, 61, 69, 77, 78, 246
Afterlife: Christianity focus on,
12, 221n.35; concept of, 151,
157, 80n.14; Paul on, 255
Amos, 117–121, 125
Apocalypse, 193–94, 265–66,
220n.19, 267–69, 292n.2,
294n.24; Daniel as, 268; writings in Judaism, 268, 293n.7
Apocrypha, 81n.1, 146, 147,
187
Apollo and Python, myth of,
283
Archetypal criticism, 42, 52n.6
Archetype, 93, 103, 107n.10
Augustine: 31–32, 43–44,
53n.10, 77
Authority of Bible, 4, 5, 30–31,
36n.13, 36n.14; dialogical
model, 30; monarchical
model, 30; natural and con-

scious literalism and, 9; as sacred in status, not origin, 30,
34, 36n.12, 36n.14; as *sola
scriptura* (sole authority for
faith and morals), 7, 9, 10, 11,
19n.4, 19n.9
Autonomy, 84n.35, 249

Babel, tower of, 77, 200
Beatitudes, 198, 222n.36
Bethlehem, 51, 117, 142n.9
Bible: accessibility and development of printing technology,
7–8; authority, 4, 5, 7, 9, 11,
19n.4, 19n.9; authorship of,
8; as both human and divine,
26–28; canonization of books
of, 28; conscious literalism,
8–9, 13, 53n.17; historical-
metaphorical reading, ix,
17–18, 33–34, 37–53; human
response to God, 21–28,
32–33, 36n.2, 36n.11,
36n.12; literal-factual reading,
ix, 4–5, 6–7; natural literalism,

I Timothy, 36n.7; authorship,
229; date, 219n.6
II Timothy, 36n.7; authorship,
229; date, 219n.6
Titus, 36n.7, 229; date, 219n.6
Torah, 58, 254. *See also* Pentateuch

Ussher, James, 59, 81n.4

Visions and call stories, 124–25,
142n.25, 230–31, 235–37,
269–70, 271–72, 293n.15

Wedding at Cana, 204–5, 206,
225n.101
Wesley, John, 32
Wisdom books (Writings or
Kethuvim), 58, 145–79;
books included in, 146; canonization, 28–29; content,
tone, form, 147–48; dating,
146; Ecclesiastes, 161–70; fear
of the LORD, 149; focus of,

146, 180n.2; Job, 170–79;
Proverbs, 148–61; Sophia,
149–51, 180n.5, 180n.6,
180n.9; way or path in, 149,
170; what is life about?, 145,
148, 165, 181n.29. *See also*
Ecclesiastes; Job; Proverbs
Wisdom of Solomon, 146, 147
Women: "alien woman" in
Proverbs, 150–51, 180n.10;
ordination, 26, 36n.9; Paul
and, 228, 258n.1, 250,
262n.64; Revelation and
misogyny, 291, 296n.54; sayings in Proverbs about good
and difficult wives, 153–54,
180n.17; Sophia as female
image of God, 149–51,
180n.5, 180n.6, 180n.9; I
Timothy and behavior or roles
of, 25–26, 36n.7

Yahweh, 82n.16

Modern Author Index

Scripture Index

Psalms: *8*, 76, 83n.22;
74.12–13, 282; *78.42–51*,
107n.21; *89.9*, 208, 282; *95.5*,
208; *104*, 83n.22; *107.25–29*,
208; *137*, 131, 143n.39

Revelation: *1.1, 3*, 276; *1.5*,
280; *1.10–20*, 269–70; *4.8*,
281; *5.12*, 281; *7.12*, 281;
11.15, 281; *12*, 284; *13, 283*,
284, 287; *13.3–4*, 286; *13.18*,
277, 294n.21; *14.20*, 291;
17.3, 286; *18.4, 289*, 295n.49;
18.7, 287; *18.9*, 287;
18.12–13, 287; *18.14*, 287;
18.16, 287; *18.19*, 287; *18.23*,
287; *18.24*, 287; *18.3*, 286;
18.23, 286; *19.6*, 281; *19.7–9*,
205; *21.1–22.5*, 289, 290,
296n.52; *21.2*, 205; *22.4–5*,
272; *22.6, 7, 10, 12, 20*, 276

Romans: *3.9, 19–20, 23*, 253;
3.24–25, 253, 257, 263n.79;
4.5, 253; *5.8, 10*, 253, 257;
5.12–21, 246, 261n.47; *6.3–4*,
249; *6.6–7, 18, 22*, 247;
7.7–24, 247, 261n.48; *7.12*,
254; *8.4–17*, 248, 261n.53;
8.35, 38–39, 251; *10.4*, 257,
263n.80; *12.1–2*, 249; *12.4–5*,
250

I Samuel: *8.4–22*, 129; *8.11–18*,
129; *9.1–10.16*, 129;
10.17–19, 129

II Samuel: *7.1–17*, 129

**Sirach (Wisdom of Ben Sira or
Ecclesiasticus):** *24*, 180n.8

I Thessalonians: *4.13–18*,
260n.39, 293n.17

I Timothy: *2.8–15*, 228; *2.9–15*,
25–26, 36n.7, 36n.8

Wisdom of Solomon: *7.7–8.16*,
180n.8; *10*, 180n.8

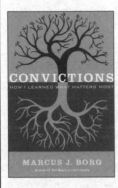

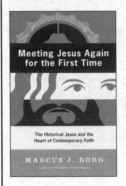

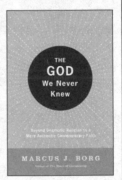